IN THE CIRCLE
OF THE DANCE

IN THE CIRCLE
OF THE DANCE

Notes of an Outsider in Nepal

Katharine Bjork Guneratne

CORNELL UNIVERSITY PRESS

ITHACA AND LONDON

First published 1999 by Cornell University Press
First printing, Cornell Paperbacks, 1999

Printed in the United States of America

Library of Congress Cataloging-in-Publication Data

Guneratne, Katharine Bjork, 1963–
In the circle of the dance : notes of an outsider in Nepal /
Katharine Bjork Guneratne
p.   cm.
ISBN 0-8014-3639-7 (alk. paper).—
ISBN 0-8014-8592-4 (pbk. : alk. paper)
1. Tharu (South Asian people)—Nepal—Pipariya—Social life
and customs.   2. Pipariya (Nepal)—Social life and customs.
3. Guneratne, Katharine Bjork, 1963–   .
DS493.9.T47G86   1999
954.96—dc21   98-32399

Cornell University Press strives to use environmentally responsible suppliers and
materials to the fullest extent possible in the publishing of its books. Such materials
include vegetable-based, low-VOC inks and acid-free papers that are recycled,
totally chlorine-free, or partly composed of nonwood fibers. Books that bear the logo
of the FSC (Forest Stewardship Council) use paper taken from forests that have
been inspected and certified as meeting the highest standards for environmental
and social responsibility. For further information, visit our website at
www.cornellpress.cornell.edu.

Cloth printing   10 9 8 7 6 5 4 3 2 1

Paperback printing   10 9 8 7 6 5 4 3 2 1

FSC   FSC Trademark © 1996 Forest Stewardship Council A.C.
SW-COC-098

To my parents,

Gordon and Susan Bjork,

who, among many other things,
have given me two invaluable gifts:
a happy childhood,
and the freedom to be my own adult

CONTENTS

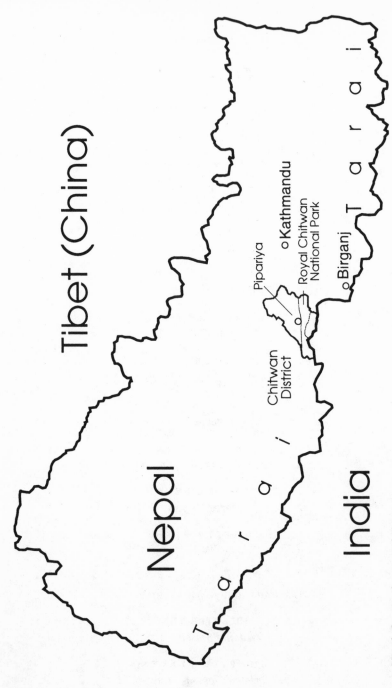

Nepal, showing location of Pipariya

ACKNOWLEDGMENTS

I regret that the use of pseudonyms to disguise the identity of people in "Pipariya" makes it difficult to properly acknowledge the many instances of generosity and *māyā* as well as the daily practical assistance and support that sustained us in the village and that, in the most basic sense, made this book possible. I hope our friends and neighbors will therefore excuse this general but heartfelt expression of gratitude for the kindness and help extended to Arjun and me during the time we spent in Nepal.

I am greatly indebted to several excellent language teachers, especially Gautam Vajracharya and Krishna Pradhan in Madison and Geeta Manander in Kathmandu. I am grateful to Satya Narayan Chaudhary for his comments on the book. Others who read the manuscript or offered advice and encouragement along the way include Marianne Alverson, Jeremy Baskes and Jane Erickson, Cathy Fisher and Barney Bate, Katherine Bowie, John Coatsworth, Kathleen Gallagher, Merrill Goodall, Laura Gotkowitz and Michel Gobat, Tania Forte, Peter Guardino and Jane Walter, Camena and Erica Guneratne, Rosalind James, Janet Morford and Jose Cheibub, Robin Derby and Andrew Apter, Cheryl Duncan and Adeeb Khalid, Shantanu Phukan, Graeme Pietersz, Ianthé Sinnathamby, Nader Sohrabi, Ariadne Staples, Julie Woodward, and Anders, Becky, Hannah, Gordon and Susan Bjork. I also thank Arjun's colleagues in the anthropology department at Macalester College: David McCurdy, Anna Meigs, Anne Sutherland, and Jack Weatherford. Jim Fisher has been a wonderful friend and colleague from Nepal to Minnesota.

My husband, Arjun Guneratne, is one of the few people whose name I have not changed. That this account owes a great deal to his knowledge and insight should be plain throughout. More than that, he has traveled every step of the journey of making this book with me. The book has been immeasurably improved by his input; without him I would never have undertaken the journey at all. His support in this, as in all the endeavors of our life together, has been unfailing, and it has made all the difference.

K.B.G.

IN THE CIRCLE
OF THE DANCE

Nak Chaina

"Tapainko bihé bhayo?" Our Nepali teacher paused in front of my desk. As always, she was smiling easily. She had worn a sari today, much to the delight of the whole class; we had seen her only in jeans. She was not tall, about five feet, but she stood very straight and moved gracefully within the arc of our desks, the loose end of her patterned sari swishing behind her.

She had arrived in Madison from Kathmandu several days earlier to take part in teaching the summer intensive Nepali language course at the University of Wisconsin. She joined two other language teachers in the Madison program. A majority of the class, all undergraduates, were planning to spend the coming academic year in Kathmandu. In addition, a prospective Peace Corps volunteer and a couple of graduate students were preparing to undertake research or work projects in Nepal. And there was me.

The teacher's red and black glass bangles tinkled as she gestured toward me and repeated her question: "Are you married?" She was using this question to introduce the past tense. I groped for the right response. *"Ho,"* I said. *"Mero bihé bhayo."* (My marriage has occurred.)

She nodded approvingly and moved on around the circle repeating the question. I was the only person in the class who was married. This was in fact at the heart of my reason for being in the class. My husband was a Ph.D. candidate in anthropology at the University of Chicago, where I was also a graduate student. He had just completed nine months of fieldwork in Nepal's Tarai plains region on ethnic identity and culture change among the Tharus, the aboriginal inhabitants of the Tarai, in the context of large-scale immigration of "caste Hindu" groups from Nepal's hills and the economic modernization of the region. Except for a brief visit over Christmas the previous year, I had stayed in Chicago to complete my master's degree in history and to take the qualifying exam for the Ph.D. program. In a few weeks we would return to Nepal together for another ten months.

Unlike my fellow students in Madison, I had not chosen to go to Nepal to study or to work. I had decided to accompany my husband because I didn't want to spend another year so far apart. I wanted to experience with him this important stage of his training as an anthropologist, this defining rite of passage, fieldwork. I wasn't immune to the appeal of taking a year off to travel and to experience a totally different way of life, but I was wary, too, wary of finding myself out of place, isolated, with nothing to occupy me and of no practical use to my husband or anyone else.

By the summer of 1990, Arjun was well established in the village of Pipariya in Chitwan District, near the famous Chitwan National Park. He seemed to have settled in with the extended family of his research assistant with whom he had been living. He was restless in Madison, anxious to get back to "the field" and to resume his work. The summer in Madison was a concession to me: a chance for me to develop a foundation in Nepali in a familiar cultural environment.

Tharu is the name used for a number of linguistically and culturally distinct groups of people who have traditionally inhabited the Tarai region of Nepal. Until the 1960s, when the eradication of malaria spurred immigration by outside groups, Tharus constituted the majority population in some Tarai districts. Although today they account for less than 13 percent of the population of Chitwan, in 1971 Tharus represented over 80 percent of the nonimmigrant population.[1]

Since the 1960s Chitwan has become increasingly integrated into the national economy and culture. While they have been affected by this "Nepalization," Tharus have for the most part remained politically marginalized in a country dominated by the high Hindu caste groups such as the Brahmins, Chhetris, and Thakuris. On the individual level, many Tharus have lost control of land or been otherwise displaced by more recent immigrants.

[1] Arjun Guneratne, "The Tax Man Cometh: The Impact of Revenue Collection on Subsistence Strategies in Chitwan Tharu Society," *Studies in Nepali History and Society* 1 (1996): 6.

In gaining acceptance into the Tharu community of Pipariya, I think Arjun had been helped by the fact that he is from Sri Lanka, an island geographically, culturally, and linguistically connected to the Indian subcontinent delimited by Nepal's Himalayan range. Part of his identity as a foreigner in Nepal came not only from being not-Nepalese but also from being not-European. To frame this in a positive sense— although identity seems most often to derive from the negation of other possibilities—Arjun shared a South Asian origin with Tharus. What this common origin actually meant was elusive and fraught with ambiguity, since many of the cultural symbols they shared were really those of a dominant Hindu Indian tradition whose relations both with the aboriginal Tharus and with English-educated Sri Lankan professionals are somewhat problematic. But there were some basic things they had in common. Arjun's hosts took one look at him and assumed he would eat rice as a major component of his diet. They were right. What would I eat? They weren't so sure. Did I live on fruit, or only on bread, as it was rumored tourists did who came to visit the national park?

Although Arjun is not personally religious, Sri Lanka's religious ties to Nepal are as old as the Buddha himself, who was born in the Tarai, in Lumbini, about a hundred miles southwest of Pipariya. Nepal is predominantly a Hindu country, but Buddhism is an accepted minority religion, and in reality, Buddhist and Hindu practices overlap. Sri Lankan Buddhists make pilgrimages to Lumbini. Nepalese Buddhists study in Sri Lanka and Hindu Nepalese know of the land of Lanka from the epic poem *Ramayana:* Lanka where the demon king Ravana fled with the kidnapped Sita.

Though I was no more outwardly religious than my husband, my Christian *dharma* was unquestionably exotic and so was viewed with some suspicion. Under the Panchayat regime, conversion to Christianity was a jailable offense. When the Democracy movement brought about the downfall of the government (and supposedly the end of religious persecution) in 1990, more than two hundred people in Nepal either were serving jail terms or had cases related to conversion charges pending in the country's court system.[2]

Race also contributed to making me feel more of an outsider than Arjun. On a landing overlooking a Kwakiutl totem pole in the anthro-

[2] Saubhagya Shah,"The Gospel Comes to the Hindu Kingdom," *Himal*, September/October 1993, 35.

pology department at the University of Chicago, photos of the department's researchers are displayed around a map of the world. Push pins indicate their fieldwork locations on the map. The photo of Arjun shows him sitting on a mat in a circle of Tharus listening to a story being told. As the anthropologist, he is the one holding the tape recorder. I remember my surprise at the exclamation of someone in the department upon seeing this photo: "He looks just like them!" Surprise first at the implied assumption that anthropologists should look different from the people they study and second because no one familiar with Sinhalese and Tharus would mistake one for the other. Still, I do think that common cultural and even physical traits contributed to Arjun's identity as foreign but familiar, whereas I, with my white skin, northern European frame, and fine, curly brown hair, was exotic.

In large part, this book is informed by the experience of being exotic while struggling to feel merely foreign. A Nepali idiom I learned in Madison is suggestive of the dilemma I faced in forging a comfortable fieldwork persona. *Nak chaina* literally means lacking a nose. When said of a person it can mean either that he or she has lost status in some way or that he or she is shameless, brazen, or impervious to (or ignorant of) social norms. Anthropology has sometimes struck me as an inherently *nak chaina* proposition.

Anthropological fieldwork typically involves a member of one culture—usually Western—living among people of another culture, learning about them through observation, inquiry, and participation. To be a successful fieldworker, one must be at least a little uninhibited about being conspicuous and unwittingly violating local norms, because the nature of fieldwork makes this virtually inevitable. I seem to be burdened by more than the usual fears of offending other people, of doing what is culturally inappropriate. In foreign countries I always have the desire to blend in, to observe unobserved. I have experienced some success indulging this predilection while traveling in the lands of my ancestors, England and Sweden. I was extremely pleased once when a train conductor confidently addressed me in Dutch in Amsterdam, and disappointed when I had to admit that I couldn't understand him. When I accompanied my husband home to Sri Lanka for the first time the year after our marriage, I felt exposed as an outsider the moment I set foot in the airport. I was uncomfortable with the feeling of being conspicuously out of place, and I did not look forward to this aspect of venturing into a strange society. I found in this respect that I differed both from my husband, who viewed his outsider status as a necessary and unexceptional part of being an anthropologist, and from some of my classmates in Madison, who seemed eager to lose themselves in another cultural identity.

One afternoon, two of the undergraduates were late returning to class after our lunch break. Giggling slightly, they walked across the room to their desks. Both young women were sporting new nose rings (*puli*), one a gold stud and the other a fine small ring, in their left nostrils, which looked a little inflamed from being pierced. Our afternoon Nepali teacher smiled when he saw them and then turned back to the blackboard. In the early 90s the craze for piercing noses (and other body parts) was just beginning on college campuses and still had some shock value. The girls sat red-nosed in their seats and whispered in answer to the questions of their classmates that they'd had it done on State Street, and that yes, it hurt. I felt embarrassed; I think we all did. Why? *Nak chaina.* They were playing with their identities, the faces that preceded them, noses foremost, as they sallied forth in the social world.

My preoccupation with how I would be perceived had a definite effect on the self I put forward in my interactions with people in Pipariya. This book details various levels of self-representation brought about by the fieldwork experience: how I defined myself vis-à-vis my anthropologist husband in the context of his fieldwork; how I portrayed myself to our Tharu hosts, neighbors, and friends; and how, ultimately, I have presented myself to you, the reader, in the narrative that follows.

The self-representation that anthropologists make in the course of putting forward their fieldwork personae are necessarily different from the ones they project in their own societies. This is not to say that fieldwork is based on a lie or misrepresentation of personality but rather that the fieldworker inevitably anticipates and accommodates reactions to him- or herself and more generally to the culture he or she represents. It was true for us, as I would guess it is true for many fieldworkers, that the question of how to represent oneself in the field is both so crucial to the success of the research and so dependent on the shifting dynamics of the fieldwork situation that it develops naturally from day-to-day interactions with people and a hundred hardly conscious calculations about perception and projection.

This book is the product of a fiction, one which I created to coax myself through the difficult first few months of fieldwork, when we first arrived in Nepal and I felt, as I had feared, out of place and aimless.

The conceit that gave me a sense of purpose was that I must pay attention to what was happening around me so that I would be able to write a book about it. I think I was more surprised than anyone when I actually sat down with my diaries at our little desk in the rooftop apartment of the United States Educational Foundation in Kathmandu during a few weeks in the spring of 1991 and drafted most of it.

Not surprisingly, the psychological motivation for writing the book has influenced the form it took. The goal of writing a book was a trick I used to force myself to participate consciously, even reflectively, in the unfamiliar world in which I found myself, so that I would be able to describe it later, capture it for a hypothetical audience "back home." The act of relating my experiences in Nepal was an attempt to render them comprehensible from the largely unexamined cultural perspective of the narrator, which she assumes will be shared by her readers. To the extent that my motivation in writing the book was not to explain or interpret Tharu culture but to accommodate myself to it by describing it, making it part of me, this book is decidedly unanthropological, or at least epistemologically naive. However, an interesting thing happened in the course of "bringing the book home," which is how I thought of the process of completing, revising, and just living with it once I returned to the United States. Certain aspects of Nepalese reality began intruding upon my experience of my own rediscovered society. For example, I found that the contrasts between Nepalese social problems, class and gender conflicts, and their American counterparts imbued familiar problems with new meanings for me. I have included some of these episodes of personal meaning-making in the book.

I first conceived of this book as a straightforward narrative of my experiences as the wife of an anthropologist in a typical fieldwork situation, an agricultural village in Nepal. As I read other works in the genre that I jokingly referred to as "anthropologist-drags-wife-to-field-and-wife-writes-book," I realized that the matter-of-fact, even social-scientific recording of day-to-day life in a strange culture interjected with the occasional reflection on feelings of alienation is a generic rhetorical formula with at least two functions. First, to the extent that this kind of book imparts information about an encounter with another way of life, this is a pedagogic device. It allows the reader to "learn" by vicariously experiencing the author's gradual and provisional accommodation to a strange culture. Second, while inviting the reader to laugh at the fieldworker's mishaps and misapprehensions, the narrative enjoys a reasonable expectation of winning the admiration of the reader for hardships endured and knowledge won. I would be deceiving myself as well as the reader if I did not admit the motivation of such desires in the narrative that follows. At the same time, my audience "back home" was not the only one I had in mind when writing of my experiences. I am aware that this book will reach Pipariya, possibly before Arjun and I are able to return there ourselves. I hope that when my English words are read aloud and translated into Tharu and Nepali, the girls who taught me how to smear cow dung *māto*, the women who invited me to sit with them on their *wosarās*, and the teachers who accepted me into their staff room will recognize themselves through the thin veil of the pseudonyms I have laid over the village and that the encounters related here will resonate with their own memories of the time we spent in "Pipariya," except, of course, that my perspective may seem—not exotic—but familiarly foreign.

CHAPTER ONE

Monsoon

Before I experienced it, the word *monsoon* merely conjured up visions of rain pelting down on verdant rice paddies and thatched huts. As a native of the northwestern United States, the idea that so much rain could be accompanied by hot weather seemed unnatural, but still within my ability to imagine. Mud, landslides, washed-out roads, disrupted communications, perpetually sodden clothes, leaking roofs, mildew, floods, sickness, even drownings—all these things I might have anticipated. What I wasn't prepared for was the forced inactivity that the monsoon brings with it.

"How can you stand just doing nothing?" I asked my husband as I got up from the hard wooden bed on which I had been sitting writing in my diary. I walked to the door of the outbuilding where we were staying and looked out into the compound. The rain was falling steadily, forming large pools in the mud. There was no one to be seen in the compound, which separated the main house of our hosts from the outbuilding, actually their old house, now used for storing grain, fertilizer, and equipment. Several school-age boys usually slept here; we had displaced them when we'd arrived in the village four days before.

Everyone was apparently inside. I looked for signs of activity in the main house opposite. Like the outbuilding, its walls were constructed out of "elephant grass," a material resembling thin bamboo, and plastered over with *māto*, a mixture of cow dung and mud. The walls and roof were supported by wood posts. The house was roofed with clay tiles, which only partially succeeded in keeping out the monsoon rains.

8

Arjun looked up from writing in his notebook. He was sitting at a small, wobbly wooden desk that had been made by the village carpenter. He had pushed the boys' school books to one side and was busy writing his field notes. The sturdy chair on which he was sitting had also been made by the carpenter. The bed, the table, and the chair were the only furniture in the room. Behind the door a couple of nails hammered through a piece of clear plastic provided somewhere for the boys to hang their clothes. Arjun seemed content, impervious to the rain even though the mud floor was becoming pitted in several places where the leaks in the roof had been dripping all morning.

"This is how it is here," he said. "People spend a lot of time doing nothing, especially now, during the monsoon. There's not very much work to be done. Everyone stays around the house, out of the rain."

As I stood restlessly at the door, a young woman darted out of the main house carrying a large cauldron full of uncooked rice (called *chāmal* in Nepali to distinguish it from cooked rice, *bhāt*, and from unharvested or unprocessed rice, *dhān*). Her name was Shanthi; she was the wife of the young Tharu university student, Surendra, who had worked as Arjun's research assistant when he'd first come to Pipariya. She had been born in a house scarcely a hundred meters from her husband's home. Their marriage two years earlier had been a "love marriage"; they had eloped. Shanthi was now about eighteen. Her face was broad and round, her nose small and flat. Above it heavy eyebrows arched across a wide forehead. Her hair was thick and black and when she let it down from the knot in which she usually wore it, it reached below her waist. Most of the time she wore a serious, almost severe expression, but when she laughed her eyes all but disappeared and her smile revealed straight white teeth. So far Shanthi had been too shy to speak to me. When I had approached her, she had run away giggling with her hand clamped over her mouth in embarrassment.

Shanthi wore a close-fitting blouse and a patterned tube of cloth, called a *lungi*. The tight sleeves of the blouse covered her arms to the elbows; the bodice, fastened with buttons down the front, ended several inches below her breasts, leaving her smooth, brown midriff bare. The *lungi*, which covered her from waist to her mid-calves was green and white with a pattern of diagonal shapes printed around the hem. She had pleated the excess cloth in the front and tucked it into a white underskirt. This was the typical dress of young Tharu women for work around the home. Older women wore a plain white cloth wrapped around the waist. In the old days, before the availability of Indian and Chinese printed cloth in the bazaars, white had been the color of dress for Tharu women, regardless of age.

At the *dhāra* I watched as Shanthi worked the pump handle on the tube well to fill the pot with water, shooing away the ducks that waddled over, craning their necks to try to get their bills into the pot. She bent over the rice and washed it by lifting handfuls of the grain and letting them run through her fingers. After washing the rice in this fashion, she would tip the cauldron and let the cloudy water run over the rocks placed around the *dhāra* for drainage. In this way she rinsed the rice three times, poured off the excess water a final time, and carried the rice back to the house. It was raining heavily; by the time Shanthi reached the house, the back of her blouse was soaked.

I remarked to Arjun that Shanthi seemed to do all the work in that house. I said I hardly ever saw her sisters-in-law, either Surendra's unmarried sister or the wife of Surendra's younger brother, going to the *dhāra* to prepare food. Arjun explained that it was Shanthi's turn to cook. The wives of the younger married sons in the household took turns, lasting two or three months, cooking for the large household, which included about twenty family members as well as servants and sometimes day laborers. Neither the wife of Surendra's eldest brother, Ram Bahadur, nor Surendra's mother nor his sister had a regular turn at cooking, although they helped with food preparation and would take over from one of the young wives if she were sick or unable to cook.

At about ten o'clock, presumably when the big cauldron of rice I had seen Shanthi washing had cooked, Surendra came to call us to eat.

Surendra was a dark, solidly built man of about twenty-eight with wavy black hair. He was in his third year at the local agricultural campus. He was always well groomed and neatly dressed. He had a quick wit and lively sense of humor and was a natural leader. He could speak four or five languages, including English. He had been Arjun's first contact in Pipariya, and Arjun still relied on his knowledge about Tharu culture and local politics although their formal relationship had ended the previous year, when Surendra had resumed his university studies.

"Arjun-sir," Surendra said, pushing open the door, "*khānā khānā jāung.*" (Let's go eat.) Out of respect for his educated foreigner status, Arjun was addressed by almost everyone as "sir." The same respect was accorded to the teachers at the local government school; the men were addressed by the whole village as "sir," the women were called "Madam" or "Miss" depending on whether they were married. I was also called "Madam," which, at least in the beginning, made me uncomfortable.

"We'll just wash our hands," Arjun told Surendra.

We dashed through the rain to the *dhāra*. We had forgotten the soap, so I went back to the room for it, leaping to avoid the deepest puddles. Arjun and I took turns washing our hands at the well while we pumped water for one another.

Surendra was waiting for us on the sheltered *wosarā*, or covered porch, of his house. Arjun had to duck slightly to get his five-foot-ten-inch frame through the door; at five-foot-six, I stepped over the threshold with no difficulty. The door led into a large room that formed the entrance to the house. Along one wall was a huge carved rectangular chest raised off the ground on blocks of wood. It measured about fifteen-by-four feet and was about five feet deep. It was used for storing some of the *dhān* kept for the family's own use. Access to the grain was afforded by a hatch in the top of the chest. The chest was also used for storing household implements, and some chickens appeared to be nesting there. At night, the family's dozen or so ducks were herded into a pen made of elephant grass just inside the entrance.

The kitchen, which ran about half the length of the main common room, was separated from it by a partition. The dividing wall was constructed, like the outside walls of the house, out of a frame of elephant grass structurally supported by vertical wood poles and plastered with *māto*. The roof was high, perhaps twenty-five feet at the apex, sloping to five or six feet where it met the outer walls. For religious reasons, as in most Tharu houses, the kitchen occupied the northeast corner of the house. Moving south, the next partitioned room was where Surendra's younger brother, his wife, and their two small children slept; then the room that Surendra shared with Shanthi; next, a big room occupied by the unmarried girls of the house. Surendra's mother, who had been widowed a few years before, slept on a bed outside this room. The *māto* partitions separating the rooms were six or seven feet high. They couldn't afford much privacy to the couples sleeping on the other side.

As usual, we were eating in Surendra's room. We took off our *chappals* (rubber thongs, or "flip-flops" as we call them in the United States)

Jimidār's house. Granary where we stayed is on the right

before entering. The mud plaster floor, which was smooth and patterned with swirling designs made by the heels of women's hands, felt cool and damp under my feet. I still hadn't overcome the feeling that it was somehow "dirty," being composed as it was primarily of cow dung.

Shanthi had spread a rough blanket on the floor for us to sit on. In front of the blanket she had set two *lotās* of water for us. *Lotās* are pewter or stainless steel vessels in which guests are served water. That must have meant another trip to the *dhāra* in the rain for her. Surendra seated himself opposite us on a low four-legged stool.

Shanthi brought two plates of rice. The plates, more like shallow pans, were made of stainless steel and had raised edges. They measured about twelve inches in diameter. The rice Shanthi had served me covered half this area.

"I can't eat this much," I said weakly to Surendra in my halting Nepali. I had to rehearse the simple sentence several times before I said it aloud.

"But that's not very much," Surendra said.

"I'm not used to eating so much rice," I explained. At home Arjun and I cooked about half this amount for ourselves.

"*Gohaurni*," Surendra yelled to Shanthi in the kitchen. Rather than calling them by their given names, Tharu husbands call their wives by the name of the village they come from. Since Shanthi had married a man from her own village, she was known as *Gohaurni*, a word apparently derived from the word for house or home, *ghar*. Women refer to their husbands as "the father of [their eldest child's name]." Tharus consider it inappropriate for married couples to address one another by their given names.

"*Kathhi?*" (What?) Shanthi yelled back.

"Take some of Madam's rice." Again that word. Madam. I squirmed but felt reluctant to broach the subject in my inadequate Nepali. I decided I would discuss the issue later with Arjun.

Shanthi reappeared with another plate onto which she removed some of my rice with her hands.

"So little rice fills you up?" she asked timidly.

"*Pugcha*," I said, which in the Nepali idiom means "it's enough."

Shanthi covered her mouth with the back of her hand at the boldness of her question and went back to the kitchen. Surendra laughed. "She's shy," he said.

Shanthi reentered the room carrying a bowl full of salty, spicy *tarkāri*. She served this onto our plates with her hands. We started eating, using our fingers.

Next Shanthi brought *sāg*. Cooked greens. Heavily salted and liberally spiced with chili peppers, the *sāg* had a mildly sudsy taste.

In spite of my protests over the quantity of rice I'd been given, I ate hungrily. Shanthi brought more rice. "*Pugcha*," I said again. I covered my plate with my hand to indicate that I had eaten enough. Both Arjun and Surendra took more rice.

"When are you going to Kathmandu?" Surendra asked Arjun. We had come to Pipariya on a sort of reconnaissance trip about a week after arriving in Kathmandu from Sri Lanka. Before we brought all our gear we wanted to see how much damage the monsoon had done to the road from the capital into the Chitwan Valley and how swollen the river was that we had to ford to get to the village.

"We're thinking of going on Saturday," Arjun said, adding, "if we can get bus tickets."

Saturday was three days away. I was looking forward to getting back to Kathmandu and having a hot shower in an enclosed bathroom, shielded from the curious gaze of Tharu children watching in fascination as I attempted to bathe like the other women in the village. I was also planning to visit some of Kathmandu's many book shops to stock up on reading material for our stay in the village. Without anything to read, I was beginning to think I'd go crazy. More than anything I was just looking forward to being alone with Arjun, not having to interact with people at every moment of the day. I liked our hosts in Pipariya very much; they had been kind and welcoming to me and I could see that they were fond of my husband, but it was just too much for me. I was feeling overwhelmed and wanted a break from the village, even if it was only for a couple of days.

"When will you come back?" Surendra asked. "As soon as we get our things, we'll return," Arjun said.

"If you tell us what day you're coming, my *dāi* will send the oxcart to meet you in the bazaar." Surendra's *dāi* was his elder brother Ram Bahadur, who had the same father but a different mother. Fifteen or twenty years older than Surendra, with four children, Ram Bahadur was the head of the household, the *ghar mukhyā*. He was also the *jimidār*, the largest landowner in the village and an important figure in local politics.

"Can the oxen cross the river now?" I asked. There was no bridge. It had been dismantled before the onslaught of the monsoon. The materials would be stored until the river had subsided again in December or January. Then the villagers who lived near the fording place would rebuild the footbridge. We had been ferried across the river on our first trip to the village in a narrow, high-gunnelled canoe.

"Oh, yes, they can make it," Surendra said, although he told us that someone from the next village—Arjun seemed to recognize the man's name—had lost his oxen crossing the river the week before. They had been swept off their feet and out of their harnesses by the current and drowned.

The early morning sounds of the household coming to life intruded on my sleep long before I actually woke up. In the cowshed next to our room, the cows, oxen, water buffaloes and goats began stirring before dawn. Shortly thereafter, I was aware of low human sounds of exhortation and cajoling as one of the boys took the larger animals out to graze in a clearing near the jungle. Through my somnolence I could hear other voices, talking, calling to one another, laughing, even singing. And then it seemed that all the roosters of the village were crowing at once.

As I gradually awakened, my senses focused on some activity that was taking place outside our room. Lying on my side, I caught a glimpse of bright colors flashing across the gaps around the door. I heard female voices, sometimes hushed and secretive, then suddenly loud and boisterous as several girls teased one another. They seemed to be moving in a circle. The colors of their *lungis* rotating across my peephole created a kaleidoscope effect. I heard a steady squelching sound as they paced round and round.

I got up, went to the door, and peered through the crack. Bhagavati, Sita, and Bikramiya were mixing *māto* with their feet. Their *lungis* hitched up above the knee, the three girls were following one another around as they trod a circle in a five-foot-wide mound of mud and cow dung. An older woman who worked as a servant for Ram Bahadur periodically dumped a new load of dung, which she carried in a shallow wooden basin balanced on her head. Shanthi worked filling urns with water at the tube well and pouring them into the mixture.

I padded back to the bed and sat down next to Arjun who was still lying on his back. Neither of us had slept very well. The bed was narrow and hard. It had been hot, and we were bothered by mosquitoes. I found the mosquitoes here particularly disturbing because of the possibility that they carried malaria. Until the area had been sprayed with DDT as part of a USAID malaria eradication campaign in the 1960s, Chitwan had been known as a "malarial jungle" and was avoided for that reason by outsiders, especially during the monsoon. The Tharus had been the main population living throughout the Tarai before the antimalaria program. Although the disease was under control, there were still occasional cases.

"They seem to be mixing up some mud plaster," I told Arjun.

"Maybe it's to do the floor of our house," he said.

This possibility hadn't occurred to me. "Do you think I should go help?" I asked Arjun somewhat anxiously.

"Sure," was my husband's sleepy answer.

"I mean, do you think they would like it if I did, or would it embarrass them?" I asked, recalling Shanthi's shyness the day before.

"I think they'd be delighted if you went to help," Arjun said, rolling over and propping himself up on his elbow.

I got dressed. I had slept in a T-shirt and slip. Over this I pulled on a below-the-knee skirt. I felt nervous about joining the young women outside in mixing the *māto*. When we had discussed what I would do when I came back with Arjun to the village, I had said I would like to participate in the work of women in the village as much as possible. I thought this would make it easier for me to be accepted as a member of the community. This seemed to be the perfect opportunity to jump in—so to speak—to involve myself in something that would afford me contact with women close to my own age. Now I was not so certain. What if I somehow offended them or if I were interfering by intruding where I wasn't wanted? And what really was the point of my stomping around in cow shit anyway? Maybe they would just think that I had something to prove, which in a sense, perhaps I did.

Unsure of my decision to join in the activity taking place outside our door, I asked Arjun for reassurance: "Are you sure they won't mind?" "What will they think of me?" "How will they react?" I went to the door again to look out.

"Don't worry about it so much," said Arjun. "It's not such a big deal. If you want to do it, fine; if not, no one's going to expect you to."

"Well, here goes," I said, aware that I was, as Arjun said, exaggerating out of proportion the question of whether to help with the *māto*.

I swung open the door and walked out into the compound. Bhagavati looked up and smiled.

"*Namaste*," I said. Except in tourist intercourse where it has acquired the same devalued currency as *aloha* in Hawaii, this Nepali greeting meaning, literally, "I bow to the god in you," was used sparingly by Nepalese in their everyday dealings with one another. I had already noticed that our frequent use of the greeting was regarded by people in Pipariya with amusement. Nonetheless, Surendra's sister Bhagavati responded easily, "*Namaste*."

I stood on our *wosarā* watching them lift their bare feet out of the muck and put them down again. Then I stepped down into the yard. "*Ma pani garchu*," I announced. (I'm also going to do this.)

The two younger girls giggled. Both were servants in the house. Sita was the daughter of a landless family living near the school. She did work around the house and agricultural labor as the season and needs of the household required. She was a *bahāriyā* servant, which meant that in return for her labor she was fed, housed, and given some clothes and spending money by Ram Bahadur. Her family received about 200 kilograms of rice a year from the *jimidār* in return for her labor. Other members of her family also worked for him at various times, such as during the harvest. Sita was a well-built seventeen- or eighteen-year old with a ready smile and a mischievous sense of humor. She seemed to get along well with the older girls in the family, and they gossiped and teased one another. The younger servant, Bikramiya, was also Bhagavati's "sister" since her father was Bhagavati's maternal uncle. Their family occupied a small hut next to Ram Bahadur's house. Both Bikramiya and Sita regularly slept with the other unmarried girls of the family in the big house.

"Don't do this," said Bhagavati, using the polite negative command form of the verb. "You'll get dirty."

"I want to learn," I said.

The girls continued stomping around in the mud. It had the consistency of wet clay.

I stood outside the circle of activity for a moment wondering how strongly Bhagavati intended to discourage me from joining in.

I stepped into the pile. The girls looked a little startled but kept lifting their feet and putting them down. The mud was slippery. I felt it ooze between my toes as my feet penetrated to the bottom of the mound. But it was not as smooth as I had expected. I felt the coarse abrasion of grass and small sticks against my feet and shins.

"What are you going to use this for?" I asked.

"We will make your floor today."

When Arjun had lived here on his own, he had slept in a hut in the middle of one of Ram Bahadur's fields. That hut had been built for one of Surendra's brothers to stay in while he kept an eye on an adjacent chicken coop. In April, when ferocious hot winds blow across the Tarai, the roof had looked like it might blow off so Arjun moved into an outbuilding belonging to Indra Prasad's house which was located in the same compound where we were now staying. Indra Prasad was Ram Bahadur's cousin; their fathers had been brothers. Ram Bahadur had promised he would have a house near his own built for us to live in by the time Arjun returned from spending the summer in the United States. Before leaving, Arjun had paid for the large supporting timbers. The labor to build the house had been provided free by Ram Bahadur's servants. As soon as we arrived in the village we'd been taken to inspect our unfinished quarters.

Our hut occupied the northeast corner of a large vegetable garden behind Ram Bahadur's house. It was about twelve by fifteen feet, with a partition dividing a sleeping room from a cooking area. The roof was thatched with rice straw. It had the same construction as other houses around us, but unlike most Tharu houses which have only slits for windows, the front room of our house had one three-foot square window meshed with chicken wire. The somewhat eclectic design of our house had caused one passerby to stop and ask: "Is it a Tharu house or is it a tourist hotel?" A pumpkin vine was blossoming prodigiously on the roof. Others in the village had expressed misgivings about the location of the hut because it was built in what was well known to be the path of a ghost. Arjun jokingly dismissed the concern about a ghost passing through our hut. He said that if the ghost showed up, he would interview it. People laughed at that, but I noticed the topic kept coming up.

The floor of the house consisted of dirt that had been shoveled from a nearby ditch and packed down with straw to create a foundation. The floor was uneven, plants were pushing up through the moist earth, and the tunneling of big worms was everywhere. The floor had yet to be given its finishing layers of straw and *māto*.

The girls had just about finished the mixing of the mud by the time I joined in. One by one they stepped out of the stuff. I followed them to the *dhāra* where I was told to wash my legs first. Bhagavati pumped water for me as I held each of my legs under the tap and rubbed with my hands. Then the others took turns rinsing the mud off their legs.

We then went to inspect the house. Bikramiya had brought what looked like a trowel with her. She used it to flatten out the surface of the hard-packed floor, scraping off uneven built-up parts and depositing the surplus in depressions, and to tamp down loose earth in other places. I asked if I could try this. Bikramiya handed me the trowel, and I set to work leveling the surface of our floor.

As I worked with the trowel, Bhagavati and Bikramiya brought armfuls of rice straw. These they spread over the leveled earthen floor. The straw was sweet smelling and pleasantly springy under the feet. I wondered where they were able to keep it dry.

The older servant, whose husband also worked for Ram Bahadur as a *bahāriyā*, brought the first load of *māto*—in a metal pan balanced on a thick woven halo of straw on her head—and dumped it with a plop in the far corner at the back of the house. Sita and Bhagavati knelt down to start spreading the *māto* with their hands. Exerting pressure with the outer finger of the right hand, they spread the *māto*, creating semicircular patterns. The wet floor had a finish like rough unset cement. Watching the deft movements of Bhagavati's large strong hands, I scooped a handful of the stuff and spread it along the north wall. As the dung mixture first touched my hand I felt a shudder of revulsion. It passed in a second, just as the sensation of cold when one first dives into a pool disappears after swimming a few strokes. My companions paid me no special attention, but after a while some other women, including Surendra's mother, came to watch the *videshi* (foreigner) at work.

The Nepalese anthropologist D. P. Rajaure, writing about the Tharu women of Dang, states that *gobar* (cow manure) is regarded by the Tharus as a cleansing and purifying substance. While this may be true in a ritual sense, I noticed that when the stuff fell on their hair or got on their bangles, the girls made a sound of distaste: "*chik!*" Much later I overheard a Brahmin guide explaining to tourists he was leading through Pipariya on a "village walk" that the Tharus used cow manure to make their houses because it came from a holy animal. When I translated his English words for Bhagavati, with whom I was sitting at the time, she hooted with laughter. "The guides tell foreigners many untrue things," she said. It was not untrue that the cow was regarded as a holy animal. During the Tharu festival of Soharāyi, Bhagavati would garland the family's cow and her elder brother would perform a *pūjā* (worship) to it. The problem was with the guide's ascribing a symbolic explanation to a practical matter. Tharus used cow manure to make their houses because it was there; it worked and that was what had always been used. At least that's how I interpreted her response.

Bhagavati and Sita worked quickly and skillfully; they seemed to be well coordinated with one another. My solitary progress spreading *māto* against the north wall was slow and halting. I was also self-conscious about what I was doing, especially as my audience expanded. Arjun, too, showed up to observe. I called to him to join us. He replied that he would like to, but people would laugh to see a man doing this kind of work. A convenient excuse, I thought! Arjun is much more fastidious than I am.

After finishing the floor inside the house and on the *wosarā*, Bhagavati brought the chair from our room. She placed it against an outside wall of the house and climbed on top of it. Bikramiya and the older servant continued bringing *māto* in metal bowls and buckets.

I scooped up as much *māto* in my right hand as I could and handed it up to Bhagavati, who, with an adroit flick of her slender wrist, slapped it onto the wall of the house and spread it evenly to create a seamless plaster over the elephant grass.

We had finished two walls in this fashion when Geeta came to call me to eat.

"Have you eaten yet?" I asked Bhagavati, whose chair was balanced precariously against the western wall.

"We'll eat later," Bhagavati said. "You go eat." She also told me to wash my hands carefully with soap first. This advice I took seriously. I regretted that my fingernails were so long; the *māto* wedged under my nails was starting to burn the sensitive skin, and scrape away as I might, I couldn't loosen all the dirt.

After eating, Arjun and I returned to inspect the morning's work. Surendra accompanied us. We couldn't go inside because the floor was still wet. We walked around the outside admiring the work.

"How long do you think it will take for it to dry so we can move in?" Arjun asked Surendra.

"It depends on the weather. Maybe a week, if we don't have too much rain. When you come back from Kathmandu, *holā*." *Holā*. The Nepali subjunctive: most easily translated as "perhaps," but more pervasive and tenuous than the meaning conveyed by any English word. I came to rely on this word a lot, but it took me a while to understand and accept the uncertainty and impossibility of predicting events or making plans that *holā* expressed.

Indra Prasad's youngest sister, Sarasvati, stood tentatively at the door looking in at Arjun and me as we sat on the bed writing.

"Didi calls you," she said. I didn't catch the words but I understood that she expected me to go with her. "Menaka has invited you to go and visit," Arjun translated for me. Menaka was Sarasvati's eldest sister who was visiting from her husband's home in the far eastern Tarai. Menaka had returned to her *maiti* (natal home) to take part in an important religious festival for women, the Jithiyā Pāvani.

I stood up and smiled. In reality I was reluctant to leave my diary to go and sit with Menaka and her sisters for possibly several hours with nothing to do. Menaka was very nice; everyone was very nice, but I still couldn't understand most of what they said to me, and I felt self-conscious under the inspection of the whole household. I put down my pen and followed Sarasvati to the other house. I wished I had brought my knitting from Kathmandu so I would have something to occupy my hands.

As we walked around the cow shelter separating the outbuilding where we were staying from Indra Prasad's house and came into Menaka's view, she greeted me enthusiastically.

"*Basnus*," Menaka said, indicating a wooden chair under the eaves of Indra Prasad's outbuilding where she, her other sister Mangala, and their nephews were taking shelter. The rain hadn't let up since morning.

I sat where I was instructed. Sarasvati settled herself on the *gundri* with the others. A few minutes later, Menaka's sister-in-law, called Baghaurni because she came from the village of Baghauda, brought me a battered metal tumbler half full of milkless tea.

I took the lukewarm tea from Baghaurni and smiled in what I hoped was a grateful way. Arjun had told me that it was not customary to thank one's hosts when given food in Tharu houses.

Baghaurni had turned around and gone back in the house, located across another compound from the shelter where we were sitting.

"How are things?" I said to Menaka, not being able to think of anything else.

"Fine," she said. "What were you doing in there?" She nodded toward the room where Arjun and I were staying. Another indication of the curiosity our presence in the village excited.

"I was writing," I said.

"A letter?" she asked.

"No . . . " I said and wondered how to explain a diary. "A sort of letter to myself," I said.

Menaka didn't seem interested in the letter to myself. She was whispering something to the girl who had met us on our way to Pipariya the first day and carried my bag, to my acute embarrassment. It had been very heavy. Menaka gave her a light push from behind and gave her the Tharu command *jau* (go). I was struck by the authority and seeming abruptness with which Menaka gave the order and the alacrity with which the young girl sprang up and ran into the house. She returned a few minutes later with two plates of popped corn. Menaka directed that one plate be given to me. The other plate was set in front of her on the *gundri*.

I stood up from the chair and moved toward the *gundri*. Menaka made room for me. "*Basnus,*" she said again. I sat down cross-legged on the mat and for a moment there was the speechless crunching of popcorn.

"What is the Nepali word for this?" I asked.

"*Makāi.*" Then Menaka told me the Tharu word, which I promptly forgot. "You must learn Tharu also," she said. "We'll teach you." I smiled and said I would like to learn Tharu, but I thought it would be confusing to try to learn two languages at the same time and I was going to concentrate on learning Nepali well first. In Nepali I could make myself understood among most Tharus. The younger generation of Tharus spoke both languages; only some old people spoke no Nepali and with Nepal's lingua franca, I would be able to make myself understood in other parts of the country as well.

When we had finished the plates of *makāi,* the girls picked up their fans again. "Are you hot?" Geeta asked me. "Yes," I said. It was a hot, sticky day. She began fanning me. I found this even more embarrassing than being given food. "Here, my turn," I said after a while.

The fans were ingeniously designed. A square of woven straw and cloth was anchored to a stick which fitted inside a hollow tube of elephant grass. With a gyrating action of the wrist, the person holding the fan could create a refreshing air movement as the fabric-covered straw rotated around the handle.

The fans were beautifully decorated with different colored fabric, yarn, and elephant grass. Geeta had sent me such a fan with Arjun when he'd returned to the United States the previous June.

"Here, look at this one," Mangala said. "Do you know what this is?" She pointed at the blue ruffle around the edge of the fan. I looked at it closely. It did look rather familiar. The girls were laughing at me.

"It's Arjun's *lungi,*" I finally blurted out. The girls hooted with laughter at my exaggerated surprise at recognizing one of Arjun's old pieces of clothing, a tube of cloth worn by men all over South Asia. It must have become so worn out that he'd left it behind when he returned to the United States during the summer, and Mangala had used it to decorate this fan.

Suddenly, Menaka started twirling her fan wildly. Her animated face brightened and she narrowed her eyes. "*Chik!*" she said. Indra Prasad's youngest son, Binod Kumar, aged 7, fixed his eyes on the *gundri* and squirmed in embarrassment. His three young aunts laughed at him. I smiled too.

A mischievous thought occurred to me. "What do you call that?" I asked, straight-faced.

My question was received with peals of laughter by all present except Binod Kumar, who looked even more ashamed.

I repeated my question. "In Nepali, what do you call this?" I compressed my lips and expelled some air in an audible—and quite authentic sounding, I thought—simulation of flatulence. Again, there were peals of delighted laughter. Menaka was laughing so hard tears appeared in her eyes. When she had composed herself sufficiently, Menaka told me the Nepali and Tharu words for fart.

I repeated both words solemnly for effect. I was not disappointed. My pronunciation of the Tharu word *padalé* was appreciated with more laughter. Periodically, Menaka would cover her face with the end of her sari and hoot, "*Padalé*, hee, hee."

After the *padalé* incident, I felt more relaxed and the conversation seemed to flow more easily. I found I could understand Menaka better than I could anyone else. She usually prefaced her comments to me with *tapain*, the respectful form of "you," and spoke in a loud clear voice in simple Nepali. She also knew quite a few English words.

The others continued to address me as "madam." I decided to broach the subject of what I should be called with Menaka.

"I don't like being called 'madam'," I told her.

Menaka nodded understandingly.

"I will call you *bhāuju*," she announced after a moment of consideration.

"*Bhāuju, bhāuju*," I repeated to myself so that I would be able to remember the word and could ask Arjun what it meant later.

"What should I call you?" I asked Menaka.

"You may call me *didi*," she said. That one I knew: *Didi* means older sister. I wondered how old Menaka was. I had assumed she was about my age, 28, possibly younger, but it didn't matter.

Geeta, who was studying English for the School Leaving Certificate, asked if she could call me by the English word *aunty*. I said that would be fine.

Later, Arjun told me that *bhāuju* means sister-in-law, older brother's wife, a close kinship relation for Tharus. I also came to be called "Srilankini," which amused me. The only association I have to Sri Lanka was through marriage. But this was of course the point.

"How is it that you and your husband married?" Menaka asked.

"Since your country is America and his is Sri Lanka?" The silence in which my answer was awaited indicated to me that it was a topic of general interest. I tried to give as many details as my limited Nepali would allow. I explained that Arjun had come to the United States to study and that we had met at the university where we were both students, and that later we had been married.

"Love marriage?" asked Menaka. The English word *love* is widely used in Nepal to distinguish matches contracted by individuals as opposed to alliances "arranged" by their families. I nodded.

I later found out that Menaka's marriage was also a "love marriage." It was her second marriage. Her first had been an arranged one with a boy in another part of Chitwan. Menaka had been unhappy with this first husband and after two years had returned to her natal home to live. Atypically, Menaka had continued studying at the local university campus even after her marriage. Her father had been furious when she eloped with her second husband and had forbidden her to come home again. Sometime after her second marriage, however, Surendra had engineered a partial reconciliation between Menaka and her father. He told Arjun how he had brought this about.

Surendra had smuggled Menaka into his house, without the knowledge of her father. She stayed in a room occupied at that time by small boys and he'd brought her food. She left the house only at night. One day Surendra noticed his uncle looking at her photo, which still hangs on the *wosarā* of their house. It is a sepia-tone portrait of Menaka and a friend of hers taken while they were students at the local campus. Surendra asked his uncle what he was looking at. His uncle responded that he was thinking he'd like to see his daughter again.

"That's not a problem," Surendra had said. "Come with me." He led his puzzled uncle to the room where Menaka was staying. When he saw her, her father became angry again and turned and walked out of the room without speaking to her. But after that day, Menaka was free to visit her family, although her father still would not speak to her and seemed not to acknowledge her presence. When Sarasvati married in 1998, however, both Menaka and her husband were invited to the wedding, signaling a reconciliation.

Menaka was the first Tharu girl to pass the national School Leaving Certificate exam in Chitwan. Only a handful of Tharus pass this exam each year. Tharus are underrepresented at all levels of education, which has traditionally not been valued as it has been by groups such as the Brahmins. The School Leaving Certificate, or SLC, is the basic credential necessary for entry into clerical jobs and university education in Nepal. Menaka had received the highest marks of any Tharu in her year, a fact she relayed to me with some satisfaction, and which had provoked some resentment and envy among the boys she'd outdone. One of them, she told me, still wouldn't talk to her.

Menaka was so quick-witted that I often felt dull in her company. She had mastered the language spoken by Tharus in her husband's district, which was different from Chitwan Tharu, within six months. But she was patient and spent long hours trying to communicate with me in spite of my inadequate Nepali and her limited English. Menaka's education set her apart, gave her special privileges, and, I later suspected, secret agonies. In any case, I was pleased that she genuinely seemed to enjoy spending time with me and sad to see her return to her husband about a month after we arrived in Pipariya.

Another reason I felt such an affinity with Menaka was that both of us were in a significant way out of sync with Tharu women our age (late 20s): We were both childless. On that first day, sitting on the *wosarā* watching the rain and crunching popcorn, more to make conversation than because I was really interested, I asked Menaka whether she had any children. I regretted the question immediately. Her normally open, animated face became clouded and preoccupied. She launched into a long explanation of how she had become very sick while studying in Kathmandu. I understood that she'd been in the hospital and had undergone surgery. She patted her belly and said *"banda cha"* (it's closed). I thought maybe she'd had a hysterectomy, but perhaps I'd misunderstood. Maybe she just attributed her difficulty in conceiving to her illness and operation. It seemed too delicate a topic to pursue.

I assumed that Menaka wanted children. Her distress at my question about children seemed to indicate this, although in a child-oriented society it could simply reflect the difficult social position a childless woman finds herself in. Certainly, life in her husband's household could become unpleasant for her if she had no children. Her husband might take another wife. Even if he were resigned to not having any, her in-laws might still criticize and resent her. My assumption that Menaka would want children was not based on her particular case. I lacked sufficient knowledge of that. It was based on stereotypes about Nepalese culture and values that I had formed even before I arrived.

I soon realized, with a surprise born of arrogance, that I was not the only one who was employing stereotypes to interpret the unfamiliar. While I possessed a store of unexamined ideas about "traditional" women in Hindu village society, I had assumed that I appeared in their midst as a unique being, an outsider free to shape my own identity. I discovered, however, that they had notions about me as well. They had observed other members of my *jāt* (caste, kind) and had drawn their own conclusions. I didn't like some of them very much.

One of my most recent predecessors in the area had been a young American woman who had lived for some time in Sauraha, a village adjacent to the National Park. How this woman originally came to Sauraha I don't know, probably as a tourist, since Sauraha is full of budget lodges for visitors who want to see the Park. Nor was I sure how long she had stayed, though it must have been several months, to enable her to learn some Tharu. The fact that she could communicate in Tharu was one aspect of the Amerikani's fame. The other, more compelling detail about her was that she had taken a Tharu lover and lived with him in Sauraha.

At first I thought that Menaka, Mangala, and Geeta were just interested in finding out if I knew the Amerikani, which was how Menaka phrased her first question on the subject. Later I decided that their reasons for telling me about her were more complex. First of all, it was clear that the subject greatly interested them. All three contributed details to the story, although, as usual, it was Menaka who took the lead.

I didn't catch the whole story the first time I heard it. I later pieced together more details that other people told me. I'm still not sure I know exactly what happened but my image of the Amerikani began to take shape that afternoon. I realized quickly that whatever the Amerikani represented to the Tharus, I also represented. At the time I felt it was an identity I wanted to distance myself from.

The Amerikani was a sexual as well as cultural adventuress. During her sojourn in the area she not only adopted Tharu dress but also "married" a Tharu. She had professed a love for Tharu food (I doubted her sincerity on this matter) and had learned to speak Tharu quite well according to Menaka. Later, someone else showed me a photograph of the Amerikani, dressed like a Tharuni in blouse and *lungi*, standing with a couple of local men outside a tourist hotel. She had long brown hair and a nice figure, which was shown off to advantage in the Tharu clothes. In the photo she is smiling expansively, in contrast to her Tharu companions who are customarily somber for the camera. She looks happy and well adjusted. As I struggled to understand what Menaka and the others were telling me, I was jealous of the admiration that the Amerikani's linguistic skills and other attributes seemed to have won.

The Amerikani's lover had a Tharu wife. I don't know what happened to her; she probably remained at home with his family, more or less aware of what was going on, but with little power to do anything about it. It was not uncommon for men working in the tourist lodges to engage in sex with foreign women tourists; I had met several tourist guides who were open (and boastful) about their exploits with foreign women. What was unusual about the Amerikani was her eagerness, at least for a time, to embrace other aspects of Tharu life. This is what made her example accessible to the people who told me about her. And what posed her as a challenge for me.

The Amerikani eventually went back to the United States; Colorado, I think. Her Tharu lover followed her there. When he arrived, he found his Amerikani living with another man. According to one version of the story, there was a fight and he returned to Nepal. Someone else told me he had visited "just as a friend." Like Surendra's story of hiding Menaka from her father, it raised a lot of questions. Had the Amerikani intended her lover to follow her? Had she helped him to obtain a visa? How did he find her in Colorado? But none of these questions was relevant to the point the girls were making by telling me this story.

"*Kasto lagyo?*" "How does it strike you?" asked Menaka when she'd finished telling the story.

My three informants waited for my reaction to their story. I found myself wondering what they wanted me to say. How did it strike me? There was apparently a moral to the story then? What was it? What would they expect me to think of the Amerikani? My real feelings were mixed. As I sat struggling to comprehend my hosts' Nepali and feeling at odds with my surroundings, I felt a slight jealous admiration for the Amerikani's ability to speak Tharu and her apparent adaptation to life there. At the same time I was disturbed by her interference in her lover's life. She seemed a dangerous model for an anthropologist's wife. On these grounds, I thought I had better reject her. I felt a need to present myself as someone trustworthy, someone whose values corresponded to what I assumed theirs to be. The values I assumed for them were "traditional" ones, not that I knew much about Tharu traditions, or even American ones for that matter. Instead, I posited for them some conservative notions about sex, about the appropriate roles and demeanor of women in their relations with men. These values were "traditional" only in contrast to my "modern" ones, again an unexamined category, but one which I felt encompassed a more open-minded and value-neutral view of sexual relations and a more egalitarian view of women's role in society than I attributed to them.

"I don't think it's good," I said. "He already had a wife and she had another boyfriend in America."

Menaka did not disagree with me, but she was grinning and her eyes sparkled with mischief. Perhaps she saw through my mock disapproval. I got the feeling that their official censure of the Amerikani's actions was tinged with admiration for her adventurousness and power. As time went on, I learned to question my original assumptions about what the Amerikani meant to the tellers of her legend, as well as her meaning for me.

That night there was a terrible storm. It had started raining in the afternoon, but it began to pour after dark. There was thunder and lightning for most of the night. We thought we had located the bed in such a way as to avoid the leaky spots in the roof. Under the assault of the lashing wind and rain, however, new leaks developed. We realized there was not a dry area in the room large enough to avoid all the drips. We huddled together on the bed, shifting as new patterns of leaks formed. It was impossible to sleep; we lay awake most of the night listening to the raging storm. In the early morning I heard a commotion from Surendra's house; I surmised that they too were unable to sleep because of water leaking through their roof. I finally fell into a fitful doze just after dawn. I woke up completely, however, when an excited Ram Bahadur barged into our room to tell us that there was a huge flood and that the village shrine was surrounded by water. He asked Arjun to bring the camera to take photos of the damage.

Ram Bahadur's house and the houses immediately surrounding it on both sides of the road were located on the most elevated piece of

land in the village. Even so, there were several inches of water standing in Ram Bahadur's yard when I opened the door and looked out.

The rain was still falling steadily. Equipped with an umbrella that
Bhagavati handed to me, we followed Ram Bahadur as he waded
through the yard and climbed up onto the road, which though muddy,
was above water. We walked east along the road, joining a throng of
people on their way to survey the damage.

One of the first people who hailed us was someone whom Arjun
and I referred to as the "man-whose-wife-beats-him." He was a gentle
man in his forties. One of his eyes was opaque with cataract and the
disease was beginning in the other eye as well. During Arjun's first
week in Pipariya the previous year, he had met this man, whose name
was Chandra Lal Chaudhary, while observing a *pūjā* at the *Bramathān*,
the main village shrine to the local Tharu gods, located under a majestic Red Silk Cotton tree. After inquiring where Arjun was from and
what he was doing in the village, Chandra Lal had asked Arjun if his
wife beat him. "No," said Arjun, somewhat taken aback. "At least, she
hasn't yet." "My wife beats me," Chandra Lal had told Arjun sorrow-
fully. He related how he had gone off to Kathmandu neglecting his
fields. When he'd returned from the city, his wife had set to and beaten
him with a stick.

Arjun asked Chandra Lal if his fields, which lay beyond the *Bramathān*, had suffered damage in the rain.

"That's what I'm going to see," he replied.

Just beyond the group of houses where Ram Bahadur's compound
was located, the road dipped down into a shallow depression and disappeared under several feet of water. A line of mud huts there were
flooded. Their occupants waded waist deep through water to get to the
road, carrying their belongings on their heads. As we walked a few feet
into the water to get a better view of the damage, a green-yellow snake,
about a foot long, swam in front of me. Further up the road we could
see that the base of the *Bramathān* was several feet under water. Across
the road from the *Bramathān*, Ram Bahadur's fields looked like a
swamp, with the tips of the rice plants barely visible above the water.

Ram Bahadur suggested that we take some photos of the destroyed
houses and the flooded fields. I felt uncomfortable taking photographs
of what was clearly a disaster for the people fleeing with a few sodden
belongings from their inundated houses. But disastrous as it was, Ram

Bahadur considered the flood a major event in the life of the village and he was anxious to have a record of it. He speculated that it was the biggest flood in twenty years.

The villagers who had gathered on the road to survey the damage were talking excitedly. They looked around at their transformed surroundings with astonishment. Those wading out of the ruins of their houses were silent. By and large they looked solemn, or perhaps they were in shock. Now and then someone would break into a brief smile, apparently in response to a comment from a bystander. There seemed to be no sense of panic, and certainly no railing against fate.

"Well, looks like we're not going to Kathmandu today," Arjun said as we returned to the house. "It must have been raining hard in the hills, too, for it to flood so badly here. The road to Kathmandu is probably washed out."

"How can we find out?" I asked. It hadn't occurred to me that the flood might mean we would be stranded in Pipariya. I realized that despite the evidence surrounding me to the contrary, I had persisted in my American assumption of human mastery over nature. We listened to *Radio Nepal* in the evening. The news bulletin began as usual with details of King Birendra's activities for the day. There was no mention of the flood.

In spite of the upset and turmoil all around us, the household routine seemed to go on as usual, at least in regard to the women's work. Shanthi was up early making innumerable trips to the *dhāra* to prepare the first meal of the day. While I ate with Bhagavati and Sita, Arjun went off to survey the damage to the other end of the village, by the school. We'd heard flooding there was even more severe, that the flood waters had coursed like a temporary river toward the Rapti a couple of kilometers to the west.

After we'd eaten, Menaka, Mangala, and several girls from the next house came by on their way to the school. Since everyone was going, except Shanthi who had to stay behind to cook, I accepted their invitation to go along.

There was so much water standing everywhere that we abandoned our *chappals*. I'd noticed that many people went around barefoot much of the time anyway. My feet were not as tough as those of my companions, and our progress along the graveled mud road was painful for me. Noticing my stooped and halting gait and perhaps the look of pained concentration on my face as I felt my way through the shallow puddles, Menaka grabbed hold of my arm. "You're not used to walking without shoes, *hola*," she said. I readily agreed that this was the case.

There were about fifteen people in our entourage, including several small children from both households. As we walked along the road, the older girls in our group exchanged greetings and comments on the flood with people we met. At first it seemed to me that people were viewing the flood as a form of entertainment: a mere spectacle. I was shocked by the damage I saw about me: houses totally or partially destroyed, wet and weary people dragging reluctant, frightened-looking cattle and oxen along the road. Only later did I realize that it was precisely peoples' shock and need for reassurance that led them to congregate, to greet one another in the everyday way and even to laugh together in their common adversity. In times of trouble they sought solace in the familiarity of their life-long neighbors and the normal patterns of interaction.

Along the road, in the opposite direction from the way Arjun and I had gone with Ram Bahadur earlier in the morning, the paddy fields on both sides were under three or four feet of water.

For the most part, the houses in our part of Pipariya had escaped significant damage. Similarly, the houses in the center of the village around the tea shop seemed more or less intact though several of the lower ones had accumulated a few inches of water inside. However, at the point where the road through Pipariya met the main road, it disappeared under water again. The dilapidated lean-to that served as the village tea shop was flooded. The old brick building housing Indrani's family planning clinic, the post office, the newly built Nepali Congress office, and the school were all cut off. The houses along this stretch of the road were partly flooded, too.

The playing field that ran along the road between this building and the school was transformed into a swamp. Only the main school building, built of brick on a concrete foundation, was above the level of the water.

At the pump in the schoolyard, which also served several houses across the road, a little girl stood in water up to her knees. She was pumping water into a metal bucket hanging from a hook on the pump's nozzle.

Beyond the school, Pipariya ended and the next village began. This was where the flood had caused the greatest damage I had yet seen. The flood waters flowed through the fields and across the road in this area like a river, flattening paddy in its path. We stopped to watch people carrying belongings and leading animals out of the water. All the houses along this stretch of the road had been damaged. The mud of the houses that were still standing seemed to grow directly out of the ground on which they were built, giving a melting effect. Earth floors and walls had been washed away. Here and there, the few damp pitiful belongings of the occupants had been brought outside, perhaps in the hope of drying them out: a battered tin box, some old bottles, bundles of clothes, and wet blankets. Over the front door of one of the houses was a collection of family photographs enclosed in a cheap wood frame. Though badly battered and hanging askew, it hung intact.

"Aye, *Bhagwān!*" Menaka repeated over and over as she looked at the destruction of houses.

One man had lost five water buffaloes (each worth over 10,000 rupees), which had been sheltered on the ground floor of his two-story house. The upper story had collapsed, trapping and drowning the buffaloes. Standing knee-deep in water, we looked through the debris of the house. Pressed against a wall, the rump of one dead animal rose out of the water. Beyond it I spied a solitary hoof.

The flood had claimed the lives of two people in our area. Arjun told me later about visiting the house where the body of one of them was laid out, wrapped in a blanket on the *wosarā*. He was a young Tamang man from the hills who was working in one of the hotels near the park. According to someone there, it would be necessary to get a *lāmā*, a Buddhist monk, down from the hills to perform the funeral rites.

A little further on we stood on the banks of what was usually a small stream that flowed into the Rapti. We looked on as a river rushed by, carrying the debris of the storm in its swift current. The bloated carcass of another dead buffalo floated by, resembling a huge black tortoise as it bobbed downstream.

On the other side of the flooded paddy fields, a cluster of about fifteen houses was completely cut off. We could see people sitting on their roofs. "They should have left those houses this morning," someone said. "They should send the elephants from the park to rescue them," said someone else. In the end, this was what happened. We stayed and watched as three elephants from the nearby National Park came trotting along the road and waded sedately back and forth through the fields ferrying the stranded people to safety. The elephants carried five or six people at a time. Upon reaching dry ground, they knelt down and the wet, tired-looking passengers clambered off. They appeared to be as terrified of the big beasts as they had been of the flood waters as they clung to the roofs of their houses. Most of the evacuees were soaked to the skin and had come away from their houses without anything. A few clutched bags or armfuls of clothes.

Having deposited another group of bedraggled people onto dry ground, the *mahuts*, sheltered by umbrellas, gave the command for the elephants to get up. Rubbing them behind the ears with their bare feet, they urged the huge animals back into the water for another load.

I asked Menaka where the people would go now that their houses were destroyed. "They will stay with their relatives," she said.

We stood on the bank of the river until all the people had been brought to safety on elephant back. The rain was letting up. The elephants seemed calmly aware that they were the heroes of the day. No one seemed to begrudge them the great swathes of green paddy and whole stalks of corn that their roving trunks pulled into their mouths as they lumbered through the flooded fields and kitchen gardens. Appreciative murmurs of "*hāthi, hāthi,*" ran through the crowd watching the rescue operation. *Hāthi* is the Nepali word for elephant.

When the elephants had completed their rescue mission, we started for home, but not before reviewing the damage done to the fields. Before we reached the school, we left the road and walked along an irrigation ditch that ran across the paddy fields. The barrier walls of the channel had broken in many places where the flood had coursed over the mud embankments. The mud on the path along the top of these embankments was slippery; I lost my footing several times and plunged either into the ditch on one side or into the paddy field on the other. We met people along the way who were salvaging building materials, wading through the water towing a log or a wood beam behind them with a rope. Everywhere I was amazed at the calm, matter-of-fact attitude of people in the face of the disaster.

In the afternoon, the other women and I came out of the house when we heard a helicopter circling overhead. "It's the King's helicopter," Surendra's mother said. After circling twice over the village it flew toward the jungle and disappeared out of sight.

Arjun, who was still out surveying the damage, told me later that there were two helicopters. They had ostensibly come to rescue people. Of course, the elephants had already done that hours before. Arjun described how the officer in charge of one of the helicopters, a well-groomed man in a neat green uniform, had questioned a group of muddy bedraggled villagers who came from all over to gather around the helicopter. He wrote some notes in a little black notebook and climbed back into his flying machine. Then some tourists appeared in the clearing. They had been staying in the lodge where the young Tamang man who drowned had been employed. They, too, Arjun said, looked conspicuous in their clean dry clothes. Their luggage was brought out from the hotel grounds on elephant back; presumably the hotel compound was still under water, or at least very muddy. The pilot motioned for the tourists to hurry up. They and their luggage were conveyed to the helicopter, and it took off again. They had a plane to catch in Kathmandu later that day.

We were not able to leave Chitwan for Kathmandu for almost a week. The road over the Mahabharat range, the main artery for transportation of goods and people from the Tarai (and from India) had been washed out in several places. It was five days before the road was opened to traffic again. Thousands of rupees worth of goods, especially agricultural produce, rotted in Mugling, the mid-point of the journey. Some buses had sold tickets for the route, but passengers had to get down and walk fourteen kilometers where the road was impassable and then board another bus to continue their journey.

A manual laborer who had been living in a makeshift shack of straw and leaves covered with plastic along the road had lost his three children when a mudslide swept their hut away as he and his wife had tried to escape with them to safety.

In Chitwan district, according to a report in the national English language newspaper, *The Rising Nepal*, that I read later, thirty-two people died in the flood and 1,035 houses were damaged. In our village over 150 houses had been destroyed or damaged.

The next day, on our way to the bazaar to get more information on the state of the road and the prospects for getting to Kathmandu, we stopped at the tea shop. Six men were discussing what to do with the body of a little girl—three or four years old—that had been found in the village after the flood waters had receded. No one had any idea who she was or where she had come from.

As far as I could tell from newspaper reports of the flood, the unidentified little girl was not counted in the casualties. The official death toll for our village was two. Had the authorities included the deaths that followed in the wake of the flood due to illness, the count would have been higher. When we returned from our postponed trip to Kathmandu more than a week later with the remainder of our equipment, we found that many people were suffering from fever accompanied by a cough. The epidemic was so bad that the *ghar mukhyās* (heads of households) of the village had decided to summon the *thūlo gurau,* a respected shaman, from a village fifteen kilometers away. The village *gurau* was not considered knowledgeable or powerful enough for this crisis. He was a general practitioner; what was needed was a specialist. The senior *gurau* met with the men of the village to discuss the problem. He performed a *pūjā* in the village and proscribed for a certain time the eating of meat, including fish, which the villagers had been catching in their paddy fields in the aftermath of the flood.

The Circle of the Dance

Soon after we returned from Kathmandu with our belongings, Arjun became ill. In addition to a horrible cough that convulsed his whole body, he had a recurrence of the giardia that had caused him to lose so much weight the previous spring, before I'd arrived in Nepal. For about a week he spent most of his time lying on the bed in our room. It was during this time that the Jithiyā Pāvani took place.

A *pāvani* is a Tharu religious festival, consisting usually of fasting, ritual bathing, and performing *pūjā* (worship). The Tharus observe many such *pāvanis* at different times of the year. *Pūjās* are performed for various gods for many purposes. The Jithiyā Pāvani lasts for three days. It is observed by girls and women, married and unmarried. Their participation in fasting, offerings to the gods, bathing, singing, and dancing is believed to bring good health and longevity to their husbands and children, or to secure good husbands for the unmarried. Women also ask for children during this *pāvani*. Most women (and some men) told me they considered the Jithiyā Pāvani the most *ramailo*, that is, pleasing and beautiful, of all Tharu festivals. Girls and women from age five to fifty enjoy taking part in activities surrounding the *pāvani*, though the formal participants are predominantly girls of marriageable age and young married women. Especially in the beginning of my time in Pipariya, this was the group I spent most of my time with. Most women my own age were busy with children and more demanding household tasks that left them less time for socializing than unmarried girls.

On the second day of Arjun's illness, I was sitting with Bhagavati, Geeta, Mangala, and a few other girls on the *wosarā* of our room, sewing and chatting. I occasionally looked in on Arjun, who was lying on the bed listening to the BBC.

Bhagavati asked me whether I thought I could *basné* (literally, sit or stay) the *pāvani*. I asked her what was involved. She recited the activities of the three-day *pāvani* with other girls chiming in details. I didn't understand a lot of the things she described, but I understood that they agreed that the most difficult part of the observance was fasting for a whole day. This was the part they had doubts about my being able to endure.

I was sure I would have no trouble going without food for a day; I was more concerned about the appropriateness of me, a non-Hindu, participating in rituals that I imperfectly understood. Aside from not wanting to offend people by taking part in religious observances which didn't belong to me, I was also concerned about whether I would appear foolish, performing *pūjās* to gods I neither knew of nor believed in. But the girls seemed eager that I should take part and repeated how *ramailo* the *pāvani* was, and I was interested to have an insider's view of things, both to satisfy my own curiosity as well as to supplement Arjun's understanding of this important Tharu festival, so I agreed to take part.

On the first day of the *pāvani*, I set off with several other girls and women from Ram Bahadur's household an hour after sunrise. Our group included Bhagavati, Geeta, the *bahāriyā* servants Sita and Bikramiya, and Ram Bahadur's elder sister, who had returned to her *maiti* for the festival. All I knew about our destination was that we were going to a stream to bathe. We were joined by women from other households in our *tole* who were also making their way to the stream. Some carried woven straw baskets on their heads or a change of clothes in their hands. Others carried plates of *khari*, the residue left from pressing mustard seeds for oil, which had dried and hardened into cakes and was used for washing the hair.

It was warm and humid, heavy and overcast and felt as if the rain that had fallen during the night might resume at any moment.

As we ambled along the road, people greeted us from their houses. Bhagavati paused numerous times to explain who I was, that I was living with them at their house, and that I was also taking part in the *pāvani*. The mood of our small party was festive but purposeful.

A boy was driving five water buffaloes across the stream to the common grazing land on the other side near the jungle when we arrived at our destination. Slipping off plastic *chappals* and hitching our *lungis* up around our thighs, we waded in the buffaloes' wake through small rapids to a sand bar in the middle of the stream. Here, people set down their baskets and we all made preparations for bathing.

Accustomed to bathing in public, Tharu women are adept at undressing under the cover of a *lungi* or an underskirt hitched up under their arms. The first object of the day, according to Menaka, who had caught up with us on the road, was to "clean well our hair." This was done by wetting the hair in the stream and then rubbing *khari* into it. Except for the young girls, everyone but me had long hair, which floated on the surface of the water like undulating black seaweed as the girls bent over the water at the waist. Some walked into the water up to their thighs and squatted down, dunking their heads under water; they reemerged sputtering and blowing their noses. Through all this, their *lungis* stayed in place. Once the hair was wet, *khari* was rubbed into it. Bhagavati offered me some of this abrasive bran from a plate she'd brought for the use of her household. I rubbed the stuff doubtfully into my curly close-cropped hair. To rinse my hair out, I followed the example of Geeta and some of the other younger girls who waded into the strongest part of the current and floated on their backs, feet first for several yards downstream, heads tipped back. When I asked Geeta later if they could swim, she said they could not, yet none of them showed any fear of the water and evidently enjoyed playing in it.

About half an hour was spent on washing hair. The rest of the bathing was perfunctory. After bathing, each girl took a leaf from a basket of leaves collected on the way. On the leaf she put a little bit of *khari.* Then, closing her hands around the leaf, she waded into the stream, faced north toward the Himalaya, and enveloping the leaf-encased *khari* in both hands, she held it aloft and dunked quickly under the water. She released the leaf into the water, where it joined a flotilla of other leaf-boats bearing their offerings downstream.

What did the ritual mean, I wondered. Why did they face northward toward the mountains? Is this where the gods they were propitiating dwelt? (This was the explanation I had heard for locating kitchens in the northeast corner of a house.) What did the offering, if that term was accurate, symbolize? What did it mean to the participants here around me, splashing and playing in the water? Even had I been able to frame my questions, I was doubtful that the answers I would receive would be consistent with the assumptions that informed my formulation of them—assumptions derived from Christian notions of worship, and the channels of human communication with God. As was often the case in Nepal, I found that while I could observe and even imitate the actions of people around me, I could not relate them to a deeper logic. That logic, or coherent system of explanation, escaped me. I was uninterested in analyzing Tharu culture in an abstract way; I was even skeptical of the possibility of doing so. I supposed that this was what disqualified me from being an anthropologist.

This is not to say that I did not seek to interpret the actions of people around me and attempt to understand their meaning, but these attempts were personal, provisional. I created my own explanations of unfamiliar customs and practices. These ran the gamut from materialist explanations of the ritual slaughter of meat animals (I found Marvin Harris on meat hunger persuasive reading while I was living on a diet of rice and vegetables!) to a more symbolic understanding of *pūjās* such as the one in which I was now engaged. But I was aware that these explanations merely translated unfamiliar experience into terms that allowed me to make sense of them and internalize them on a practical level. I felt I had no analytical tools for understanding what things meant for Tharus.

After finishing the offering, we all put on the clean dry clothes we had brought with us. I alone had brought a towel. The others just put the clothes on their still-wet bodies. When everyone was dressed, and the belongings had been bundled up and restored to baskets, we started for home, again at a leisurely pace, greeting people we passed on the road.

That morning we ate our first special meal of the *pāvani*. The six of us in Ram Bahadur's household who were observing the *pāvani* sat on a rough cloth folded and laid out for us in the main room of the main house. Instead of the usual metal plates, Bhagavati prepared banana leaves. The banana tree is sacred to Hindus. "Plates" were made by overlapping two square sections of a banana leaf which was cleansed with water by the person who would eat from it. Before we ate, an ember was brought from the kitchen onto which we each dropped some fragrant wood chips. Shanthi brought rice and *sāg* and then hot buffalo milk, which she ladled onto the rice.

I asked why Shanthi wasn't taking part in the *pāvani*. Geeta told me that the household god did not favor the participation of the young married wives of the family in this *pāvani*; indeed, the only participants from Ram Bahadur's household were unmarried girls and his married sister, who was in her forties. And me. Perhaps an anthropologist would have followed up the information on the god's preference for unmarried girls taking part in the ceremony, but I am not an anthropologist. I rather prided myself on this distinction between my husband and myself. This was the personality aspect of my abstention from what I thought of as "anthropologizing": attempts at systematic analysis of the society in which we were living. Of course, I could never do what he had done, that is, present myself to a community such as the one we were living in with the publicly stated intention of studying it.

When I first joined Arjun in Pipariya, I found that I was creating all sorts of elaborate mental images of myself to convince others—and myself—that our role in the village was a legitimate one. Later, when I became caught up in day-to-day life and had established relationships with people, this became less important. I don't think identity was ever an issue for Arjun, however. This is not to say that he didn't have a special fieldwork persona. He did. Arjun's Pipariya self was a public one, outgoing, gracious, expansive, even jovial; in short, what I sometimes viewed as a stage personality in contrast to the private, reserved, stay-at-home, even stick-in-the-mud husband I was used to. But both of them were authentic.

In contrast, my reaction to being an object of curiosity in the village was to project as little personality as possible. I concentrated myself on the role of wife, telling myself that nothing was expected of me personally, only as Arjun's wife. This was partly a coping mechanism, but also a cop-out. And since it took me a while to figure out that my preconceived notions of the role of a Tharu village wife were flawed to the point of caricature, it dawned on me relatively late that the role I thought I was conforming to was one that didn't exist for Tharus.

Like many American women of my age and class, brought up by liberal parents in the era of "Women's Lib," I was nurtured on the principle that, in all important respects, men and women were equal. Our capacities for intellectual endeavor and for employment were the same; in a democratic and just society, therefore, our opportunities would also be the same. I had a dim historical awareness, similar to my awareness of the Vietnam War, that this happy equality had not always been enjoyed by American women and, of course, I knew that in less developed countries than the United States, women were still treated as inferior to men.

My first inkling that the sexual equality I had been brought up to believe in was, at best, an unrealized ideal, came when I went to Dartmouth for college. The last all-male bastion in the Ivy League, Dartmouth had first admitted women in 1972 (when I was nine). The decision to admit women was still being hotly debated by the alumni of the college when I arrived on campus ten years later. I don't mean to blame my disillusionment and the ensuing confusion over the issue of sexual equality on Dartmouth. I believe I would have had a similar experience at almost any institution that herded together several thousand young adults, men and women, to socialize them for adult roles in our sexist society. I have the perspective to see now that, like the cleaning closet converted into a bathroom on the ground floor of the library, with "janitor" rubbed out and "women" painted over it, the college, and similarly the larger society, could not realistically be expected to fit women into spaces designed for men. But I couldn't see it then; I was blinded by my desire to believe in an idealized equality.

By the time I arrived in Nepal I had abandoned the belief in equality that was part of my youthful feminism, but I retained the ethnocentric conviction that if things were not perfect for women in the United States, they must necessarily be even worse (meaning less equal) for women elsewhere. My standard for judging women's status remained an idealized equality with men.

The rhetoric of equality is part of the legacy of Enlightenment political thought. While the word has enjoyed a great deal of currency in contemporary Nepalese political discourse, the philosophical premise seems often to be an irrelevant, even alien one, at least with respect to women's rights. In a speech published in the English-language newspaper, *The Rising Nepal,* the leader of the Nepali Congress Party argued that "mere talk about equality between men and women will not have any meaning because nature itself seems to differentiate between men and women; their physical anatomy and every behavior are totally different from those of men . . ."[1] In the same article, another Nepali Congress leader condemned "the tendency of snatching away the rights of men," as if the balance of rights between the sexes was somehow a zero-sum game. Of course, with speeches such as Tipper Gore's at the 1992 Democratic National Convention urging that women not be alienated from their "essential natures," we would soon see

[1] "Women Told to Strive for Rights," report on speech of K. P. Bhattarai, *The Rising Nepal,* 9 March 1991.

mainstream American political discourse reevaluate the sexual equality paradigm, but in Nepal, the premise of such equality has always been a nonstarter.

After the meal, we tossed our "plates" into the ditch behind the *dhāra*. The ducks finished off the leavings from the first meal of the *pāvani*.

The second night of the *pāvani*, it rained heavily. In the morning we congregated on the road by the banana trees to wait for women from other houses to join us. After the rain, the ground was wet and pungent; the air heavy with moisture. In the distance, clouds hung low over the jungle obscuring the Churia hills to the south. We squatted on the road. Women talked and laughed. The mood was celebratory but relaxed. Walking to the stream early in the morning to bathe together was indeed *"ramailo."*

When we reached the stream on the second day, it was swollen. A channel had broken through the sand bank from which we'd launched our bathing the day before. The current was swift. Bhagavati bent over and delivered some rapid instructions to five-year-old Suneetha— each sentence punctuated by the Tharu *"ho"* seeking the hearer's compliance with the directions being given. Suneetha nodded seriously in response to her aunt's orders. Suneetha and the other small girls remained on the bank as the older girls and adult women made their way through the fast current.

I thought it ironic that although I was probably the only one there who could swim, Bhagavati and Menaka grabbed hold of both my hands to help me across the stream. With her other hand, Bhagavati steadied a basket of clothes balanced on her head. I was carrying a camera around my neck. The rocks on the river bottom were hard and sharp under my feet. Several times I thought I would be knocked off balance by the current. We all made it to the sand bank mid-stream, which had been diminished in size by the rain during the night.

We returned home to eat a meal off banana leaves. This was preceded by an offering of wood chips, rice, and yogurt from our banana leaf plates. After the meal we got ready for a trip to the bazaar.

For work and everyday life around the village, Tharu women wear *lungis* and tight-fitting blouses. But for special occasions and trips to the bazaar, they put on saris. They urged me to wear a sari, too, but I said that if I went to the bazaar in a sari, people would stare at me. They sympathized with this and told me they too got stared at in the bazaar. *Pahariyās* (Tharu term for people from the hills) pointed them out as Tharus and made comments about their appearance, dress, and especially about the elaborate tattoos that Tharu women traditionally wear on their legs, arms, and even their backs. Several girls told me the main reason they hadn't had tattoos done was because they didn't like being stared at and ridiculed by people of other ethnic groups. They also said the tattoos were painful to have done, causing several days of inflammation and fever; one or two told me quietly that they thought tattoos ugly.

The bazaar was a six-kilometer walk, on the other side of the Rapti river. It was a dirty, shabby strip of small shops and stalls along the east-west highway. We set off in a party of fifteen. The girls looked beautiful in their brightly colored, gauzy saris as we walked along the muddy road between undulating fields of ripening rice.

I marveled at how they managed to walk in their plastic *chappals* without getting mud on their clothes. Before we were even out of Pipariya, the back of my skirt was speckled with mud flicked up by the heels of my *chappals* as I walked.

We washed our feet and legs in the Rapti, and Bhagavati helped me wash mud off my skirt. There was a crowd on the banks of the river waiting to be ferried across in the long dugout canoe, so we had to wait. Finally, we clambered in and squatted down in the tippy boat. Some men hauled their bicycles in and stood with them as the boatman, standing in the narrow stern, maneuvered his craft deftly through the strong current using a long pole that he shoved against the river bottom. The boatman was paid by all the households of the area in grain, or other commodities, for ferrying them across the river when it was too full to ford. Nonresidents in the area paid one or two rupees to take the boat across. There was some discussion about my status in the community when we reached the far side of the river, but Bhagavati prevailed. She said I was living with them so I shouldn't have to pay extra.

It started to rain. We had three umbrellas among fifteen people. We all got wet.

The walk to the bazaar was a journey away from the closeness of the trees of the jungle toward the mountains. Fields of waist-high green rice surrounded us on all sides. We walked through both Tharu villages and *pahariyā* settlements. All along the road, my companions were greeted by friends who asked, "Where are you going?" or "Where are you coming from?" These questions, I realized, constituted the real Tharu greeting, not the hackneyed "*namaste*."

As we walked through the populated area and the ramshackle

Canoe ferrying people across the river

shops at the near end of the bazaar, the attitude of the girls I was walking with seemed to change. Confident, exuberant, and uninhibited in their actions in their own village, here in this town of a few thousand they seemed shy and uneasy. They walked close together and cast their eyes down when we met other people on the road. At the same time, I could see that they were interested in looking around, studying the clothes of other people and seeing what was going on up and down the road.

We turned onto the east-west highway that runs through the bazaar. This macadam road reaches from Kakarbhitta in the east to Nepalgunj in the west. Eventually, it will be extended to Nepal's western border. Its construction has been supervised and funded in segments by various foreign governments. We happened to be walking on the section built with development assistance from the United States. Only a few cars passed us on this stretch of road, but there were lots of lorries, brightly painted with pictures of gods, animals, and flowers, most of them bearing the English legend "Horn Please" on their fenders. One truck bore the motto "work like a koolie; live like a king" painted in uneven lettering on its side. Bicycles passed us coming and going. There were almost as many bicycles, seemingly all ringing their bells, as pedestrians. Beside the paved road was a muddy rock- and rubbish-strewn strip onto which the shops opened out.

East-West highway through the bazaar

We walked along the highway to the far end of the bazaar. Here Bhagavati ducked into a shop that displayed red tassels for braiding into the hair. Inside, the walls of the narrow space were lined with glass bangles, gaudy earrings and other jewelry, cosmetics, and imported toiletries such as shampoo. We all crowded into the small space. The girls barraged the proprietors with questions about the price of nail polish and *bindis,* the round dots of adhesive felt that Hindu women wear on their foreheads.

After making our purchases at the bangle shop, Menaka and Bhagavati bought some apples from a woman selling them out of a basket. These, I was told, were for the *pāvani.* I bought a kilo, too, thinking I could contribute to the celebration. Next we went to a stationer's store. Here, Bhagavati inspected several copybooks, rather haughtily I thought, especially considering she could not read. She was buying some school supplies for one of her younger brothers. It seemed to me at the time that all the girls were ganging up to harass the shopkeeper in the stationery shop, demanding to look at all manner of merchandise and then tossing it contemptuously back on the counter, and badgering him to tell them the time. When she found a copybook that met with her approval, Bhagavati dropped a 100-rupee note disdainfully on the counter. The copybook cost five rupees. The shopkeeper asked if Bhagavati had any change. "Don't *you* have change?" she retorted. He rustled around in a plastic bag full of small notes and shook his head. I was just about to offer my own five-rupee note when Menaka pointed at a large locked wooden box. "Look in there," she commanded. The shopkeeper fumbled with his keys and after a few seconds spent wrestling with the padlock, opened his cash box and handed Bhagavati the change. The girls tittered triumphantly. The shopkeeper looked flustered. I was surprised by the girls' behavior, which seemed rude to me. It was only much later, after going to the bazaar in the company of one or two girls, that I realized what kind of mistreatment and ridicule the Tharus were often subjected to. Their cavalier treatment of the shopkeeper was probably a form of getting their own back.

The rain had stopped and we started for home. It was a relief to be out of the noisy, dirty bazaar and on the open road walking through the glorious rice paddies, heading south toward the dense dark jungles shrouding the Churia hills. By the time we reached Pipariya, our clothes were dry again. I found Arjun sitting up but feeling weak and feverish. I had become so caught up in the *pāvani* that I had forgotten about his illness.

In the evening, after another meal eaten off banana leaf plates, Bhagavati spread a cloth over a bed on the *wosarā* and bade me sit. From the next house Menaka, Sarasvati, and Mangala came with a little jar of a brownish substance that they had bought earlier that day in the bazaar. It was *mehedi,* used for beautifying the hands, especially of brides in India according to Geeta. Bhagavati brought an oil lamp, and, holding my left hand close to the flame so that she could see, Menaka began daubing the brown stain onto my palm with a matchstick. The stuff smelled like shoe polish. The other girls crowded around, commenting on her design and giving suggestions. In the center of my palm, Menaka painted a leaf bordered by a zigzag design. The undersides of my thumb and fingers she decorated with flowers and designs composed of diamonds, bars, lines, and dots. Finally, she capped each finger with a daub of *mehedi* that covered the nails. "These are like little hats for the fingers," I said. Everyone laughed. I felt happy sitting there on the *wosarā* having my hand decorated, feeling the gentle pressure of the matchstick on my palm and sharing in the atmosphere of *māyā* (love). The rain had started and stopped again. Every once in a while, a flash of distant lightning crackled in the western sky. As always on a clear Chitwan night, the stars were bright and seemed close.

While Menaka was making the intricate design on my hand, Surendra was writing the names of several little girls in Roman script on their hands. It was interesting to see my language system being turned into a kind of decoration. The other girls took turns staining one another's hands with flowers and geometrical patterns. Some of the patterns were designed around swastikas. The word *swastikā*, of course, comes from the Sanskrit for well-being; this symbol is a common sign of auspiciousness in Nepal.

I was given strict instructions not to peel the layer of *mehedi* off my hands for several hours so that the design would "come out well." In the morning, the girls assured me, my hands would be beautiful. I was more concerned about the inconvenience of preparing for bed and sleeping with the smelly goop all over my hand. In spite of the happy congenial mood I had shared in kneeling on the bed, I went back to our room and complained to Arjun, who was dozing fitfully: "How am I supposed to get undressed with this junk on my hand? I can't even bend my fingers!" The *mehedi* was like plaster, immobilizing my fingers. I also complained that I would have to get up at one in the morning to eat my last meal of the day. On the third and final day of the *pāvani*, Bhagavati had explained to me, we could neither eat nor drink after the first cock's crow in the morning. One o'clock should put us well before the first crow, I told Arjun wryly.

I set our travel alarm clock—the possession that had generated more interest than anything else we'd brought with us to the village— for one o'clock. When I woke up, a little before the alarm, it was raining. I got up and stood at the door, picking at the caked *mehedi*, which flaked off my hand like dried bread dough, and wondered what to do. I peered out at the big house. Were they awake? Should I go over there? My indecision was arrested by Geeta and Bhagavati who brought an umbrella across the compound to get me. "Let's go eat," they said. On the way to the house, Geeta told me that after eating they would sing a long song. She put the emphasis on the word *long*, and seemed to relish giving me this information. Maybe she guessed that I was less than enthusiastic about getting out of bed for these nocturnal meals and activities.

Before eating, I was given a twig with which to brush my teeth and directed to cleanse my mouth with water. Tharus use the twigs to clean their teeth. They chew on the end until it frays, creating a bristle effect. Then they rub the surface of their teeth with this. The beautiful smiles and generally healthy looking teeth of most Tharus I met seem to suggest that this is an effective method of tooth cleaning. Or perhaps their good teeth are attributable to the fact that Tharus rarely eat sweets.

We never did sing, much to my secret relief. We sat for a while after eating, waiting for the rain to ease. But it didn't. So I went gratefully back to bed until it was time to bathe for the third and final time at the stream.

On the last day of the *pāvani*, the girls performed an elaborate *pūjā* at the stream. After bathing, they knelt and formed about a dozen mounds in the sand. These they sprinkled with flower petals, rice, and *dal*. Then a small group of girls holding leaves sprinkled with water from a *lotā* waded into the stream and, facing north toward the mountains, held the fistfuls of the fragrant leaves (*pakadi*) over their heads, dunked their whole bodies under the water, and released their offerings into the current.

When one group had returned to shore, another group of three or four would perform the ritual. When everyone, including me, had made her offering, we got dressed to return home.

Today was the day of fasting. Instead of eating when we returned to the house, we joined some other girls and old women who had not been to the stream at the foot of a tree in approximately the same spot from which the elephant rescue had been mounted the previous week. After some animated discussion and laughter, the twenty or so women assembled began to sing. The singing was high-pitched and repetitive. It had an eerie, piercing sound. Meanwhile a dozen young girls climbed into the trees and picked armfuls of the same fragrant leaves that had been used for that morning's *pūjā*.

Arjun appeared with tape recorder and camera to document this part of the *pāvani*. Becoming aware that he was recording their voices, the women covered their mouths with their hands, a Tharu gesture of shyness or embarrassment. The singing and leaf-picking lasted for less than an hour.

The dancing began in the compound of the house of the man-whose-wife-beat-him. Ten girls formed a circle and, continuing to sing as they had around the tree, moved their feet more or less in unison and circled counter-clockwise. The dancers were divided into two groups, roughly corresponding to two arcs of the circle. They took turns singing verses of the song. While one group bent at the waist and clapped their hands just inches from the ground, the other half shuffled their feet and clapped their hands with straight backs.

After a little urging from Surendra and beckoning from Bhagavati who was in the circle of dancers, I joined in. I had been watching their movements for some minutes from the *wosarā* of one of the surrounding houses. The movements were slow and regular. Still, it took me a few rounds before I felt in sync with the other dancers. And I couldn't even guess what the Tharu words they were singing were.

Surendra had told us that Tharu women used to do this kind of dancing more often, as a way to relax after working in the fields all day. As I went through the slow relaxed motions of the dance, I could see how it might help to stretch tight muscles in the back and arms after bending at the waist all day with a sickle.

Both the form and, apparently, the function of women's dancing differed from the dancing I had seen performed by the men in the village. In the first place, dances by men were performances; the women's circle dance seemed more like a participation in a ritual. Women danced at times and in ways that accorded with ceremonial occasions. The circle dance was plodding, inward turning, repetitive, monotonous. The music that accompanied it was produced by the dancers themselves. In contrast, men's dancing was individualistic, innovative, and aimed at impressing and entertaining an appreciative crowd of onlookers, largely but not exclusively other men (and wide-eyed little boys). Men's dancing incorporated new moves or styles observed in the Hindi movies shown in the bazaar. Though not essential, a cassette player blaring Hindi film music was a much sought after accompaniment for the staging of men's dancing. Emboldened by the throbbing of the film music, men took turns getting up to perform their dances, which were by turn lascivious, comical, and just plain exuberant. They incorporated some elements of Western rock dancing. Indrani's nine-year-old son managed a fair approximation of Michael-Jackson-style moon-walking. Even the most self-assured young men felt (or feigned) some shyness when they stepped into the middle of a circle of their peers to perform.

Suddenly the circle disbanded. I rejoined Arjun who was sitting on a twine bed with Surendra. He was out of bed for the first time in three days, looking weak, but better. Surendra complimented me on my dancing. "Just like a *Tharuni*," he said. I smiled. I asked him what would happen next.

"Now there will be some more singing. In Indra Prasad's house. Tonight there will be a big *pūjā* in our yard."

Arjun and I went back to our room. I lay down on the bed. I felt weary. It also seemed to me that I had not been alone with my husband for days. I was being absorbed into the women's life in the village, which especially during this festival was quite separate from men's activities. I had expected before I came to Nepal that my main associations in Pipariya would be with women of more or less my own age. But I found the reality that this interfered with the time I was used to spending privately with Arjun frustrating, especially when he was sick and I was feeling overwhelmed by cultural differences. I was just beginning to explain some of these frustrations to him when Sarasvati appeared at the door.

"*Bhāuju*, they're going to start singing," she informed me. "Come."

"Here, take the tape recorder with you," said Arjun.

There was a ground cloth spread over the floor of the outbuilding where I had sat many times in the last two weeks with Menaka and her sisters, eating and chatting. The area was already full of females of all ages, many of whom I did not recognize. There was no singing as yet, only conversation and laughter.

A place was cleared for me near the center of the group. I set the tape recorder down carefully on the cloth in front of me. Women craned their heads and half stood to look at it. There was some discussion amongst them, which I took to concern the small machine's function. I picked it up, pressed the eject button, flipped over the tape, and rewound it. Then I played the recording of the earlier singing session by the tree. Women smiled and laughed in delight. They teased one another, apparently able to distinguish the familiar voices of friends and relatives.

Mangala brought several bottles of *rakshi* (distilled rice liquor) from the house. These were lost from my sight in the mass of people. Presumably some of the assembled singers wanted to fortify themselves for the singing.

Again, discussion and laughter preceded the singing. Finally, eyes downcast and with their hands or shawls in front of their mouths, two groups of women took turns singing. Occasionally the singing would stop because they had forgotten the words. An old woman would then instruct the younger women and the high-pitched intoning would begin again. Nonsingers like Geeta shushed the little girls who were talking in the periphery. It was clear that this was out of consideration for the tape recorder. It was my first indication of a concrete way in which my participation in the *pāvani* had altered it. The singers were now not only singing for themselves and the gods but also for a little black plastic box with a flashing red light and a whirling ribbon inside.

This singing session lasted for over an hour. I was well into the second side of my ninety minute tape. Then, as unceremoniously as they had begun, the women stopped singing and the group disbanded.

"*Bhok lāgyo?*" Bhagavati asked me. (Are you hungry?)

"No," I said, quite truthfully. My diet and eating schedule had been so affected by travel and sickness that I seldom felt hungry. Partly, I thought this was a psychological response to the knowledge that I couldn't eat when I wanted to anyway.

"Oh, I am so hungry," Bhagavati said, holding her stomach. I realized with surprise that I was probably much more used to going without food than the Tharus, at least the relatively affluent ones like Ram Bahadur's family, who were accustomed to eating rice whenever they felt hungry throughout the day.

In the afternoon, Bhagavati and Geeta came to fetch me to dress me in a sari again. They were already draped in floral saris. They had put on makeup and done their hair carefully. Bhagavati had braided some false hair that she'd bought from the bangle seller the previous day into her own tresses to make them fuller. The final touch was a *bindi* or "*tikā*," a sticky red dot of felt with a gold design on it, which Sita pressed into the center of her forehead.

Carrying metal plates containing rice and *dal* and the fragrant *pakadi* leaves the girls had picked in the morning, we walked toward the tree that had been the site of the singing. Geeta was carrying a colorful woven basket decorated with shells. Bhagavati was carrying a small lamp filled with mustard oil. I was surprised when we turned off the road and walked toward the fields; I had thought we were going to do a *pūjā* at the *Bramathān*. I asked Menaka about this. She said we would go to the *Bramathān,* but first we would do a *pūjā* in the paddy field. I reflected again on how little I understood of what was going on. Off the road, the ground was still wet and muddy from the flood. I was flicking mud onto my sari with my *chappals*. Again, Bhagavati showed me how to fold my petticoat protectively up over the sari. All the girls did this. Legs bared to the knee, with the colorful ends of the saris thrown over their shoulders, carefully coifed black hair shining in the sun, our group proceeded single file along the narrow ridge that served both as a barrier between paddy fields and a path to walk above them. Then, at a certain point, the leaders in the group stepped off the raised path and plunged into the water of the paddy field, which reached to the knees. The rice plants were chest high. I, too, waded into the paddy field, wondering as I did so what sort of parasites were lurking in the silty mud that oozed between my toes.

All around me girls splashed in the paddy field. The bright colors of their saris against the green of the ripening rice was breathtakingly beautiful. And all around me Tharu faces beamed with joy. Without my realizing it, the *pūjā* had begun. Bhagavati doled out fistfuls of the various grains that had been brought as offerings. Girls from other families did the same thing for their households. Mustard oil lamps were lit. Girls tossed their offerings into the water of the paddy field. "Grow well, and give us a good harvest," they said in Tharu. Since I hadn't been able to master this phrase in Tharu, Menaka had suggested that I say it in English. She had translated it for me as "I want to be very rich." The final part of the *pūjā* in the paddy field involved the participants sprinkling water on one another's heads. This was accomplished with much laughing and joking. The scene was indeed *ramailo*. It was also characterized by an unceremoniousness that did not accord with my idea of religious ritual.

We climbed back onto the path between the fields and continued on our way to the *Bramathān*. Paralleling us on the road was another group of fifty or sixty Tharu maidens and matrons. We all converged in a festive group at the village shrine.

In bunches of twenty or thirty, loosely divided into family groupings, the assembled took turns circling the imposing Red Silk Cotton tree that dominated the area of the *Bramathān*, pausing at the four shrines of the different gods to do *pūjā*. After all had circumnavigated the tree in this fashion, we formed a circle just to the east of the tree and danced again, this time singing a song about the legendary Ram and Sita. Although I did not know the words, I managed to hit the same pitch and intoned the song along with the other women. We danced there for about half an hour.

When we got home, we all bathed again. This time I bathed with Menaka at Indra Prasad's pump. I was given a twig with which to clean my teeth. After a peremptory bath, Menaka helped me redrape the sari. It was now almost sunset. We joined the girls from Ram Bahadur's

Jithiyā Pāvani, *pūjā* at the *Bramathān*

house in the next compound, where Surendra was helping some men erect a huge leafy branch to make a symbolic tree in the center of the courtyard. As it began to get dark, girls and women from other houses in the village arrived with baskets of fruit, mostly bananas, which they set around the "tree." Plates of the fragrant leaves, rice, and *dal* were placed with the fruit. Participants in the *pāvani* sat in a circle facing the tree and the fruit. I sat between Bhagavati and Menaka. They were again complaining of being hungry. I was beginning to feel a little light-headed, too.

To the north of our circle, a smaller area was defined by spreading *gundris* on the ground. This was for the teller of the Jithiyā Pāvani story, or *kathā*. This story, which lasted more than two hours, was told by a Tharu man in his late forties. Younger men, including Menaka's brothers, sat around him listening and chiming in with what sounded like agreement or encouragement. I couldn't catch more than a few words of the story, and none of it made sense to me anyway. More interesting to me was the fact that although this appeared to be the culminating ritual of the Jithiyā Pāvani, none of the girls around me seemed to be paying any attention to the story. Menaka occasionally played with the piles of rice and *dal* set on a plate in front of us. Other girls lolled on the ground; some had fallen asleep. People talked quietly to one another. The animation and absorption with which the girls had entered into the activities at the stream and in the paddy field were gone. The focus of the *pāvani* had shifted outside the circle of women. Men were in control and the women had become silent observers.

I asked Bhagavati if she'd heard the story before. "Yes," she said, "It's a very long story." She said she was bored. And sleepy. And hungry, very hungry. I understood that we wouldn't eat until the story was finished. I started listening for signs in the teller's tone of voice or the pace of the story that might indicate it was nearing the end.

At one point I thought the story might be about to end because all of a sudden, reacting to some cue from the storyteller, everyone around me grabbed a handful of rice, *dal*, and leaves and flung them toward the "tree" at the center of our circle. Then we settled down again and the interminable storytelling resumed. A short while later, Menaka nudged me and told me to get another handful of rice ready. A few moments later we repeated the action of pelting the tree with grain. And again and again, interspersed with storytelling. We threw the rice into the center about five times. Then I thought I detected some restive anticipation among the assembled. Sure enough, before long, one man got up and entered our circle. He was carrying a small bow and arrow. He walked around the circle once or twice pointing the bow at the girls and saying something that made everyone laugh. After the man with the bow and arrow had made his rounds, everyone got up and moved to the center. People gathered up their baskets and quickly departed.

At Ram Bahadur's house, the beds were moved off the *wosarā* into the compound. A gunnysack was laid down for us to sit on against the wall of the house, and again the banana leaf plates were prepared for our meal. Then Surendra's mother served us fruit: bananas, pears, apples, and cucumbers. And yogurt. We made an offering of yogurt and bananas mixed together on the ember that was brought from the kitchen. The fruit was very tasty; I enjoyed this meal more than any I had eaten in Ram Bahadur's to that point. We wolfed the food, tossing peels and other debris onto the floor of the *wosarā*. It was swept off after we finished eating, and the beds were moved back onto the porch.

The next morning we went to bathe at the stream for the last time. On this final day of the *pāvani* the girls got dressed in saris on the banks of the river. Menaka had brought one of her saris for me to put on. She and Bhagavati helped me to drape it there on the banks of the stream. I felt a little self-conscious about returning along the road wearing a sari, but everyone else was dressing up, so I submitted to Bhagavati's expert adjustment of the pleats in the front and to her instructions about how to protect the garment by folding the underskirt up over it when walking through mud on the road.

I was particularly reluctant to walk past the tea shop where I would feel the gaze and imagine the ridicule of men sitting and chatting over a morning cup of tea. I did in fact hear the conversation die down as our gaily dressed group neared the shop. I looked down at the pink folds of my sari and thought with embarrassment how foolish I must appear: an American woman dressed up to take part in a Tharu festival. As we passed the thatched lean-to, someone called out, *"Namaste, didi."* Literally, "I bow to you, (older) sister"; a respectful, friendly greeting. I lifted my head and smiled in gratitude in the direction of the tea shop. I found invariably that if I was feeling defensive or awkward about my status as a foreigner in Nepal, some unexpected—and quite often anonymous—comment or gesture such as this greeting would disarm and put me at ease in this unfamiliar place.

At the house, a place was quickly prepared for us to sit and eat. For the last time, we performed the offering on the smoldering ember. First we ate *chiurā* with bananas and yogurt. This was followed by rice, bowls of soupy *dal,* and *tarkāri.* And meat: a chicken had been killed for the breaking of our fast which further set the meal apart as special, since meat is a rare commodity. I was ravenous, and everything tasted good. I mixed the bananas into the rest of my food. This helped to ameliorate the saltiness of the food and enabled me to continue eating beyond the point when I was full.

And then the Jithiyā Pāvani was over. We tossed our banana-leaf plates behind the *dhāra,* and I sat for a while on the *wosarā* in companionable and satisfied silence with Bhagavati and Surendra.

CHAPTER THREE

On My Own

About a month after we returned to the village from Kathmandu, Arjun went to witness the *thūlo gurau* perform a special *pūjā* in another village. We discussed whether I should accompany him and decided that, given my still-inadequate Nepali, the fact that I didn't know any-one in Parsa, and my lack of enthusiasm for religious rituals, I would probably be happier staying in Pipariya even though I would be on my own.

Still, I was apprehensive as I watched him walk out of the com-pound with one of Surendra's younger brothers who was to act as his guide. I realized how much I depended on Arjun, not only to do the talking for me but to interpret situations as well. My feeling of be-ing cut off was intensified because, with other people present, there wasn't even an opportunity to talk privately before he set out.

Arjun left in the late afternoon. The *pūjā* was the next day. He would spend two nights with the *gurau*. In addition to observing the *pūjā*, he wanted to interview the *gurau* about Tharu religious beliefs and prac-tices, including the meaning and background of the particular *pūjā* he would see performed. Noting the gloomy expression on my face as he told me his plans, Arjun said, "I'll try to be back as early as I can in the morning, day after tomorrow."

"OK," I sighed.

"It won't be so bad, Kate," Arjun had tried to reassure me. "You know people here now. They'll take care of you."

I watched Arjun out of sight. No one else took any notice of his departure. I returned to our little room, sat down on the bed, and wondered how I would keep myself occupied for two days while he was gone.

"Well, I might as well make an effort," I thought. I got up and peeped through the slit in the wall above the door frame into the courtyard. Bhagavati and Geeta were sitting on a bare bed frame that had been hauled off the *wosarā* into the middle of the compound. They were both engaged in crocheting lace, or, as they called it, "less." I picked up a needle, some thread, and the pajama-style pants to my *surwal-kurtā* that had ripped along the seam in the seat when I squatted in the dugout canoe the first time it had ferried us across the Rapti. I went out to join the girls.

When they saw me heading toward them, both girls smiled broadly and naturally. Geeta got up and fetched a blanket, which she spread on the bed.

"*Esma basnus,*" (Sit on this) she said.

I sat.

They resumed their crocheting and I became absorbed in figuring out how to stitch the seat of my pants back together. Some of the little girls from the next house came to lean on the bed and watch me at work. When I caught their eyes, they smiled shyly and ran away. Some boys were playing "badminton" with shuttlecocks fashioned out of feathers plucked from indignant ducks. They used their *chappals* as rackets. I had also seen marigold blossoms used to play this game. Fascinated by the dexterity of Bhagavati's flashing crochet hook as she worked on a fine yellow circle of lace, I let my own needle dangle from its thread and watched her.

"Do you know how to do this?" she asked; literally, "does it come to you?"

"No," I shook my head. "It's very beautiful. I would like to learn."

Counting out the stitches in Nepali, Bhagavati slowed the work of her fingers and demonstrated for me the three components of the circular pattern.

She handed the hook to me. "Here, *bhāuju,* you do it," she said.

I held the hook awkwardly in my hand. I had forgotten the first step of the pattern already.

"Make a string: ten stitches," Bhagavati instructed. I was beginning to regret my display of interest in learning the skill. Neither choreography nor needlework has ever come easily to me. Bhagavati was a patient and encouraging teacher. With her constant corrections, I managed to complete one round of the pattern.

I was so engrossed in the needlework that I didn't notice the arrival of Tulsi Prasad Ghimire in the yard.

"Hello, Madam," he said in his gruff hearty voice. Tulsi Prasad was one of the longtime *pahariyā* residents of the village. He was the brother-in-law of Ram Bahadur's family's Brahmin priest. The relations between this leading Brahmin family and that of the Tharu *jimidār* were cordial and even close, but their contact with one another was largely confined to ceremonial occasions. One of the most educated men in the village, Tulsi Prasad taught math and science at the local high school. He also gave "tuition" at his house for students preparing for the School Leaving Certificate exam. Tulsi Prasad was studying for an MA in economics at the local campus. He was one of the half a dozen men in the village (there were no women) who could speak English reasonably well. A big man, with a hint of a belly and a full face and classic Brahmin nose, Tulsi Prasad was known as something of a joker. In a letter to me before I had joined him in Nepal, Arjun had related one of Tulsi Prasad's witticisms. Shortly after he'd met Arjun, learning that he was married to a white woman, Tulsi Prasad had quipped: "you and your wife are like a black and white photograph, but when the children come, they will be in Eastman color." Eastman color is the sepia film used in old Indian movies. Another game that Tulsi Prasad enjoyed playing was to mix Nepali and English words to produce an amalgam he called "*Nepangreji.*" (*Angreji* is the Nepali word for English.)

"Where is Arjun-sir?" Tulsi Prasad asked, seating himself on the blanket next to me. I tried to respond to his English question in Nepali. He looked puzzled at my response and turned to Bhagavati. He repeated his question in Nepali. Bhagavati repeated that Arjun had gone to Parsa to observe the *pūjā.*

Tulsi Prasad turned back to face me. He looked disappointed. "I have come to invite both the couple for our Dasain," he said.

Then he told Bhagavati to bring him some water, which she did, in a rounded brass drinking vessel with a spout. Tulsi Prasad put the spout to his mouth and drank. I had never seen anyone touch his lips to a drinking vessel. Nepalese, including Tharus, regard a drinking vessel that has touched the lips of another person as *jutho,* that is, polluted. Perhaps, since the vessel had been brought and offered for his exclusive use, this did not matter.

Putting the half-empty water-vessel under the bed and standing up, Tulsi Prasad said authoritatively, "Let us *jaung*." I laughed at his *Nepangreji*, but ignored the suggestion that we leave. I was enjoying sitting in the yard with my "sisters" as dusk approached. All I knew about the Dasain festival was what I had read about its celebration in Kathmandu where for ten days hundreds of goats, sheep, and buffaloes were sacrificed at temples around the city. I had heard that during Dasain the streets literally ran with blood. I had no desire to leave the companionable sewing session to witness unknown bloody Dasain rituals. Also, I couldn't help feeling that I was an inadequate substitute for Arjun-sir's company and that Tulsi Prasad was only inviting me out of politeness because my husband was not around.

Tulsi Prasad must have thought I hadn't understood him. "Let us go," he said in clear English. I stood up reluctantly. "I have to put these things in the room," I said to him, picking up my mending. "I'll come in a minute."

As we strolled through the village to Tulsi Prasad's house, he told me about Dasain. "It is the greatest festival of the Nepalese," he said. "Like your Christmas." He pronounced Christmas as it is abbreviated in advertisements; for the first syllable, he said the letter *x*.

"It is the celebration of Ram's triumph over Ravana. . . .Do you know *The Ramayana?*" I told him I did, but his interpretation of the meaning of the Dasain festival didn't match what I had read about it in my guide book, which described Dasain as the celebration of triumph of the goddess Bhagwati over the demon Mahisasur. "It is the triumph of good over evil." Tulsi Prasad concluded.

He also told me that they had butchered eleven goats in his *tole*, or group of houses. He had been feasting on goat's meat all day.

When we reached Tulsi Prasad's house, I was offered a chair. Shortly thereafter Surendra arrived carrying our short-wave radio slung around his neck. This he had appropriated when Arjun went to Parsa. It was blaring the popular Hindi movie songs that Surendra loved to listen to. I didn't have the heart to ask for it back, though I would dearly have liked to listen to the BBC. Surendra had seen Tulsi Prasad and me walking on the road when we passed the Nepali Congress office. He had been sitting on the porch of the office playing cards with some other young men of the village. Another chair was brought for him. We sat in the courtyard of Tulsi Prasad's house. It was a beautiful evening, warm and still; the heat of the day just a memory hanging in the air. Looking west, across the verdant richness of the paddy fields, beyond the Rapti, the sky was awash with blue, purple, and pink as the sun set over the jungle.

After Surendra's arrival, the conversation reverted to Nepali and I had trouble following it.

Tulsi Prasad's middle daughter brought me a *lotā* of water, which she set at my feet. I didn't drink it, of course, as my most strictly observed rule of conduct in Nepal was "don't drink the water." (Because we asked Surendra's family to boil water for us to drink, the rumor had gone around the village that we only drank hot water.) I felt bad about letting this gesture of hospitality go unappreciated, but Arjun had told me that it wasn't necessary to drink the water; offering it was a way of welcoming guests. It was the provision of the water, not its consumption, that was important.

I caught a glimpse of Tulsi Prasad's wife looking out at me from the kitchen located at the rear of the two-story mud plaster house with a straw thatch roof. She was an attractive woman with a serious expression. I guessed her age to be mid-twenties, although I could not be sure. Her husband was thirty, he'd told us. Like most Nepalese women, she favored the color red and even if her sari and blouse were of another color, I never saw her without red *sindoor*, the mark of a married woman, in the part of her luxuriant black hair that hung in a long braid down her back and was plaited with a red tassel to add extra length and decoration. On this festival day, she was wearing *tikā* on her forehead: a small clump of rice grains stained red with vermilion and held together with yogurt. This mark had been made by a priest, in this case probably her brother-in-law who lived next door. When she noticed me looking at her, she smiled self-consciously and backed over the threshold into the shadows of the kitchen where my eyes couldn't follow her.

"How do you celebrate *x*-mas in America?" Tulsi Prasad wanted to know. Again he pronounced the *x* prefix.

Words failed me to adequately convey the lavish and expensive rituals with which our secular and materialistic society ostensibly commemorates the arrival in the world of a baby born in poverty, in conditions much closer to those in present-day Nepal than in the affluent West, whose life and teachings eschewed worldly wealth and ostentation.

"Families get together," I began uncertainly, adding that in America it was not common for the members of a family to live in the same house after the children had reached adulthood and that sometimes members of one family lived several days' journey from one another. "For example," I said, "For me to visit my family, it takes two days on the train, or five hours in an airplane, but Arjun and I always go to stay with my parents at Christmas. My brother and my two sisters live closer to home. They can drive their cars there in several hours."

"People give gifts to their friends and family," I continued. Again, I was struck by the gap between the meaning that my words suggested in the Nepalese context and the visions that came into my mind as I spoke of gift-giving. I thought of my parents' living room in California, knee-deep in crumpled and torn wrapping paper, with our gifts to one another, whose value I had never even bothered to speculate on, but which must have totaled many hundreds of dollars, strewn about the room as we reveled in an orgy of unwrapping our presents on Christmas morning.

"What are the presents?" Tulsi Prasad asked, reminding me of our recording of Dylan Thomas' poem "A Child's Christmas in Wales," which is also a tradition at our house at Christmas.

"We give presents of new clothes," I said, thinking of the sweaters, skirts, coats, and pants that my mother usually orders liberally from catalogs for everyone in the family. New clothes are also bought in Pipariya during Dasain. Most new clothes seemed to be acquired during festivals, I noticed, when girls would go to the bazaar to buy three quarters of a meter of Indian-made cotton to have a new blouse stitched, or buy a new lungi, or less often and with much more excitement, purchase a new sari. Men also bought new clothes during festivals.

". . . and books," I said, consciously editing out mention of cameras, ski equipment, tennis rackets, and now that we children were setting up our own independent households, blenders, coffee makers, and other such domestic gadgets.

"And we eat special food," I said. This, I realized, was the aspect of our Christmas that was most translatable to my hosts. I tried to describe the kinds of food we eat at Christmas in my Swedish-American-English home, including such traditions as the heavy nut-and-citrus-studded fruitcake that my English-born mother makes and the purchased jars of pickled herring and the garlic-and-dill-flavored Swedish meatballs (made from, eek: hamburger!) that are part of the contribution of my father's heritage to our Christmas dinner. Forgoing the complications of explaining the ancestry of our holiday fare, I resorted to generalizations. "In America, at Christmas, we eat turkey."

There are no turkeys in Pipariya, although I once spotted one in Kathmandu. My audience was very interested in my description of a "kind of large duck" and downright astonished when I said that one bird might weigh seven or even ten kilos and that we bought them already killed, cleaned, and frozen.

"And people sing special Christmas songs and go to the Christian temple to do *pūjā*."

My discourse on American Christmas had continued as Tulsi Prasad's wife brought out three plates of *chiurā*, a kind of rice that had been soaked in water and then beaten or pounded so that the grains were flattened, and then dried. It vaguely resembled rolled oats. *Chiurā* is eaten as a kind of snack food, in place of *bhāt*, which has to be cooked. The mound of *chiurā* on my plate looked enormous. There was also a small serving of potato *tarkāri* and half a dozen large pieces of goat's meat. Tulsi Prasad's wife returned a few minutes later with a metal bowl from which she took a few more pieces of meat and put them on my plate. Then she poured some gravy from the bowl onto my plate, where the *chiurā* absorbed most of it.

The meat was good and I found to my surprise that I was enjoying it. I did find it a little difficult to swallow the large pieces of skin that had been served to me, presumably as desirable morsels. Several of the pieces were from the goat's organs, one I thought might be a bit of the heart. I reflected on how strong food taboos are: one moment I was thinking that a piece of meat was delicious, the next moment I was feeling sick when it occurred to me that I was eating the heart of a goat. I had felt the same way eating the fish heads (especially the eyes!) that had been served to us since we arrived in Pipariya.

Dasain is a festival that lasts for eleven days. The normal life of Nepal gives way to feasting and celebration. In Kathmandu, government offices and many businesses close down. Foreigners complain that it is "impossible to get anything done." As the festival nears, children playing with new toys, especially colored balloons, are a common sight along the filthy, twisting, narrow streets of Kathmandu's old residential areas. Hovering, dipping, diving, and getting caught in power lines and trees all over the city, kites are flown with a passion that approaches obsession by young boys from the flat rooftops of their houses or from any other piece of high ground that affords them access to a bit of open sky.

In the village, if one were not familiar with the everyday appearance and routine of life during the rest of the year, I can imagine that "the greatest festival of the Nepalese" might escape the notice of any but the most observant outsider.

Even though I'd lived in Pipariya for almost a month, I still didn't notice the signs of Dasain at first. But after starting to look for them, I found evidence of the festival all around. Some people were wearing new clothes. Balloons and plastic toys were less conspicuous than in Kathmandu, but there were some to be seen, in the wealthier houses. But quite apart from the new clothes, toys, decorations, and special food, I thought I could detect something else, something intangible: the same kind of excitement with which I anticipated and savored Christmas as a child and the indescribable specialness of the occasion that set that day apart from all others.

The most exuberant expression of Dasain high spirits was "playing *ping*," an activity in which people of all ages participated. Everywhere the *pings* (swings) appeared. Humble *pings* were fashioned out of a piece of homemade rope and hung from the roof beams of someone's *wosarā*. Others were suspended from trees. One family had lashed two saplings together to hang a *ping* between them.

After I had finished, with some difficulty, the large plate of *chiurā* I'd been given and had refused Tulsi Prasad's insistent offers that I take more, his wife brought out a heaping plate of cooked rice. The *chiurā* had apparently been a snack to tide me over until the real (rice) meal was ready.

"No, no," I pleaded. "I'm really full." Tulsi Prasad also declined the *bhāt*; by his own admission, he'd been eating all day. Only Surendra accepted. The rice was accompanied by more fatty chunks of meat and the salty *tarkāri*. When he had finished eating, we got up unceremoniously and walked home in the dark to the accompaniment of the radio, still playing Hindi film music.

Geeta met us as we walked into the compound. Had we eaten? "Yes," I groaned.

"Was the meat good?" she asked.

"*Mītho thiyo*," I said. (It was good.)

Surendra went into the house. I stayed outside in the moonlit compound with Geeta.

"Are you going to sleep alone (*eklai*) or with a friend (*sathi sanga*)?" Geeta asked. Both Tulsi Prasad's mother and our neighbor Jamhaurni had asked me the same thing. After a little consideration, I told Geeta I would sleep *eklai*.

"Aren't you scared, aunty?" Geeta asked, adding, a little mischievously I thought, "There's a ghost." I pretended to ponder this for a moment.

"How many ghosts?" I asked. "One, or many?"

"Just one," said Geeta. She added that she was afraid to sleep by herself.

I assured her that I wasn't afraid and went to the *dhāra* to wash the grease from the goat's meat off my right hand. Tulsi Prasad's daughter had poured water over my hands after I'd eaten, but they were still covered with a film of grease, like vaseline.

I was sitting on the bed writing in my diary by the light of my little oil "lamp," which was a medicine bottle half-full of kerosene with a wick in it. The door opened and Bhagavati, Geeta, and Bikramiya entered the room. I invited them to sit on the bed. After a few questions about the Dasain feast at Tulsi Prasad's, they got to what seemed to be the main point of their visit: Was I going to sleep by myself or did I want a *sāthi* to sleep with me? Bhagavati indicated that she would come to sleep with me if I wanted her to. I thought seriously about the offer this time. They seemed genuinely concerned about my sleeping alone. I appreciated their concern. I was also anxious to do what was proper. Was their expressed fear of ghosts a cover for a fear that I might be attacked in the night? Was it improper for a woman to sleep by herself alone in a room? Or were they just, as Arjun had promised, "taking care" of me? I almost accepted Bhagavati's offer. How was I to tell them that I didn't know how to sleep with a *sāthi*, someone other than my husband? The bed was narrow and the pillow was smaller still. Was it acceptable (or even expected) that one touch one's *sāthi*, or even lie close together for warmth during the coolest part of the night? I might be so nervous and unsure of what I was supposed to do that I would be unable to sleep.

"No, it's really all right," I said. "I'm not afraid to sleep by myself."

Then I changed the subject. Was Shanthi ready for me to put *aushadi* (medicine) on her feet?

Bikramiya said she didn't think Shanthi was done with her work, presumably cooking and serving food, and that she would probably come to call me when she was ready to have the *aushadi* (hydrogen peroxide and Neosporin ointment) put on the fungus that was eating away at the skin between her toes and fingers.

Shanthi came to call me at about half past eight. I opened the rectangular white plastic file box that contained our "medical kit" to check our supplies before following Shanthi across the yard. Already the basic first aid supplies that had been intended to last us the year were almost gone. Bandages had been dispensed, along with solemn injunctions to keep wounds clean, to women for cuts sustained in cooking and to youths for soccer injuries. Our aspirin had gone for headaches and toothache; Arjun explained that the aspirin wouldn't cure the problems that caused toothache, only ease the pain.

We had also been approached for medicines for stomach ailments, a constant and widespread problem in Nepal among the indigenous population as well as the scourge of tourists. We had in our kit several courses of a drug called Tiniba, a strong remedy for giardia. We had given some to an old woman who came to us complaining of giardia-like symptoms. When the medicine proved effective in her case, we had more requests for Tiniba than we could meet.

At first I was happy to give out our medicines, bandage cut fingers, and swab infected wounds with antiseptic. Here at last was something I could do for the people who housed us, fed us, and welcomed us among them. I was calmly confident of the superiority of our drugs over the amulets and prescriptions of the *gurau*. And it was such a relief to be in the position of giving instead of taking all the time. I felt magnanimous and, in a small way, powerful when I unlatched our mysterious plastic box and authoritatively bestowed some minor remedy on an appreciative patient.

Shanthi led me into the partitioned-off room where she slept with Surendra. She brought me one of the low stools and told me to sit. She sat on the bed and put a small kerosene lamp on the floor by her feet. Her feet were clean, in fact, still wet. I was sure this was part of the problem. When it was her turn to cook, Shanthi's feet and hands were in and out of water all day as she washed rice and vegetables and carried water back and forth to the kitchen. I thought I could smell rotting flesh.

She didn't flinch as I swabbed the open sores on her feet with the hydrogen peroxide. "Does it hurt?" I asked.

"Just a little at first," she said.

I felt noble sitting on the little stool in front of Shanthi, playing doctor; it was only later that I began to have doubts. Our supply box was small in the face of a village full of people with chronic gastroenteritis and myriad other ailments. Even if we were able to refill the supplies in the box frequently at the bazaar, we would be leaving the village soon. Where then would the Tharus get bandages, cough syrup, and the hydrogen peroxide that fizzed so impressively when it was used to clean a wound? They wouldn't. And would it matter? Not much. The Tharus, like most Nepalese, lacked adequate medical care. Our white box could do nothing to change that. Without articulating this conclusion to one another, Arjun and I let our supplies run down. When asked, we began to say that we had no medicine for such and such an ailment, that we had run out of bandages. We had succumbed to a common compulsion among anthropologists (and their spouses) who set up house in poor Third World communities where they have little of practical value to offer their neighbors and "informants," yet they have every desire (and need) to be accepted on good terms.

When I had finished putting the ointment on Shanthi's feet I sat for a while with her and Surendra, who had come into the room and was sitting on the bed listening to the radio.

"You are sleeping alone," Surendra observed in English. "Are you frightened?"

"No," I said.

"If you are frightened, Bhagavati can sleep with you," he said.

"Thank you," I said. "That's very nice, but I'm all right."

"OK," said Surendra, letting the subject drop.

From the other side of the six-foot *māto* partition that divided Surendra's room from where the unmarried girls slept together, I could hear them talking and giggling.

"*Aunus, Didi,*" I heard and then some more giggles.

"Sita is calling you," said Surendra.

I went into the next room, slipping off my *chappals* at the door, as I had before entering Surendra's room.

The four girls—Bhagavati, Geeta, Sita, and Bikramiya—were lying on their stomachs on several blankets spread over *gundris* on the floor. Geeta was writing in a copybook by the light of a flickering bottle lamp. I lay down on the edge of the blankets beside Bhagavati.

The conversation was of films and film stars. As different songs came on the radio in Surendra's room, the girls would pronounce them good or bad and comment on whether they'd seen the film in which the song debuted or not. It was companionable chatter. I felt very comfortable lying there on the mat close to Bhagavati. I was loathe to go back to my room across the compound by myself. Once again I considered and rejected the idea of asking one of them to sleep with me.

As I walked across the moonlit compound calling good night to my friends in the house, I wondered if the "fear of ghosts" that played such a big role in the concerns about my sleeping by myself were not just a symbolic form of an aversion to being alone that I had observed among Tharus, an aversion the girls assumed I would share.

Or maybe it's just a matter of being susceptible. In any case, something happened that night that never happened before, nor after, as long as Arjun and I slept in that room. In the early hours of the morning, I was suddenly awakened by the sound of the door flying open and banging against the wall. I sat up in bed, fully awake but a little disoriented. In spite of my deep-rooted skepticism, I found myself peering into the night for the ghost. When I told Arjun later what had happened, he merely said, yes, it had been a windy night in Parsa, too.

The feeling that I had experienced the night before while lying with the girls in their sleeping room listening to the radio, of being content and at ease in the company of my new companions, had vanished by the next morning. I woke up with a sinking feeling when I remembered that I was on my own. A whole day to get through without Arjun loomed before me. I lay in bed without the least desire to leave the room and interact with the village world outside. I looked at our travel alarm clock. It was 6:45. I decided I would lie in bed and write until 7:30. With my left arm folded on the pillow and the notebook I used for my diary on the bed to the right of the pillow, I rested my head on my arm so that if people looked into the room they would not be able to tell that I was awake. I could hear the voices of Geeta and her mother, Indrani, right outside the door; it sounded as if they were on the *wosarā* outside the room.

After half an hour of writing like this, my eyes began to feel strained from being too close to the paper and I was getting a stiff neck. Besides, I had begun to feel that I was behaving in a foolish and cowardly fashion. I threw off my sheet and stood up. I was already dressed. I brushed my hair hurriedly and stepped onto the *wosarā*. Indrani and Geeta had by this time moved off the *wosarā* and were washing their hair at the *dhāra*. They called for me to join them. I mumbled something about it being too cold. "*Jāro chaina*, aunty," said Geeta, meaning that the water wasn't cold.

My immediate need was to go to the latrine. I went back inside our room and fetched our little blue plastic jug and put some toilet paper in the pocket of my skirt. Since toilet paper isn't used by Nepalese villagers, I always felt shy about carrying it around and usually kept it concealed. Nepalese use water for washing themselves after defecating. I filled our blue plastic jug at the dhāra and headed for the latrine in the field behind the house.

Latrines were a new feature of life in this village, and they still were not used by the majority of people. Many people still preferred to squat on a raised path across the fields or next to an irrigation ditch. In Nepal, river banks are popular places for this purpose because of the convenient availability of water to clean oneself afterward. This of course creates a serious health problem, especially since many people drink water from streams and rivers without treating it first.

Coughing to announce my approach in case someone else was already in the latrine, I carried my jug of water toward an elephant grass screen, protected somewhat from the rains by a sheet of plastic draped over the top. Over the pit, which was smelly and fly-ridden, even at this early hour of the morning, two pieces of wood had been laid across the hole. Placing one foot on each of these unpeeled logs, I squatted inside the makeshift structure. A burlap sack was hung as a door. Pulling it aside slightly, I had a spectacular view of the Himalaya: clear, snow-capped, and looking so close across the green plain dotted with banana trees and darkening into the purplish-grey hues of the Mahabharat hills. The view made up for the stench of the latrine, which I was able to diminish somewhat by pulling my T-shirt collar up so it covered my nose. The odor from my body wasn't pleasant either, but at least it was my own smell. I decided to go back and bathe with Indrani and Geeta.

As I had expected, Indrani and Geeta were still bathing at the *dhāra* when I returned. During my brief visit to Pipariya the previous Christmas, I had been even more self-conscious about bathing at the well in full view of anyone who cared to look than I was now. But I still tended to try to get my bath over with as quickly as I could. The Tharus, on the other hand, especially the girls, took a long time to bathe. At first I had thought they were just using the daily ablutions as a way to spend time pleasantly and possibly as a way to forestall returning to work. They appeared to have a good time together, gossiping, laughing, scrubbing one another's backs; however, the longer I stayed in the village the more I came to appreciate that it just takes a lot of time to stay clean. And Tharu girls like to be clean.

Having finished washing their hair, Indrani and her daughter were squatting around an old mill-stone scrubbing clothes. Still reluctant to get under the cool water so early in the morning, I brought out some clothes to wash, too.

At about 9:30, just as I was finishing with my bath, Bhagavati walked out of the house and bade me to come eat.

"*Aunus, bhāuju, khānā khānus.*"

"I'll come in a minute," I told her.

Instead of leading me into Surendra's room where Arjun and I usually sat to eat, Bhagavati spread a folded blanket on the floor of the big entrance hall and I sat cross-legged with my back against the partition of the kitchen. Bhagavati went back into the kitchen and returned with two round metal plates heaped with rice. She placed one of these in front of me and squatted across from me with her plate in front of her.

Shanthi brought us potato *tarkāri* which she served onto our plates with her hands. Then she brought another bowl of *sāg.* We ate in silence for a while. I was careful to eat several handfuls of rice before mixing any *tarkāri* into my food. I had discovered that the rice was less filling when it wasn't combined with other things, and in order to get through the huge quantity of rice I was always served, I had to rely on this strategy. I had also noticed that the Tharus ate less *tarkāri* and more rice than we did. This, I thought, might explain why they could tolerate so much salt and chili in their food—they used the *tarkāri* to season the rice.

When we had assured Shanthi that we didn't want any more food served to us, she came and squatted with us.

We looked up as a figure moved into the door frame blocking the light that was coming into the windowless room from the outside. It was Jamhaurni, Ram Bahadur's neighbor to the north. Our new hut backed directly onto her compound.

"Have you finished eating?" she asked.

"Yes," I said. I was resting my right hand on the empty plate waiting for Shanthi and Bhagavati to finish eating.

"I've come to invite you," Jamhaurni said.

"Go," said Bhagavati, excusing me. "Here, wash your hand."

She pushed a *lotā* of water toward me. I poured some of the water over my hand onto the plate. I stood up and bent over to pick up the plate. Usually, Arjun and I just left our plates on the floor after eating, to be picked up and washed by one of the girls. This time I thought maybe now that I was eating with the other young women, the courtesies extended to me as a guest (as Arjun's wife) might be relaxed a bit.

"*Chor-dinus*," Bhagavati said. (Leave it. We'll do it.)

I left the plate and followed Jamhaurni out of the house. I stopped at the *dhāra* to wash my hand properly.

I thought I knew what I was being invited to Jamhaurni's for. A few days earlier, Arjun and I had got caught in a downpour and had sheltered on her *wosarā*. At that time she had told us that their buffalo had recently given birth. The calf had died immediately, but the buffalo was giving milk.

Jamhaurni's house was smaller than Ram Bahadur's but better maintained. Jamhaurni's husband, a thin taciturn man, was a drunkard. His eldest son had told me that his father didn't know how to "drive his life" and that due to bad management they had to sell a lot of the land that had belonged to the family in his grandfather's time.

Jamhaurni led me to an enclosed room with two windows adjoining their cattleshed. A small wooden table piled with books with a bed on either side suggested that the room was occupied by students. When I speculated on this, Jamhaurni confirmed that her two youngest sons slept here.

Jamhaurni told me to sit on the bed. She went into the house. A young woman entered the room and swept out some vetch and grasses that seemed to have been stored there. She made no sign of noticing me.

Jamhaurni returned with a metal tumbler full of piping hot buffalo's milk. An ant had come to an unhappy end in the milk and was floating on the thin skin that had formed on top. I blew into the glass and sipped the milk, prematurely it turned out: I burned my tongue.

Jamhaurni sat on the bed next to me. "How's the milk?" she asked.

"*Mītho cha*," I responded truthfully. The milk was delicious: rich, sweet, with the slightly smoky taste that distinguishes it from cow's milk. Now that it had cooled slightly, I drank it greedily. Last of all I slurped the skin, ant and all.

"In Tharu, we call our friend *sanhatiyā*," she told me in Nepali. "*Aré, sanhatiyā, yeté yao.*" ("Hey, friend, come here.") She demonstrated this use of the word for friend. She repeated the sentence. I tried it. My attempt to get my tongue around the Tharu words was greeted by children's laughter alerting me to the fact that I had an unseen audience.

Jamhaurni called to one of the boys outside: "*Aré, Bikana, yeté yao.*" I repeated the phrase after her. A boy of about eight or nine sheepishly rounded the corner and hung on the door frame staring at me. "*Aré, Bikana, yeté yao,*" I repeated, but he didn't come any closer. A few seconds later he was off.

"He's afraid," I said.

"He's shy," said his mother.

Jamhaurni had taught me the Tharu words for calling one's friends and children. I asked her how she would call to an older or respected person.

"*Yébehun,*" she said. In practice, though, I never heard this formal command used.

Then she taught me how to say, "Hey, mother, eat rice." She also taught me names for various family relationships, and I puzzled anew over the cultural meaning of the fact that the words for brother and uncle's son were the same.

It dawned on me that I was having my first Tharu language lesson. Jamhaurni was a natural teacher. She pronounced words clearly and slowly, repeated sentences several times, and started with simple sentences and only gradually increased their complexity. She also made me understand new words by her use of gestures and expressive body language.

She told me to call to the children who were still hanging around outside the cowshed, telling me each of their names in turn. Upon being called, the two little girls and one remaining boy—Bikana was nowhere to be seen—came inside. I commented on their mirth.

"They're happy," Jamhaurni said.

She said she was happy, too, because I had come to her house. When she told me that I tried to look as happy and pleased as I felt. I was touched that these people were happy because of my presence there; I made a conscious effort to show it. At least I could smile; I had noticed that Tharus smiled more often and easily than I was generally used to, or would be considered "sincere" in the United States. I thought about saying that I was happy, too, to be there, but worried that it might sound artificial, although it wasn't. As long as I stayed in Pipariya, even much later when I felt more confident of my ability to interpret personal interactions with people and surer of what was appropriate and expected behavior on my part, I never lost the feeling of having to act, of needing to exaggerate my feelings and responses to people in order to demonstrate them. By acting, I do not mean that I was pretending feelings; I do not mean that I felt I had to act in a false way, but rather that I felt that I had to overcome cultural differences in expressing emotion.

The happy children were overcome with excitement a few minutes later when the infrequent sound of a vehicle passing on the road through our *tole* gave way to the even rarer sound of the engine being killed—right here in the village—signifying that a visitor had arrived in a car, a noteworthy event indeed in the life of Pipariya.

"A car, a car," chorused the children. They ran out of the cowshed. I heard the sound of the doors of the car slamming shut. The sound of well-fitted metal cushioned by rubber was an alien sound in the village.

Curious to see who the visitors were and thinking it not unlikely that it was someone looking for us, I announced to Jamhaurni that I was going. "*Mui jai,*" I said in Tharu. And I followed the children through Jamhaurni's vegetable garden.

Just as I entered Ram Bahadur's compound, I met Bhagavati. She was coming to fetch me. "Madan-*dai* has brought someone to meet you," she told me.

Surrounded by some small boys and a few servants from Indra Prasad's household, a white Toyota Landcruiser was parked in the yard.

Madan Chaudhury and a white man were occupying two chairs on the *wosarā*. I saw from the two *lotās* at their feet that they had been welcomed in the traditional way. Madan was a successful businessman, one of a few Tharus. He was also a self-proclaimed leader of his community, and was always talking about uplifting and advancing Tharus.

As I approached, Madan was talking animatedly with Indrani and Ram Bahadur. The foreigner was seated somewhat apart, taking in his surroundings with quick, darting glances as he drew nervously on a cigarette.

Madan greeted me and asked jokingly how my Tharu was coming along.

"*Aré, Madan, yeté yao!*" I said, demonstrating my newly learned phrase. He said something in Tharu, which he then translated into English as, "I am sitting here; I will not come there."

He turned to his companion and said, "I'm a very good language teacher. I can teach Tharu and Nepali language very well." The white man nodded. Madan was something of a braggart. But he was good-hearted and generous, and I was prepared to believe his claim that he did a lot of good for the Tharus in the area. He was certainly a popular figure in Pipariya.

"Where is Arjun?" he asked. I told him he'd gone to Parsa for the *pūjā*.

"This is Bogdan," he introduced me to the foreigner. "Her husband is the anthropologist," he informed Bogdan.

"Oh, really?" Bogdan lit another cigarette. "What's his field?"

I wasn't quite sure what he meant. "Cultural anthropology," I said, and gave a brief description of Arjun's research.

Bogdan told me that he, too, had training as an anthropologist. He said he'd done research in Khumbu on Sherpa traditional healers. There were only eight healers left in the region, he said. He had become interested in finding ways to reintegrate what he called "Sherpa medicine" into mainstream Nepalese health care. Now he was working for a British development organization that focused its attention on women's development. I asked him the name of the organization. I didn't recognize it. It was a small one, he said. He spoke English well, but with a trace of an accent. With his sharp features and fair skin I wondered if he were a Russian émigré. Yugoslavian, he told me, but he'd been living in Britain for fourteen years. He had studied anthropology at an English university.

Putting out another cigarette on the mud floor of the *wosarā*, Bogdan turned to Madan. "I hate to hurry you," he said, "but Pokhara calls."

The two men stood up and walked to the car. Bogdan climbed behind the wheel.

"We're going to the clinic," Indrani said to me. "Come with us."

"*Huncha,*" I said. (OK.) I followed her to the vehicle where she opened the rear door and climbed in, arranging her sari before sitting down. Indrani always wore a sari. She was a community worker for the Family Planning Association of Nepal. She was also the wife of the *jimidār* and an important woman in the village. Indrani's son Hari Prasad climbed over me to sit by his mother.

Bogdan started the engine. The boys who had been running their hands appreciatively over the shining paint of the hood of the car drew back. Bogdan backed out of the yard coming very close to hitting one of the roof beams of the carpenter's house as he did so. It was the first time I had ridden in such a comfortable—and insulating—vehicle in Nepal.

As soon as I climbed into the Landcruiser and shut the door, I felt a very different relationship with the villagers we passed on the road. Perched high on my comfortable seat, I looked down on the people who stepped off the road to stare at the vehicle as we drove along the route that I had walked so many times. As we slowed down to negotiate a piece of the road that was muddy and worn away by the rains, Madan asked Bogdan if the vehicle had four-wheel drive. It had; we got through the mud without difficulty.

We passed the Nepali Congress Party office. Surendra and some other young men were playing cards outside. They looked up with interest when they saw Madan ride past in the white Toyota. Madan shook his head sadly. "Very much unemployment in our Tharu villages," he said. Bogdan nodded in thoughtful sympathy. Madan turned and looked at me. "Did you mark how many of our Tharu boys are unemployed?" I nodded uncertainly; it was the first time I had thought of the young men we had passed as unemployed. I thought of them as students, farmers, and tourist guides, enjoying a card game when there was no work to do. My sense of perspective shift was reinforced. Here I was seated in a powerful high-riding vehicle looking out through the clear glass windows at what Madan called "idle youth," wasting their time in playing cards. Previously I had viewed their games as a form of harmless entertainment and a way to enjoy the companionship of friends in their leisure time when, as now, their labor was not required in the fields, or their campuses were closed for Dasain. But maybe I had been wrong. I suddenly wondered if I had been romanticizing the difficult economic situation of the Tharus, their lack of economic opportunities and their frequent displacement by other *jāts* and immigrants, as "leisurely." I was confused: Was Madan's interpretation of the situation in the village accurate? Or were my previous assumptions right?

We stopped at the crumbling *Panchāyat* building, the seat of local government administration under the old regime, which had been overturned by the Democracy Movement the preceding April. We went into the "family planning clinic" where Indrani worked. It was a single small room decorated with nutrition posters and exhortations to breastfeed babies. It was here that Indrani came a few days a week to give advice on family planning and to dispense contraceptives, including condoms and Depo Provera as well as an erratic supply of other medicines such as penicillin and analgesics, to anyone who came to the clinic for help. As a "community health worker," Indrani's job was to "motivate"—the word had passed into the Nepali lexicon —villagers to follow the various programs of the Family Planning Association. These programs included sterilization for men and women as well as implanting intrauterine devices (IUDs). Indrani accompanied groups of motivatees to a regional family planning clinic for sterilization. I happened to know that she had recently escorted Madan and several of his friends to get vasectomies at the clinic. To dull their fear of the operation, the men had got drunk together before showing up at the clinic. But the doctor said he wouldn't perform the operation unless they were sober, and they had been sent home.

Bogdan, as it turned out, organized Yugoslavian mountaineering expeditions in Nepal. In return for this, the expeditions donated some medicines that Bogdan distributed as he saw fit.

"I tell them what medicines to bring; when their climb is over, they give me what's left over to do what I like with." Bogdan looked at his watch. "The Mount Everest expedition should be down in a month," he said.

Bogdan told Madan he'd like to donate some medicines, disposable syringes, and other supplies to the Pipariya clinic "to help Tharus."

He also asked Indrani, through Madan, whether there were any traditional midwives in the village. Yes, said Indrani, women from all over the area called for a woman who lived in our *tole* to help deliver their babies as well as to treat some ailments. Bogdan expressed an interest that other *jāts* besides Tharus also used her services.

"Right," said Bogdan to me. "I might see you again when I bring the medicines in a month or two." He was clearly intending to bring more than a first aid kit. He folded his hands together in *namaskār* to Indrani, got into the jeep, and drove off with Madan.

Indrani, Hari Prasad, and I walked home, answering the questions of people we passed about the *videshi* in the white car. Surendra also questioned me about the Yugoslav's visit. I asked him what he thought of the man's plans for helping Tharus. "I think it is better for Tharus to get their own medicines," he said.

Arjun returned from Parsa the following morning. He was disappointed to have missed Tulsi Prasad's Dasain invitation and interested to hear about the Yugoslav's visit. I was happy to be reunited but also felt the two days on my own were a milestone in my adaptation to life in the village.

CHAPTER FOUR

Setting Up House

"Does every family in America have a cow, or only some families?" Baghaurni asked me one afternoon about a month after Arjun's visit to Parsa. I was helping her prepare a kind of wide, flat bean for cooking. She was seated on a sack made of hemp. I was sitting on one of the low four-legged stools commonly proffered for guests in Tharu houses. Between us were a knee-high basket full of freshly picked beans and a *nanglo* (a flat traylike basket used for winnowing and sifting grains and flour). We tossed the beans onto the *nanglo* after snapping off both ends and tearing the larger ones in half.

I had to think for a moment before I could answer Baghaurni's question. It reminded me how different the organization of our respective economies and the symbols of wealth were between our two societies. Baghaurni knew that America was a wealthy country. She had asked me a question aimed at translating the meaning of fabled American riches into Nepalese terms.

In Pipariya, as throughout rural Nepal, cows and buffaloes are a source of household income. They are also a status symbol of sorts. We had been told by older members of the community that in the past Tharus had owned many cattle, and milk had been a regular part of their diet; now there was less land to graze cattle on, due to the creation of the National Park and immigration into the area. The size of people's herds had decreased with the shrinking of available pasture for them. Now Tharus kept only a few cattle, or a single buffalo, if any.

I explained to Baghaurni that although most Americans drank milk, few actually kept their own milk cows. I told her that many cows were kept together on large dairy farms and that the milk they produced was then sold through stores. She asked me, for the fourth or fifth time, whether Americans ate cows.

"Yes, American people eat cow meat, " I said.

"Do you eat it?" she asked.

I responded that in America I ate beef, but in Nepal I didn't. For Hindus, beef is taboo. In Nepal it is illegal to kill a cow. It was neither the first nor the last time that I encountered a kind of horrified fascination when I admitted that I had eaten beef.

"In the bazaar they make *momos* out of buffalo meat, " Baghaurni told me distastefully. Had I eaten them?

"I've eaten *momos* in Kathmandu," I said a little evasively. In fact, the first thing Arjun and I usually did when we arrived in Kathmandu was to head for a restaurant called Ringmo's in Lazimpat where we ordered large plates of these delicious Tibetan spicy steamed meat dumplings. Sometimes I had mouthwatering visions of *momos* on the bus to Kathmandu.

I asked Baghaurni if she had ever eaten *momos*. Once, she said. "*Mītho lagdaina,*" she said. She hadn't found them good to eat. "Our *jāt* considers buffalo meat to be dirty," she told me.

Baghaurni's prized she-buffalo, which had been given to her by her mother and which had already borne one female calf, was about to calve again. I had been hearing for about a week that the calf would arrive "*bholi, holā,*" (tomorrow, maybe). The advent of the buffalo calf and, more important, the flow of milk it heralded, was of no less interest to us than it was to the rest of Indra Prasad's family. We also had been promised a share of the rich milk.

That evening, Indra Prasad summoned one of the teachers from the school. He and this Brahmin man were *mīts*. This meant they had entered into a special relationship of ritual friendship. The teacher also owned six buffaloes. Indra Prasad asked his *mīt* when the calf would be born.

"Tomorrow," he said authoritatively. No *holā* about it.

Indra Prasad's faith in his *mit*'s expertise proved justified. The calf was born the next morning. I was hanging up some clothes to dry on our line when Arjun came back to the house and announced the news. He had come back for the camera.

"You're really going to take pictures?" I asked. "People will laugh at you."

"So what? I can get some great slides of the birth."

As it turned out, no one laughed at Arjun's desire to record the event on film. In fact Baghaurni and Indra Prasad, who were both at the cowshed when we arrived, asked him to take a photo of the small animal as it first struggled to its feet.

However, I was partially confirmed in my prediction that the birth would seem much more routine and less interesting to our neighbors that it did to us. Surendra was sitting outside his house in the sun listening to Hindi music on the radio. I passed him on the way to the cowshed.

"Are you going to see?" I asked.

"I've seen it, oh, many times before," he said.

Except for Indra Prasad and Baghaurni, the audience consisted mostly of small children.

At first only a glistening protuberance of mucus was visible at the entrance of the buffalo's straining vulva. Then the calf's small bony head poked through and two surprisingly long forelegs dangled from the mother's rear end. The buffalo, tethered on a short rope to a supporting post of the shed, shifted her hind quarters uneasily from side to side.

Within minutes the calf slithered into the world, landing on some straw. The mother slowly turned around, nuzzled the calf briefly, and began to lick her offspring. The afterbirth hung like a sodden bloody scarf behind her. Arjun waited for the calf to stand up for the requisite photograph, but when the calf showed no signs of rising for almost an hour, I lost interest and went back to my clothes washing.

When I passed the shed later in the day, I saw Baghaurni prodding something in the straw with a long pole. She had a look of distaste on her face. It was the placenta, which the buffalo had finally expelled. It had fallen onto the dirt floor of the shed. Mangala stood watching nearby. After several attempts, Baghaurni managed to hook the pole under the mass of bloody tissue. She called to one of her sons to bring a hoe. Moving slowly she walked with the afterbirth balanced on the pole. She headed toward the vegetable patch behind the house. Without putting the pole down, she directed the boy to dig a hole. After the boy had had a brief turn with the tool, Mangala took over. She finished digging a hole about two feet deep. Baghaurni dropped the afterbirth into the hole and shooed away a dog that came up sniffing in interest. "If the dog eats this," Baghaurni said, "the buffalo won't give milk."

That afternoon Baghaurni sent her son to call us to eat a special preparation that could be made from the milk that the buffalo gave during the first two days after calving. The milk was heated on the stove, sugar was added, and, as the milk began to boil, it separated into something resembling curds and whey. They also made a custard with this first milk. Both these special foods were treated as delicacies and were parceled out to all family members and some of the neighbors. Arjun and I also enjoyed the treat. I once re-created the curdlike substance unintentionally while boiling some milk I'd purchased in a plastic bag from a "cold store" in Kathmandu. In the city, we found the resulting curds utterly unappetizing. As I threw out the uneaten remnants of my accidental concoction, I wondered how we could have found it so delicious in the village.

In one of his visits to Arjun and me on his way home from teaching in the upper school in the next village, Tulsi Prasad Ghimire had complained of how the social value placed on keeping a number of dairy animals was creating an "uneconomical" condition in his household. He said that because he was an educated man, studying for his MA in economics, he had many ideas about "reforms" that he would have liked to introduce into the farming of his land. He also told us that he would like to get rid of some of their livestock.

"We have too many cows and buffaloes," Tulsi Prasad complained. "We are importing milk and exporting *ghee*," he quipped.

Tulsi Prasad claimed that the food for animals cost him 10,000 rupees a year. Furthermore, a lot of household labor was taken up with gathering grass for them. His wife, he said, had to spend all her time collecting fodder. He said he would like to take her to visit other parts of the country, but the animals had to eat every day; therefore his wife had no holidays.

"Every day is Sunday and Monday," Tulsi Prasad said. "There is no Saturday for them." (Saturday is a holiday in Nepal; Sunday is a working day.)

"Every day is spent picking grass for the cattle, cleaning their residence. Then life is over," he said mournfully in his peculiar English.

The three of us laughed.

"Why don't you sell them?" I asked. "You could raise a lot of money that way and invest it in some other enterprise."

"I know," groaned Tulsi Prasad. "I would like to sell them. But my mother will not allow this. My mother is the Iron Lady of my house."

(This was a reference to then Prime Minister Margaret Thatcher, who was one of the world leaders in whom Tulsi Prasad took an active interest.) He explained that both his parents, who lived with him, were conservative. Like other Nepalese of their age and experience, they saw cattle as a form of wealth and security and were reluctant to try new methods of farming or to change the organization of their household. When Tulsi Prasad challenged his parents' traditional views by suggesting changes, his parents would threaten him, he said.

"How do they threaten you?" asked Arjun.

"They say, 'we are old now, and useless; we will go off and leave you, your wife, and our grandchildren to yourselves.'"

We all laughed again.

"That's what we call moral blackmail," said Arjun.

Tulsi Prasad looked puzzled. Arjun explained the unfamiliar term in Nepali. Tulsi Prasad sighed and, shaking his head, laughed again.

"Yes, yes, my mother is doing the blackmail," he agreed.

After Baghaurni's buffalo gave birth, we were invited regularly to drink its milk at her house.

"Come in the evening, after you've eaten rice and I'll give you milk to drink," she'd say. Accordingly, we would make our way to Baghaurni's house after dark. She would lead us into the main bedroom, lit only with a few flickering medicine bottle lamps, and direct us to sit on one of the four large bedsteads arranged around the room. Here she, Indra Prasad, their children, and Indra Prasad's younger sisters slept together. Then Baghaurni would disappear into the kitchen. We would sit in the darkness with the soothing sound of peoples' low after-dinner conversations enveloping us. Sometimes we would be joined in the bedroom by Indra Prasad, who sat without speaking, crunching his areca nut and smoking a cigarette. Usually we were under the shy gaze of their two youngest sons, already lying in bed though not yet asleep.

Baghaurni would return with two steaming metal beakers of rich smoky-tasting milk, which we sipped with silent appreciation. Placing the empty tumblers on the floor after we'd drained them, we would return to our hut, warmed by the milk and the quiet Tharu hospitality.

Some mornings, one of Baghaurni's sons or their young *bahāriyā* servant girl would appear at the door of our hut with tea made with buffalo milk. "Bed tea," Ram Bahadur called this. I regarded it as the greatest luxury of living in Pipariya.

The buffalo milk tasted so good, especially given our diet of rice, vegetables, and *dal,* which was otherwise very low in fat; we couldn't get enough of it. Baghaurni was extremely generous in giving us milk. In fact, I sometimes worried that we might be depriving other members of their large household by our consumption.

Before Baghaurni's buffalo began giving milk, we had occasionally bought half a liter of milk from a Brahmin family living just beyond the tea shop. When Baghaurni had found out about our purchase of milk, she had asked me how much we took from them. I told her. "When our buffalo starts giving milk, I will give you that much milk every day. Don't buy milk from the *pahariyās,*" she said. "Take it from me."

This generosity touched me, but I was not about to take so much milk from them for our own use. This put us in a strange position. We would have liked to drink more milk. There were people in the village, like Tulsi Prasad, who had surplus milk and who would have liked to sell it to us. But if we bought milk in the village, it would suggest that her generous gifts of milk were not enough and we might offend her if we got our milk from another house.

Instead we bought powdered cow's milk imported from India. This was not nearly as tasty as buffalo milk, and it had none of the fat that we craved in the fresh milk. Nor did our purchase of it contribute anything to the local economy.

Milk, milk everywhere, nor any drop to drink!

We didn't move into our own hut until after we returned from Kathmandu. On the day that we judged the little house to have dried out sufficiently to inhabit, Bhagavati, Geeta, Surendra, Arjun, and I carried our belongings from the outbuilding we'd been staying in to the hut, about fifty meters away. Our things consisted of a backpack full of clothes and personal effects; two aluminum boxes containing tapes, paper, and books; a year's supply of batteries of various sizes; a tape recorder, short-wave radio, camera, and other photographic equipment. We had made an effort to limit the things we brought to the field so as not to appear ostentatious. In the village it still seemed like a lot of stuff. Ram Bahadur's two male *bahāriyā* servants picked up the wood frame bed we'd been sleeping on and carried it on their shoulders to our hut. They set the bed on pieces of wood embedded in the *māto* floor so that the legs would not gradually sink into the ground.

Shanthi followed them with our bedding: a *gundri,* a pink patterned Chinese-made cotton sheet that we'd bought in Kathmandu, and a *sirak* (quilt) encased in the same thin, soft, gauzy cotton. The nights were still too warm to want anything but the sheet over us. So far we had been sleeping on top of the *sirak,* using it as a kind of pad. I was getting used to our hard bed. I had even become accustomed to the sound of the rats scurrying around in the granary next door at night; their skittering and squeaking had ceased to disturb me.

Soon after our return from Kathmandu, we had bought a small Indian-made kerosene stove in the bazaar, as well as two metal plates and tumblers. Even after we moved into the hut, however, we continued eating with Surendra in his house for several weeks. We used the stove only for boiling water.

It proved surprisingly difficult to initiate cooking for ourselves. When Arjun had lived in the village the previous year, he had taken all his meals at Surendra's house, and now, Surendra's family expected us both to continue this tradition, although we had said from the start that we intended to do our own cooking.

"Why do you want to go to such trouble?" Surendra's mother asked. "Why don't you just eat in our house?"

"Don't be in such a hurry to split the household," Indrani joked. Splitting the household occurs when an extended family divides into two or more groupings, each living in its own house, doing its own cooking, and managing its economic affairs more or less separately. In the old days, we were told, Tharus had very large extended families, with several wives of the head of the household as well as their children and daughters-in-law living in the same house or at least eating out of a common kitchen. Before Surendra's father, the old *jimidār,* had died, the families now headed by Ram Bahadur and his uncle had lived together as a joint family. After the old *jimidār's* death, they had separated into the two households as they were presently organized. They had also divided the land between them. Now Tharu households tended to be smaller; few men could afford more than one wife and people were having fewer children. In other parts of the Tarai, Tharus still lived in big joint families. We had visited one family in the remote western Tarai that was comprised of over fifty members.

Every time we announced our intention to begin cooking for ourselves, a reason was found for us to delay just a little longer. First of all it was *Tihār,* or rather the corresponding Tharu festival called *Soharāyi,* and we were invited to eat special meals with Surendra that included meat. After that we delayed cooking for a few more days when we found that we lacked a gadget necessary to clean our little kerosene stove so that the gas flame would burn evenly. Finally, Arjun laughingly but firmly informed Surendra that we would really begin cooking for ourselves the following day. "All right," sighed Surendra. "You must do what you want."

Arjun was responsible for producing our first meal in our new house. I returned one afternoon from the local primary school where I had started teaching English after the Jithiyā Pāvani was over to find him lying on his stomach on the bed, writing.

"Hello, my lazy husband," I teased him. "Let's make lunch; I'm really hungry."

"Yes, I've just been lying here all day," Arjun said. I didn't catch the playful sarcasm in his voice. If I had, I might have guessed what he had been up to. I put down the satchel I used to carry my schoolbooks and walked into the back room.

"I'll make some rice," I said. Then I saw one of our new aluminum pots sitting on the kerosene stove on the floor. I lifted the lid. A delicious smell of curried vegetables sharpened my pangs of hunger.

"What is it?" I asked.

Arjun had cooked a potato and tomato *tarkāri, dal,* and rice. As we served ourselves and sat down on the bed to eat the meal, Arjun told me about the interest that its preparation had aroused. Surendra's mother in particular had been almost beside herself with curiosity. She had first caught sight of Arjun cooking through our window, while she was at the *dhāra.* After starting for her own house, she had turned and resolutely struck off for our hut. Finding Arjun squatting over a pot on the tiny stove, she had demanded to see its contents. A little while later one of her younger sons showed up at the house with a small metal bowl. He asked Arjun for some of the *tarkāri.* Arjun asked him who had sent him, and he replied that his mother had sent him because she wanted to taste the *tarkāri.*

I asked her later how she had found my husband's cooking. "*Mītho cha,*" she said. She'd found it tasty. However, it seemed that the initial taste of Arjun's curry had not satisfied her curiosity, but only piqued it. Over the next few days, the old lady was frequently hovering around our house, peering through the wire mesh of our window. Carrying her small grandson on her hip, she would come into the kitchen to watch over the preparation of our food. And she was by no means the only one who took an interest in our cooking during the first few weeks. As we were struggling to figure out our temperamental new stove and to arrange the tiny back room so that we could cook in as efficient and convenient a manner as possible, it seemed to me that all the women of the village came trooping through our kitchen. I tried to remain relaxed and remind myself that they were only interested to see how we did things. Moreover, their curiosity was no different from our own, probably more intrusive, anthropological investigations aimed at discovering how their households worked, who cooked, what they cooked and how. Nevertheless, the intrusion on our privacy bothered me. Having all those people in the house made me nervous. I began trying to prepare food at times when I thought others would be busy. I chopped up vegetables inside the house instead of outside on the *wosarā*, which was where Tharus prepared their vegetables for cooking.

The stress of having to display our culinary skills in front of an appreciative audience took its toll on both of us. One evening, with Bhagavati and Geeta ensconced on our bed watching me cook, I burned my thumb. I was already feeling annoyed with myself for leaving the cooking so late. It was dark when I had begun washing the rice and *dal* at the *dhāra* because I had been occupied before that talking with several people who had stopped by. And I felt flustered with the girls watching me and frustrated that my language skills weren't better so that I could have talked more with them. I couldn't seem to cook and speak in Nepali at the same time. After we'd eaten, I lay down on the bed and licked my burned thumb. I complained to Arjun that my back was aching from all the bending over I'd been doing, sweeping and cooking.

Arjun turned down the radio. He observed that I didn't seem to be enjoying life in Nepal very much.

I was surprised by this. I said, on the contrary, I had been thinking only earlier that day how happy I was here. I recited the things I liked about our life in the village: sitting and talking with people, having so much time to be with him without the pressure of studies or a job, even taking care of the house gave me a lot of pleasure.

"You've said nothing but negative things recently," he said.

I thought about this criticism for a moment and realized it was true. I had been complaining a lot, even about the things that I had just

The sleeping room of our house

claimed made our life in Nepal enjoyable. Then I realized that this was perhaps not such a contradiction as it first seemed.

"I am happy here," I told him. "Surprisingly happy, but I have a lot of anxieties about my relationships with people in the village, and about what is expected of me. And you're the only one I can tell these doubts and frustrations to. That's why it seems like I'm always complaining to you, Arjun. There's just no one else."

If the Tharus were curious about our cooking and concerned about our diet, they were downright dictatorial when it came to other housekeeping details, such as keeping our cooking utensils in good condition and sweeping the house and yard properly.

At least in the beginning, I took sole responsibility for washing our pots and plates at the *dhāra*. This was as much to safeguard my *ijjat* (honor) as that of my husband. For what kind of a wife would sit by shamelessly while her husband scrubbed the pots and pans? On the occasions when Arjun did venture out to the *dhāra* with dirty utensils in hand, they were taken from him as he squatted scrubbing away at them with dirt and straw. Giggling, Shanthi or Sita would relieve him of whatever he was washing. After some time, however, they became accustomed to his doing it and left him alone.

The first day I brought a charred pot to the *dhāra* for scrubbing, Shanthi clicked her tongue critically. She told me I should put a layer of *gobar* (cow manure) on the bottom to protect it from being charred by our stove. One day, more to humor her than because I was interested in this method of preventing our pots from becoming discolored with soot, I asked Shanthi to teach me how to put the *gobar* on the pots. My request for instruction was open-ended: whenever you have time, I said. She said she would show me how to do it then and there.

First she took the pots—two aluminum pans that we used for boiling water and making tea—and scrubbed them thoroughly to remove the charred marks from the outside. After thus cleaning them, we moved over to the mound of dirt in the yard where *māto* was mixed for house repairs and other purposes such as this. Shanthi turned the pots upside down on the mound of dirt and asked me to give her some water. She scraped off a layer of dirt from the mound and expertly mixed it into mud with her right hand. Then she stood up, took a few steps over to the cowshed, picked up a small cowpat, and dropped it into the mud she had just mixed. She kneaded this in, too, squeezing it through her fingers to work out the lumps. Then she scooped up a handful of the stuff and delicately spread it over the base of the larger pot. Watching her carefully, I copied her motions and smeared the smaller pot. When we had achieved a thin even layer of *māto* on the bottom of both pans, we left them, upside down, to dry in the sun. When the first layer had dried, we smeared the bottoms of the pots twice more. I was pleased with my handiwork when I placed the larger of my newly protected pots on the stove that evening. When the flame touched the *gobar*, it gave off a slightly sweet, acrid scent. And sure enough, the *māto* layer absorbed the soot from the flame. I had to be careful not to get the bottom of the pan wet when I washed it, until the stuff had baked on for a few days. I also found that the *māto* acted to distribute the heat from our erratic burner more evenly, so that food cooked without burning.

In retrospect, it seems to me that at least part of the curiosity about what we were cooking arose out of concern that we would not be able to feed ourselves properly. For Tharus, this primarily means eating enough rice. Even before we began cooking for ourselves, several people had asked me whether Americans ate rice, or only fruit. At first I was puzzled by this image of my compatriots as a nation of fruit eaters. Then I reflected that Americans on holiday in this area, concerned (with good reason) about the safety of eating local foods and surrounded by a plentiful and, by dollar standards, cheap supply of tasty tropical fruits, probably did subsist largely on bananas, oranges, papayas, and other fruits during their stay, thus creating the impression that this was their natural diet.

The other thing that Nepalese know (or think they know) about Americans is that we eat a lot of bread. Bread is not considered real food in Nepal. It is at best a snack to be taken with tea. It certainly should never replace rice in a proper meal. We quickly discovered that our original idea to eat bread with jam or a boiled egg if we didn't want to take the time to cook would be viewed critically by our neighbors. When Arjun asked Ram Bahadur casually where one could buy bread in the village, Ram Bahadur responded by asking what did we want to be eating bread all the time for. There was *chāmal* (uncooked rice) in his house and we should take as much of that as we wanted.

The morning following our exchange with her father, Geeta strode purposefully over to our house and demanded to know whether we had eaten *bhāt*. She was clearly on a mission.

Feeling flustered at my manifest inadequacy as a cook and provider of proper food, I said no, we were eating another kind of grain that morning. We would cook rice later, I hastened to add. Geeta was not to be deflected from her errand. She took a sample of the wheat-meal cereal I had made for our breakfast in her hand. "What is it?" she asked. I took its plastic package out of the metal box where we kept our perishable goods away from the mice and rats. I was careful not to let her see our instant "chow-chow" packets, the Nepalese equivalent of ramen noodles. "If they catch us eating that for dinner," I told Arjun, "We'll be in real trouble!"

"It's the same stuff bread is made out of," I said.

As soon as I'd uttered the word *pauroti* (bread), I knew I'd confirmed her worst suspicions. Geeta took a sample of the wheat mush and marched back to the big house to show her mother.

In spite of offers of rice from both Ram Bahadur and Indra Prasad, we continued to buy rice at the bazaar. We did this surreptitiously, carrying the rice concealed in a backpack amongst other purchases. Since rice was usually in the largest bundle, this was difficult; I don't think we really deceived anyone, except, partially, ourselves. I was used to other people peering into the pot in which I rinsed the rice at the *dhārā* and exclaiming at how little we ate. One day Indrani leaned over my pot as I was swishing the rice around with one hand under the spout of the well.

"You bought that rice in the bazaar," she accused me. There was nothing I could say. I blushed.

"Why did you buy rice?' Indrani asked. "Why don't you take rice from us? We have plenty of rice."

I tried to reply honestly. "I know that, Indrani-ji," I said. "But we are embarrassed to be eating your rice all the time."

"There is no cause for embarrassment," said Indrani. "Just come and ask in the kitchen for rice. We like it when you take our rice."

A few days later, Indrani walked into the kitchen in the morning with a large woven basket full of rice. I estimated the amount to be about five kilos. There was nothing to do but smile and accept the gift graciously, as it was offered.

One of my most embarrassing memories of life in the village is of being discovered by Indra Prasad during one of his evening visits. Arjun and I were squatting in the kitchen in the dark eating bread and packaged soup because we were both too tired to cook. Taking in the shameful meal with one disdainful glance, he barked, *"bhāt khānu-bayo?"* Have you eaten rice? In Nepali, eating is virtually synonymous with eating rice.

I was too ashamed to say anything.

"We've eaten," said Arjun. "But not rice." An oxymoronic statement.

About once a week we made a trip to the bazaar to buy kerosene, vegetables, and other supplies. Frequently either Arjun or I would borrow a bicycle and ride the six kilometers to the bazaar. Sometimes we went together.

One Saturday in November, we walked to the bazaar carrying our empty five-liter plastic jug for kerosene. We had a few other things to buy, too, but we went first to the far end of the bazaar to the "petrol *tanki*," where about twenty people already stood in line waiting for their ration of kerosene. A young man in a *topi* was scooping the clear liquid out of a big drum. Joining the queue, we asked how much they were giving that day. Petrol and kerosene distribution is under the auspices of the government in Nepal. Nepal imports all its oil, which is transported overland from Calcutta, in trucks. During Iraq's occupation of Kuwait, petroleum products were in short supply; rationing was imposed and people frequently had to stand in line for an hour or more to get a liter of fuel. Or none at all.

Today we were lucky, we received two liters of kerosene: one per person.

Carrying our kerosene jug we walked into the main area of the bazaar. At the intersection of a north-south road and the east-west highway, people were selling all manner of produce and goods from makeshift stalls. I squatted to inspect some tomatoes piled in a woven basket on the ground. A dark, wiry man wearing a *lungi* sat under an umbrella watching me scrutinize his produce. He looked like a Madeshi, someone from the outer Tarai, possibly from India. Madeshis represented a significant portion of the population in the area. Many of them rented small pieces of land, sometimes only a fraction of an acre, to grow vegetables. Tharus told stories of the incredible sums of money that the Madeshis were able to make from selling their produce in the surrounding bazaars. I had heard of people who'd earned 18,000 or 20,000 rupees, twice a civil servant's salary, by growing vegetables on small plots of land. The other thing the Tharus said about the Madeshis was that they worked very hard. "We could never work like that," was a frequent judgment.

"How much for the tomatoes?" I asked.

He seemed to consider my question for a moment. "Twenty rupees a kilo," he said. We had bought tomatoes from a man who came through the village with produce on a bicycle on his way to sell to the tourist hotels for seventeen rupees several days before.

"Too expensive," I said. "Give them to me for fifteen." When I had first arrived in Nepal, I had been embarrassed that Arjun would bargain when buying fruit in the bazaar. "What does it matter?" I'd say. "We have plenty of money. We can pay a few more rupees than other people." After several months in the country, my attitude had changed. I had no desire to exploit these small vendors, but I had come to resent their trying to get more money for their produce simply because I was a foreigner. While I still didn't mind paying an extra rupee or two, I did not want to be "ripped off" by shopkeepers. I didn't want them to think I had no idea of the going market price for things or that money had no value to me.

"These tomatoes are very tasty," the man countered. "They are very good ones." We finally settled on eighteen rupees.

"You certainly have changed your mind about bargaining," Arjun said with a smile as we walked toward a dry goods shop run by a Tharu man. Although Tharus accounted for 30 to 40 percent of the population of that area, few of them had businesses in the bazaar. Besides this shopkeeper, we knew only two other Tharus with businesses in the bazaar. One was Madan Chaudhary, who had brought the Yugoslav to meet us; the other was a man who fixed and sold bicycles. The same was true of the tourist trade. Of thirty or so hotels and lodges in the area, only three were owned and run by Tharus. Among Tharus there seemed to be a certain ambivalence about doing business. When Arjun had told Surendra that he intended to buy a bicycle from the Tharu bicycle mechanic in the bazaar, who happened to be one of Surendra's relatives, Surendra had offered to inspect the bicycle before Arjun bought it to make sure he was getting a good deal.

"Do you think your own uncle would cheat me?" Arjun asked Surendra jokingly.

"Businessmen are always thinking about their profits. Farmers are always thinking how to have food to eat and how to have the happy life," Surendra responded.

I had heard other Tharus express the opinion that shopkeeping was not good work because the shopkeeper buys something for nine rupees and sells it for ten; this is viewed by some Tharus as a form of cheating.

When we arrived at his store, the Tharu shopkeeper was seated cross-legged on a low table, doing some accounts in a ledger. Arjun greeted him in Tharu. The man looked up from his work and beamed. Like most Tharus, he was delighted to hear a foreigner speaking his language. He addressed a few words to me, but I reminded him in Nepali that I couldn't speak the language. His wife came into the shop through a door leading into the back. She also greeted us. She asked if we had eaten. I wondered if she intended to invite us to share a meal with them. We assured her we'd eaten and she disappeared.

The shopkeeper bade us sit down on two stools, and we told him what we wanted to buy from him: a big box of matches, a kilo of onions, two kilos of rice, and a kilo of *dal*. He put our purchases into plastic bags and added up the total. We chatted for a few more minutes and took our leave.

It was late afternoon by this time. "I hope it's still light enough to cook when we get back," I said to Arjun. We divided up the things between us. I carried the grains and the onions in a backpack; Arjun carried the kerosene in one hand and the bag of tomatoes in the other.

As we walked past a mill on the outskirts of the bazaar, a voice called out to us in Tharu, "*Aré, sanhatiyā!*" It was our next-door neighbor Jamhaurni. She was sitting on two sacks of grain atop the family oxcart, which was parked on the edge of the road. The oxen were munching on rice straw nearby. We crossed the road to talk with Jamhaurni. She had come to the bazaar with three of her male relatives to bring some grain to be milled. The men were still in the mill. She asked us what we had been doing in the bazaar. Arjun held up the kerosene bottle and the tomatoes in response.

"Why don't you ride home in the cart with us?" she offered.

We readily agreed. An oxcart is not the way to travel if you're in a hurry, but it sure beats walking when you're tired. We put our bags into the front of the cart and climbed up beside Jamhaurni. Oxcarts in Chitwan have only one axle. The yoke that fits over the oxen's shoulder humps was resting on the ground; this meant that the cart and all its contents and occupants were tipped forward at about thirty degrees. The cart was homemade. Its high sides were carved and painted. Tharu carts tended to depict animals that could be found in the jungle: rhinos, deer, peacocks. They invariably bore the artist's rendering of the English word "wel-come" somewhere on them.

We had been sitting talking with Jamhaurni for about half an hour when the others emerged from the mill with two sacks of grain, which they hefted up on the cart with considerable effort. The sacks must have weighed over 100 pounds each. The oldest of the three men said a few words to Jamhaurni, and they walked off down the road into the bazaar.

"Where are they going?" I asked, hoping that their errand wouldn't take long.

"They're going to buy some pumpkin seeds," Jamhaurni sighed.

We sat in the cart for an hour with Jamhaurni. It was getting dark. The last of the winter's warmth went with the sun. I was wearing only a T-shirt, a light skirt, and rubber *chappals*. I was beginning to feel cold. Every once in a while someone would stick a head out of one of the upper windows of the house opposite. They must have been wondering why we were staying there so long.

Arjun and I got down from the cart and paced around on the road. I said I wished we had walked. We would have been home by now.

"They've probably gone out drinking," Arjun said. "They've sold some rice to the mill and now they're having some *rakshi* in a hotel."

"Where did they go to buy the seeds?" I asked.

Jamhaurni shrugged. *"Thaha chaina,"* she said. She didn't know.

We climbed back on the cart and sat down. We had run out of things to say and sat silently listening to the houses around us making the transition to night. It was a comfortable silence. Still, I found myself casting around for topics of conversation.

"It's taking them a long time to buy the seeds," I commented, not for the first time.

Jamhaurni agreed with me. She did not show any signs of impatience, however. She was used to waiting.

"Having bought the seeds, maybe they are planting them," I said. To my surprise, Jamhaurni apparently found my sarcastic comment funny. She laughed at the thought of the men buying and planting the seeds at dusk. I was pleased that I had succeeded in amusing her and decided to play the idea for all it was worth. "Perhaps they won't come back before harvesting the pumpkins," I said. Again, Jamhaurni laughed uproariously.

We sat in the cart a while longer. I speculated several more times on the progress the men might be making with the pumpkin seeds and each time Jamhaurni laughed appreciatively.

Finally, Arjun said, "Here they come." Jamhaurni and I looked up the road and, sure enough, walking toward us out of the dark were Jamhaurni's three kinsman. Two of them were walking with their arms about one another's shoulders. They all looked slightly unsteady on their feet. Arjun was right. They had been drinking.

They were smiling expansively when they reached the cart. No one said anything about their taking so long and leaving us there to wait in the cart while it got dark. They began to harness the oxen for the trip home. This activity was performed with a lot of boisterous comments flying back and forth between the brothers. (The precise relationship of the three was unknown to me, but they were all members of the same *patidār,* or patriline.) When the hand-carved yoke had been lifted onto the shoulders of the oxen, and we had arranged ourselves on the cart for the journey home, Arjun inquired innocently whether they had bought the seeds.

"No, no," said the man who was driving, sitting on a narrow plank of wood that joined the cart with the yoke and steering the oxen with a stick that he used to prod them in the sides. Another man, picking up the joke, chimed in that they hadn't been able to find any seeds to buy. At this point, Jamhaurni told them what I had said about planting the seeds. They laughed even harder than she had, their enjoyment of my wit enhanced by the liquor.

The oxen, reflecting the drunken guidance they were receiving from their driver, were wandering from one side of the road to the other. "At least drunk driving is less dangerous in an oxcart than in a car," I said to Arjun, hoping the animals knew better than to take us into the ditch.

Every once in a while we met another oxcart coming along the road. I was surprised that so many people were on the road at night. Our high-spirited companions called out greetings to those they recognized. Several times it seemed to me that our carts scraped by one another on the narrow road bordered by a ditch on either side. The most frightening moments came, however, when a motor vehicle overtook us on the road. Luckily they were few and far between. The night was dark, with only a hint of a moon; the headlights of oncoming cars were visible a long way off and blinding as they flashed past. They came relatively fast along the rocky road and rushed past us in a cloud of dust. They seemed somehow sinister, as they raced effortlessly by, propelled by some supernatural force, their passengers comfortably ensconced and impervious to the night world of the villages and countryside they roared through. How strange to think that I was accustomed to riding in such vehicles!

Jamhaurni and I perched on a sack of grain just behind the men who occupied the front section of the cart. Arjun sat in some straw behind us. Shivering, I clasped my arms around my knees. Jamhaurni noticed this and wordlessly put one end of her cotton shawl around my shoulders. I moved closer to her and gratefully pulled the thin cloth around myself.

When we reached the river, the driver reached out and grabbed both animals' tails. He shook them and shouted at the oxen. They reacted by setting off down the inclined sandbank at a gallop. This was the way drivers usually negotiated the river crossing. I suppose the animals had to run faster than the cart down the incline or the yoke would slip over their heads. Tonight we were hurtling into darkness, bouncing around on the sacks of grain. I could just make out Arjun's face in the darkness. He wore a sober expression.

The oxen stepped gingerly into the river. I wondered for a moment if they would balk at crossing in the dark. But they were only pausing for a drink. After a few moments, Jamhaurni's relative slapped the oxen's thighs with his switch, and the wheels of the cart ground slowly forward through the small rocks of the shallow water.

Suddenly, the cart felt stuck. I looked over the side; the water was swirling around the wheels. It seemed we were in a deep part of the channel. I thought back to the stories I had heard about oxen being swept down this river in the monsoon. Why had I never before thought to wonder what had happened to the people they were pulling? The men were all standing, the water was coming into the cart. The driver caught hold of the oxen's tails and jerked them as if they were reins. He yelled at them and whacked them on the rear with his stick. They strained forward and the cart began to move again. I sighed with relief.

I thought our experience might have sobered our drunken friends a bit, but apparently not; as the oxen pulled the cart up the opposite bank, they broke into song. I smiled in spite of myself. At least we were across the river now, and we would reach Pipariya in another half hour or so. Maybe someone in Surendra's house would give us something to eat. I was meditating on this cheerful thought when the cart suddenly listed to port. With a shout, the man who had been sitting on the left side of the cart half jumped, half fell over the side. He landed in the ditch. It took me a moment to figure out what had happened: we had gone off the road. The left wheel of the cart was in the ditch. The ox that had been walking on the right had slipped out from under the yoke. While his *dai* ran after the escaped ox, the driver tried in vain to get the remaining ox to pull the cart back onto the road. Instead the animal took another step into the ditch. The driver hopped down and took the yoke off the ox's neck. The floor of the cart was now at a forty-five degree angle pointing straight into the ditch. The sacks we were sitting on started to slide. I clambered over the side of the cart. When I looked back there was my husband, one hand on the side of the cart with his body spread-eagled over two sacks of grain. In spite of his valiant efforts, he and the sacks were sliding inexorably toward the front of the cart. He just managed to scramble off the side before the sacks slid into the ditch.

"The tomatoes!" Arjun said. We had put our bag of tomatoes on the floor of the cart. When it had been upset, they had all rolled out of the bag into the ditch. We searched around, but we could only recover a few of them. Arjun put them in the pockets of his trousers.

One man came back with the runaway ox. We helped the other two maneuver the cart out of the ditch and push it up onto the road. The men reloaded the bags of grain.

As we climbed back on the cart to continue the journey home, Arjun let out a sound of exasperation and faint disgust. He had put one of his hands into his pocket and discovered the tomatoes again—rather the worse for his efforts to get the cart out of the ditch and reload the rice. We made it home without further excitement, though Arjun and I decided to walk the last few hundred yards to our house where the road narrowed and the ditch was rather deep on one side.

Later that week we transplanted some 200 tomato plants that we had grown from seeds. We had also planted some carrots and some spinach. We looked forward to the time when we could harvest some of our own vegetables and would not have to go to the bazaar to buy them.

CHAPTER FIVE

Kathmandu

More than anything else, our periodic trips to Kathmandu meant anonymity and the privacy and freedom that escaping the intricate web of relationships in the village afforded us. In Kathmandu I was just another Western tourist to be hassled by brazen hustlers hawking carpets and wildly colored sweaters in Indra Chowk, to be served imitation Western food with good-natured deference in one of Thamel's many restaurants, to be outrageously overcharged for fruit in Asan tole, to be leered at and "eve-teased" by teenage boys on New Road.

At first I resented the assumption that I was just another tourist. I tried to behave in a way to convince myself—if not other people—that I was different from the other foreigners I saw on the streets of the capital. I responded in curt Nepali to the sidewalk carpet-seller's rasping "like to see carpet, Madam . . ." followed in the same breath but a few decibels lower: ". . . change money?" Months later when I had renounced my superiority as a resident in the country and merely affected, like other weary wanderers of Kathmandu's streets, a determined aloofness, I was ridiculed by one young carpet salesman (and would-be black market banker): "*Pardaina, chaindaina malai,*" he would taunt me as I passed his shop. (I don't need or want [carpets].) I had to smile at the self-righteous and rather foolish image of myself suggested by his parody.

In the beginning I somehow thought that my long-term status, my understanding of the language, and interest in the culture ought to exempt me from the vulgar ogling of young men, the "hellow, one rupees," of insolent schoolchildren, the importunate begging of old men, and most of all, the nonstop badgering of street vendors. Occasionally, walking through Thamel at night, Arjun and I were offered "smoke" or "hashish" by a figure leaning out of the shadows. All this I found distasteful, but I eventually came to question my annoyance and was forced to confront the fact that part of what disturbed me was that I didn't relish the intrusion by real people into my fantasy version of Nepal, a world in which I was the star protagonist—the searching, sensitive, inquiring, sympathetic Westerner who was vastly superior to the preoccupations of the average tourist. I also had to come to terms with the fact that to a large extent I had to inhabit a role that had been defined for me by the thousands of other foreigners who had come before.

If our stay in Kathmandu was a short one—to get immunizations or to attend to some business—we stayed in a room reserved for Fulbright scholars on the roof of the United States Educational Foundation (USEF) office in Thamel. The room at the USEF was long and narrow. It was just wide enough to permit the length of a bed at one end. At the other end of the room (only a few feet away) was a desk. Two chairs and a chest of drawers were also provided for our use. The room opened out onto one of the flat concrete roofs on which so much of Kathmandu's life takes place: clothes drying, food preparation, rug-making, kite-flying.

On a clear day in the fall or winter we could see the hills ringing the valley and the dome of the Buddhist stupa of Swayambunath to the west. We could also look down into the lanes of the neighborhood at women scooping water from pipes that ran under the streets. They filled plastic and clay vessels with water to carry home. Women also brought plastic basins and washed clothes there on the spot.

Next door to us, in a position to look down on our clothes washing activities, the huge brick house of a prosperous Newar grain merchant loomed over the USEF building. From early in the morning we could hear the sounds of carters throwing all their strength behind flat wagons loaded with sacks of grain to get them up the slight incline at the top of our unpaved little lane. Their grunts and exhortations to one another were interspersed with the ringing of a bell in the temple across the way as people performed their morning *pūjās*. Sometimes I would catch a glimpse of a teenage girl dressed in Western clothes leaning over the parapet of the grain merchant's house talking on a cordless phone. The image of someone using a cordless phone in Kathmandu struck me as incongruous. But when I saw an old lady, perhaps the girl's grandmother, dressed in the traditional Newar black-and-red sari with long, gray tresses hanging down her back clasping the receiver to her ear and talking animatedly while hanging out the washing one day, I realized that I had been romanticizing a dichotomy between the modern and traditional that didn't necessarily exist.

Staying at the USEF reminded me of a book that had caught my fancy as a child, called *From the Mixed-up Files of Mrs. Basil E. Frankweiler*, in which a brother and sister had run away from home and had gone to live secretly in a museum. During the day they hid their belongings and mingled with groups of schoolchildren who visited the museum on field trips. At closing time when the guards checked to make sure everyone had left, they stood on toilet seats in the bathrooms to avoid discovery. At night they bathed in a fountain and collected small change to buy themselves food. At USEF we confined our activities to the roof during the day, venturing into the downstairs rooms only after office hours. We had use of a kitchen on the second floor where the offices of the director and accountant were located. Since the kitchen was only accessible through the accountant's office, we didn't like to use it during office hours. We would fix ourselves tea and a quick breakfast early in the morning, snack on fruit and biscuits during the day, and cook dinner after the staff left at 5:30.

After months of struggling with our temperamental kerosene stove in Pipariya trying to maintain an even flame long enough to cook a meal, the automatic glow of the coils in the electric burner produced by a flick of the wall switch seemed magical. And preparing food on counters at waist height instead of squatting or sitting on the floor of our hut was luxury itself. However, we were both amused one day when I remarked to Arjun, quite seriously, that a good coating of *gobar* would put an end to the tendency for rice to burn on the bottom of the pan where it came into contact with the electric coil of the burner. "Where are you going to get cow shit to smear on our pots in Chicago?" he teased me.

One of the things I looked forward to about coming to Kathmandu was the hot indoor private shower at the USEF, also located on the second floor and used only after hours.

In the evenings we would descend to the comfortably appointed second floor offices, make ourselves a hot cup of Horlicks, and sit under the fluorescent lights reading English language magazines and writing letters.

During one of our longer stays in Kathmandu, USEF arranged for us to rent a *derā,* (apartment) in Patan, one of the three ancient kingdoms of the Kathmandu valley. Our neighborhood was dominated by the headquarters of various international aid agencies. At one end, Save the Children and the Japanese Volunteers organization; at the other end, the Embassy of Myanmar (Burma).

Our *derā* was on the second floor of a four-story house. The landlord lived on the top floor; he invited us up several times to sit on the roof with him and watch the planes taking off and landing at Kathmandu's Tribhuvan airport. On a clear day, we also enjoyed a beautiful view of the Himalaya to the north. The apartment was new, convenient, well lit, and, except for the infrequent and exciting roar of planes landing, quiet.

It also came with a *didi. Didi* means elder sister in Nepali. It is also the term used to refer to a woman who is hired to clean house and cook, as well as to perform other household tasks such as shopping. In other words, a servant.

I was uncomfortable with the idea of having a servant. "We don't need any help with the housework," I protested to Arjun when he told me the arrangements USEF had made for us. "There are only two of us. We are used to doing everything for ourselves, and I'm not even working here. Why don't you just tell USEF we don't want a *didi?"*

Arjun pointed out that that wouldn't be fair to the *didi.* She was used to working for whoever rented this apartment.

"Well, we can do our own cooking," was my final comment.

The day after we moved into the *derā,* Didi showed up. She was a middle-aged Newar. She was dressed in a red sari. Her yellowed teeth and persistent cough suggested that she smoked, but I never saw her with a cigarette. She was friendly but deferential. She addressed Arjun as "sir" and me as "memsahib," which I hated. Memsahib reeked of colonialism and conjured up images of brown men in turbans bowing and scraping before the frivolous and plaintive demands of Victorian ladies. I considered asking Didi not to call me that, but I didn't know how to explain why I found the word so objectionable or what she could substitute for it. More than that, I thought, what right did I as a short-term resident have to attempt to restructure her relations with expatriate white women? Wasn't that really more presumptuous than trying to accept and adapt to the relationship that Didi thought appropriate, however foreign it might seem to me?

As I reflected more on my interactions with Didi, I realized that my aversion to dealing with a servant was as much cultural as it was personal. It was not the economic relationship that I disliked. We were paying for her help in the house, not directly, but through our rent. I found that if I thought of Didi as an employee providing remunerated services to an employer I felt better about the relationship, although I still felt uncomfortable having a stranger cleaning up after me. If I could somehow reduce Didi's cooking and cleaning to the status of a mere job I had no problem with it.

It was the social relationship that I found uncomfortable, the way that class (and racial) hierarchies were manifested in the house. I couldn't reconcile the image I had of myself and my presence in Nepal with my image of someone who had a servant.

On the one occasion when Didi did cook for us, she served us our food at the table in the dining room. She ate, after we had finished, squatting in the kitchen. Since I had embarrassed her earlier by offering her a seat when she first arrived at the house, Arjun warned me not to repeat the mistake by inviting her to eat with us. Months later, as I squatted with my own plate of food after having served a guest in our hut in Pipariya, I smiled at the recollection of my horror at walking into the kitchen with my dirty plate and fork to find Didi squatting in the corner eating rice with her hand.

One day, just before we left to go back to Pipariya, Didi arrived later than usual. She had come over sick the previous night, she explained. She was still feeling sick and weak. In fact, her hands were shaking as she described her symptoms to us: nausea, fever, and headaches. She had had to take a "tempo," one of the numerous Indian-made small motorized three-wheeled vehicles that serve as taxis in Kathmandu. She asked us for fifteen rupees to cover the fare; Arjun gave it to her.

"You shouldn't have come," we told her. We suggested that she go home and rest; we assured her that we didn't need her help that day. In fact, we were finished with our morning meal and, since we were leaving the next day, were almost out of food; we had cooked and eaten everything and cleaned up the kitchen.

Didi said she was going to meet the USEF accountant later to get her pay; that was why she had come. She would work *bistaré, bistaré,* (slowly), she said. Again we urged her to rest but she seemed determined to get on with her tasks.

She asked us if we wanted her to make us some tea. It occurred to me that she probably wanted a cup of tea herself. Apologetically, I told her that we had used up the last of the tea, as well as our milk, that morning. What about food? Would we like her to cook for us?

My satisfaction at having finished our meal before Didi arrived so as to avoid the issue of being served by her vanished as it struck me for the first time that by cooking for us she also got to eat.

"Have you eaten?" I asked her.

"No."

Our efficiency had deprived her even of a cup of tea. I felt mean.

Although we had never stopped at the place, I had noticed a tea stall just beyond the intersection of our narrow lane with the main road to Patan. Taking a jar, I hurried up the road. It took me about ten minutes of fast walking to reach the tea shop. As I sped along on my errand to bring tea to my sick servant, I felt righteously confirmed in all my egalitarian objections to having servants. How ironic, I thought. Wasn't having a servant supposed to free up one's time, save one work and bother, and make life easier? This was the opposite situation. I was vindicated in my objection to Didi and her intrusion into our life, our privacy, our established self-sufficient routine. I disliked her subservience, which was only a ploy, anyway, wasn't it? I mean, she could call me "memsahib" all she wanted, but here I was going to fetch her tea!

At the tea shop I asked for two cups of tea, indicating that I wanted to take it away in the jar. I waited impatiently for a few minutes as the tea shop owner pumped up his kerosene stove to heat the brew. Then I returned with the steaming hot glass.

It was mostly downhill on the way back, but I couldn't walk as fast because I was carrying the jar full of tea. As I picked my way carefully along the rocky path, I thought about my indignation at being imposed upon by Didi. I had been thinking of the relationship in primarily economic terms. She was the servant; I was the employer. She should work and get paid; I should be responsible for paying her for the work (and nothing else—no bus fare, or medicine) and receive the benefits of her remunerated labor. Her health was her problem, not mine. But in a society where what we might call "personal" problems are not mediated by impersonal institutions such as insurance companies or state-supported medical care, are not the personal problems of the servant actually the responsibility of an employer? By the time I had reached the house, having sloshed only a little of the tea out of the jar, I was feeling more kindly disposed to poor Didi, who was after all sick; bringing her a cup of tea seemed the least I could do.

I poured some of the tea into a glass and set it in front of Didi. "This is for you; drink it," I said.

"I have caused you so much *dukkha* (trouble)," said Didi. "You drink some, too." She looked around for another glass.

"No, no," I assured her, still a little self-righteously. "We drank lots of tea this morning; this is all for you." So she drank the tea and said she felt better for it.

After living in Pipariya and visiting other Tharu villages in the Tarai, our interactions with people in Kathmandu often seemed artificial. The city seemed corrupt and our relationships with people merely commercial or downright confrontational, determined by patterns of contact conditioned by the tens of thousands of other foreigners who passed through the valley each year.

Whenever I got to feeling that Kathmanduites were jaded, unfriendly, or impolite, in marked contrast to the Nepalese I had encountered in my travels to other parts of the country, it seemed I would be treated to an experience that flew in the face of this harsh judgment on the capital's inhabitants and restored my conviction that a good-humored generosity was the fundamental characteristic of all Nepal's people. One such incident happened during Indra Jatra.

Indra Jatra is an eight-day festival falling in August or September. It commemorates the visit of the god Indra to the valley, where he was kept captive after he stole some flowers from a garden. In return for freeing him, Indra's mother agreed to take the souls of all those who had died the previous year to heaven and to provide dew and mist to ensure a good harvest. The celebration of her gifts to the valley is accompanied by dancing and visits to temples. The highlight of the festival is the procession of the living goddess Kumari through the city's streets in a chariot. This is called the Kumari Jatra.

During Indra Jatra, the King receives *tikā* from the Kumari, a young girl chosen from the Newar subcaste of Sakyas. This year Indra Jatra fell during the interval between the time that the King had promised that a new democratic constitution would be forthcoming and the date, more than two months later, when it was actually promulgated. The King's procession was from the new palace at the top of Durbar Marg to the throne room in the old palace, Hanuman Dhoka, from where he would witness the procession of the Kumari and two young boys who serve as her escorts, the living Ganesh and the living Bhairab in their respective chariots.

The uncertainty surrounding the appearance of the new constitution meant that this Indra Jatra festival was taking place in an atmosphere more tense than usual. I was curious to see how the Nepalese who lined the King's route along New Road would react to the monarch against whom they had recently risen up. What was the nature of the authority of the King in the aftermath of the *jana andolan* (People's Movement) the previous April when he had capitulated to the demands of the successful democracy movement that he lift the ban on political parties? Would it make any difference that the King was riding among his subjects as a constitutional monarch for the first time in Nepal's history? I thought I might glean some answers to these questions by gauging the responses of spectators waiting along the parade route.

Arjun and I had tried to push our way into the crowded Hanuman Dhoka area so that we could watch the King's arrival, but there were too many people with the same idea. So we stood along the railings on the slightly less congested New Road and watched the crowd and the uniformed police and mounted soldiers patrolling the area.

The King's entourage was late. It was beginning to rain. We had just about decided to give up and head for home when the police at the Thundikel end of the street started blowing their whistles and waving their arms. Cars carrying ambassadors and Nepalese ministers of state had been driving past us the whole time we'd been standing there. They had driven slowly, or at least conservatively, through the crowd. The King's motorcade on the other hand, drove by at top speed. First a white-suited military guard whizzed by on a motorcycle. Following him, several jeep-loads of police rushed by at intervals of a few seconds. Directly preceding the King's black stretch Mercedes Benz, another car sped by with flashing lights. This might have been a security measure. In a country where the most common kind of vehicle is an oxcart, however, the very speed of the King's twentieth-century chariot seemed symbolic of the degree of his difference and isolation from his subjects, as if not even the same physical laws applied to his move-ment among them.

The King and the Queen were seated in the back of the Mercedes. They were visible to the crowd but seemed utterly oblivious to it. As their car sped to Durbar Square they looked neither left nor right at their subjects who had been waiting for a glimpse of them. I was struck by how much they looked like their portraits, which hung in every village school and tiny shop in the kingdom. They looked like three-dimensional versions of their pictures; they didn't look like real people at all. As they passed in front of us, a slight ripple of applause went through the crowd. Then people drifted away. The spectacle, at least where we had been standing, was over.

It had begun to rain quite hard. Folding our arms across our chests and hunching over to try to keep dry, we hurried, along with a mass of other people, toward Ratna Park to catch our bus back to Patan Dhoka and the shelter of our *derā*.

Then it started to pour. We were walking along a little lane off New Road. We stopped in a doorway to a staircase leading up into a resi-dence or business. Sitting on a box in a tiny opening in the wall, which was actually the stairwell of the stairs we were sheltering in, an elderly woman was knitting as she kept an eye on the jars of homemade pickles (*achar*) that stood on a table on the street in front of her stall. I leaned against the one side of the stairwell, and Arjun against the other. The old lady looked up from her knitting at the rain pelting down on her jars of preserved fruits and vegetables.

"*Pāni*" (water, rain), she said, reaching behind her into her closet of a shop and pulling out a stool, which she handed to me. "*Basnus*" (sit), she said.

I smiled appreciatively. I asked her what she was knitting. A sweater for her granddaughter, she said. How did I know Nepali? I explained that I was living in the country. On hearing that I was teaching English in Chitwan, she asked how much I was being paid and seemed dis-pleased to hear I was not getting a salary for my work. There were many schools in Kathmandu that would pay well for a foreign English teacher; why didn't I try one of them? She asked me whether Arjun was from Japan, which threw me for a moment. When I mentioned that I could knit, she wordlessly handed me her needles. There was a look of challenge in her eyes. I tried to replicate her pattern and made a mistake that caused her to break into a wide, toothless grin of triumph.

She was from the Punjab, she said. It was beautiful there, she told me, adding that the Punjabi milk was the most delicious in the world. Had I tried it? Had I ever been to India?

"No."

I should go.

Meanwhile Arjun was engaged in conversation with a doctor from Bir Hospital who had also taken shelter from the rain in the stairway. Every once in a while, they had to step aside to let someone pass out from the stairs. The doctor was expressing interest in Arjun's research on Tharus and suggested that Arjun visit his village in Dang in the far Western Tarai. Before darting off to the hospital through the rain, he wrote down the address of friends and relations to contact in Dang if we went there as well as his own phone number at the hospital, where he invited us to come and visit him, "but not as a sick," he joked in English, before taking leave of us.

We waited a while longer in the company of the old lady and her pickles. Although none of us spoke much more, it was a companionable silence. When the rain had let up enough for us to continue on our way, the old lady rustled around in the back of her little cubby hole and brought forth a plastic bag. "*Pāni*," she said again, pointing at the notebook I was carrying with me. I smiled and gratefully put my notebook and pen into her plastic bag. Unlike in the United States where plastic bags are given out free of charge, they are used sparingly by shopkeepers in Nepal. I've had a shopkeeper transfer my purchases out of a plastic bag into a homemade paper one (usually constructed out of pages torn from children's used copybooks) when I decided I wanted two rather than four eggs. Frequently street vendors charge a rupee for such a bag.

As we walked away, I reflected that the old lady had offered all the hospitality it was within her power to give the two strangers who had taken shelter near her stall. She had cheerfully shared a dry place with us, given me her only stool to sit on, and provided a plastic bag for my notebook. As we walked away I said happily to Arjun, "She gave me a bag."

"I know," he said.

"But isn't that nice!"

Most of Thamel's begging children seem to congregate along the narrow street leading to the Kathmandu Guest House. There they importune tourists to "give one rupee" as they emerge from boutiques selling silver and turquoise jewelry, *"rangi-changi"* (many-colored) sweaters, and loose tie-dyed pants or from restaurants serving Asian imitations of French pastries, English cakes, and American "home-style" egg breakfasts.

Sternly informing a ragged boy with a runny nose that we were not going to give him one rupee, and furthermore that "begging was not good work," Arjun and I turned into a staircase leading up into Alice's Restaurant, a second-floor restaurant overlooking the psychedelic Thamel street scene.

We have a policy of not giving money to children in Nepal. The act of begging, unless it is sanctioned for religious or social reasons, as in the case of *sadhus*, (holy men) asking for alms, is degrading. This is especially the case when children exaggerate their vulnerability (or are actually maimed) to exploit the pity of adults. We observed that begging corrupted children who might otherwise pursue some other kind of work. We found that when we visited places where tourists didn't regularly go, there was no begging among children. Where tourists went, the children had learned to beg, suggesting a phenomenon that has grown up largely in response to the tourist presence in the Kathmandu valley.

Entering Alice's is like walking into a cafe in Berkeley or Chicago's Northside, only not quite. We pause at the front counter stocked with Western music tapes to pick up a newspaper to read over breakfast. I choose today's *The Rising Nepal*. Arjun selects a few recent issues of *The International Herald Tribune*. An espresso machine hisses as we head for a table overlooking the street. Alice's, as usual, is full of Westerners. My husband is the only Asian who is seated at a table. Three young Nepalese men make their way between the closely spaced tables, pouring coffee and taking orders for croissants, pancakes, and steak (buffalo) and egg breakfasts.

When I'd first arrived in Nepal, this self-contained tourist world of Thamel had seemed so strange to me, catering to the gustatory whims of homesick travelers, like some kind of Platonic parody. Now I am more or less used to it and enjoy having omelets and "home fries" served to me while I sip coffee and read the newspaper.

I skim the front page of Nepal's only English language daily, mostly culled from AP reports. I steal glances at my fellow breakfasters. They are mostly young, mostly male trekker types, some with long hair, many with beards. Almost all are sporting *rangi-changi* sweaters and cold-weather-trekker appetites. Here and there a solitary tourist sits absorbed in a book, picking away at Alice's breakfast fare. One twenty-ish woman in a tie-dyed skirt with close-cropped hair and a nose ring sits absorbed in Salman Rushdie's *Midnight's Children,* hardly touching her bowl of yogurt and muesli.

I am surrounded by my countrymen. At the table next to ours is a convert to Buddhism from Vermont. He's telling an older woman about a retreat he's just returned from, "um, like above Pokhara," where some *lāmās* had said some things he "really needed to hear," and he'd had some "real moving experiences." The older woman nods. She orders another glass of fresh-squeezed orange juice.

At the table by the next window, which should have been out of earshot, a voluble young woman is terminating a "relationship," while continuing to endorse "friendship" and telling a silent and crestfallen young man that she's enjoyed the time they've spent together, but that she "just can't commit anymore," at least not until she can get back to the United States and "get her head together."

Behind me I hear a sun-browned sinewy middle-aged man ordering his breakfast. He enunciates carefully and omits most articles in the exaggerated way that Americans speak English to foreigners. When the waiter has taken his order to the kitchen, the man remarks to his female companion that he never drinks milk in his coffee at home. Or sugar. "I usually drink lattes," the woman responds. "But I've started mixing some decaf beans in with the regular."

The guilty twinges I felt dodging past the boy begging outside to reach the safe haven of Alice's Restaurant are rekindled by a story on Kathmandu's street children in *The Rising Nepal.* The author of the full-page article reckons their numbers to be 5,000. Some of these children are described as "rag-pickers" and pickpockets. Others, like the boy on the street outside, make a living by begging money from tourists. The article includes several case histories. One of them is about a little girl whose father died of tuberculosis. According to the article, she now contributes the money she receives from tourists to help support her mother and siblings. They live in one of Kathmandu's filthy slums. How can I, I wonder, feel righteous about refusing money to such children?

Once, as I was walking from the USEF to the Peace Corps headquarters to collect some English teaching materials, I met a man, wrinkled, weather beaten and stooped, who was carrying a limp child on his back. The little girl, who may have been five or six, showed no signs of consciousness; her head was buried in the man's neck. He stopped me and silently handed me a prescription from Kalimati Children's Hospital. He said it was for some *aushadi* (medicine) for his daughter who was sick. I had no doubt that his plight was real, although I couldn't read the prescription, which was scrawled in handwritten Nepali. As I stood staring at the piece of paper I couldn't really read, the man told me the medicine for his daughter cost 120 rupees, about four dollars. "I don't have 120 rupees," I lied. In fact, I was carrying over 200 with me. I handed the man a ten-rupee note and walked off, telling myself that he could collect money from other tourists in this same way (ignoring the fact that he hadn't spoken any English with me) and assuring myself that ten rupees was a generous sum to give to a perfect stranger. But as I walked past the government dairy and along the wall surrounding the royal palace, I wondered if I hadn't just acted to avoid involvement in the old man's problems and any kind of responsibility for his daughter's illness, whatever it was. On the other hand, I thought, if I hadn't been here, if the man had not had the opportunity of asking a foreigner for help, what would he have done then? As I so often did in Nepal, I was contending with a feeling that I wasn't really here. I wasn't really part of the Nepalese reality; I was just a phantom, a voyeur, aloof and uninvolved, immune in a sense, to the consequences of my actions in this alien land, exempted from any lasting effects of my fleeting presence in this country. Sometimes my experiences in Nepal seemed so far out of my real existence, my American reality, it was as if I had been transported to Nepal by some kind of time machine. If I did anything that really affected people here, I'd be stuck. To be really fully here was just too scary: there were too many sick, hungry, needy people.

Of course to be really fully here in the United States, at least in our large cities, is to be confronted with our own beggars, "the homeless," as I was reminded when I paid a visit to my parents in southern California on my way back to Chicago from Nepal. Not that I have ever encountered any beggars in the suburb where my parents live, but one Saturday afternoon we drove into Los Angeles to see a play at the Music Center in the heart of downtown LA, which seemed, at least on this Saturday, to be populated exclusively by homeless people. When we parked our car in a parking structure and walked the four blocks to the theater, we were besieged by requests for money from the people we passed. Dressed up for the outing, we seemed to be the only theater-goers on the street. Everyone else had apparently taken advantage of a shuttle bus between the garage and the Music Center.

Compared to the beggars I had become accustomed to in Nepal, the people importuning us, black and white, young and middle-aged, seemed relatively well dressed and outwardly healthy. Most noticeably, they all wore shoes. Yet strangely the fact that my countrymen appeared in absolute terms better clothed than Nepalese beggars engendered in me not less pity for them, but more. I realized that there were few instances when I had truly identified with Nepalese beggars. They had always seemed completely other. But here were other Americans, people who lived in my country and spoke my language, and they were in need. Perhaps not as great in absolute terms, but compared to the resources of the country, greater relative deprivation, than beggars in Nepal. More striking to me than their outward appearance was their attitude in asking us for money. Below the superficial attitude of deference and subservience of the Nepalese beggar, one is aware that he or she is making a socially legitimate claim on the greater resources and status—and therefore responsibility—of the person being asked for money. Begging invokes a social relationship in Nepal. In contrast, I felt that the beggars in LA had no social claim on us. We had arrived from the suburbs in our car and after the play we would return. In spite of the nagging tug of common citizenship, I felt in no way part of the same community, the same social fabric.

When my mother told one young black woman that we'd just given the last of our "spare change" to someone else, she responded cheerfully, "God bless you for giving to anyone!"

This was my initial reintroduction to begging in the United States. When I returned to the Hyde Park neighborhood of the University of Chicago it seemed to me that there were more homeless people than I had remembered, but maybe Nepal had heightened my awareness in some way. It also struck me that the tendency to lump all the people who beg on the streets of our cities into the category "homeless" underscores our desire as a society to avoid the social relationship implicit in the act of begging by shifting the focus from the act of begging, which is a form of social interaction, to a more abstract lack of housing, which is a material fact. Homelessness means exclusion from such social relationships. But as I resettled into my life in Chicago again, I ceased trying to compare the homeless with beggars in Nepal; I just sought to avoid them.

When we spent a longer time in Kathmandu, one thing that spoiled my enjoyment of walking the city's streets by myself was the "eve-teasing" that I was regularly subjected to. Eve-teasing is the practice of men, usually young and in groups, making comments or gestures to women on the streets. The term originated in North India, where the phenomenon is even more prevalent and has provoked protest marches on the part of beleaguered and fed-up women. I am prepared to admit that this kind of public intimidation of women in Nepal is relatively mild, compared with many other countries of the world, but it's still annoying to be leered at and catcalled after on the streets. As a foreigner, one already feels exposed, and as a Western woman in Kathmandu, one is more likely to be a target of obnoxious looks and comments from young men, mostly from middle-class families.

Having made, as I felt I had, every reasonable personal effort to dress and behave in a way that would not be considered immodest or inappropriate according to local standards, I resented that these expressions of Nepalese beliefs about Western women—that we are sexually promiscuous, irresponsible with money, and stupid—were aimed at me.

I found that the annoyance of American women who spent a long time in Kathmandu with these perceptions was nearly universal. "It's just a huge misunderstanding," one of my friends who had spent almost as long as I had in the country said. She was agonizing over a slap in the face she had delivered to a kid who had pinched her on the rear. "It was automatic," she said, "but I shouldn't have hit him." I disagreed. I thought that her action had been the culturally appropriate response. When I asked the other women teachers in the school what one should do if one were insulted by a boy, they both responded without hesitating, "hit him." But as my friend pointed out, "these kids probably see some tourist pinch his girlfriend's ass in Thamel, and then she kisses him."

"It's not the same," I maintained. "It doesn't translate into what happened to you." But we both agreed that the revealing dress and violation of sexual decorum by Western tourists did adversely affect respect for foreign women.

Still, I couldn't agree with people (usually men) who diagnosed the phenomenon as having been caused solely by the dress and behavior of Western women. That was only part of the story of cultural misunderstanding. I became angry with a Swiss tourist who was holding forth on the treatment of Western women in India. "If they dress modestly, there's no problem," he asserted. I knew from my experience in Nepal that this was untrue. An individual's actions and appearance, no matter how circumspect, could not deflect and certainly not reverse stereotypes determined on a larger cultural level. I knew that what my friend described as a "huge misunderstanding," was more complex than that. In the first place, "eve-teasing" is not a plague on foreign women exclusively. Nepalese women are also subjected to unwelcome comments and touching in public. To some extent this behavior can be correlated with dress and behavior; women in Westernized dress out alone attract more attention than accompanied women in traditional attire, but again, individual modesty and propriety don't protect Nepalese women from abuse any more than they do Western women. And factors seemingly unrelated to eve-teasing or sexual relations generally seem to affect them. For example, one respectable middle-class Newar woman in her early thirties told me that during the tense period leading up to the general elections she had been subjected to more eve-teasing than usual when she went out. She felt that the increased political uncertainty contributed to the eve-teasing. This suggests some interesting and troubling connections between men's general sense of anxiety or unease and their tendency to channel such tensions into intimidating and harassing behavior toward women.

I tried to puzzle out exactly what was going on with this "teasing" with my friend Martha, an American who had lived and studied in Nepal for over three years. In fact, the subject seemed to come up whenever we got together. Martha shared my impression that boys engaged in this kind of behavior primarily (though not exclusively) in groups, not on their own. Her observation was that the eve-teasers were usually middle-class and had some education. Neither of us had ever been hassled by someone who looked like a laborer. She linked the phenomenon to urbanization and exposure to Western culture, especially in the form of videos, but she didn't think direct observation of tourists in Kathmandu was as important as people assumed. She made some observations about caste: Brahmins and Chhetris were less likely to engage in conspicuous teasing; their behavior in public was more constrained than that of Newars, for example. She also thought that Tibetan peoples such as Sherpas, sometimes teased differently— with a little more finesse. Not "fuck you, American," but "would you sleep with me?" She speculated that this may be because Tibetans and Sherpas grow up with sex; it is not taboo in the way it is for the Hindu caste groups like Brahmins and Chhetris. Another group that was particularly prone to harass women were the sons of "Gurkhas," Nepal's mercenary soldiers who serve in the British and Indian armies. Drawn primarily from the Magar and Gurung ethnic groups, the behavior of the children of these "Lahurees" (from Lahore, where the British traditionally recruited Nepalese hill people for their Gurkha regiments) may result from exposure to Western lifestyles, relative wealth and prestige in Nepalese society, a deemphasis on education, and possibly from the disjuncture between military and civilian culture.

I also wondered what it was that bothered me about the comments. Why couldn't I just ignore them and walk on by as I would at home? I came to the conclusion that it was not only my foreigner status, but also the social context in which I experienced the insults that made it different. In Nepal, insulting words pose a very real threat to respect, which I came to think of as a kind of social glue, providing some cohesion for a diverse society, perhaps also keeping its members in hierarchically determined places, but nonetheless keeping people from one another's throats. Paradoxically, the fundamental importance of respect for the conventions of social distance makes it more difficult to ignore unwelcome comments from strangers in Nepal than it would be to shrug off the analog in the United States, say, catcalls from construction workers. If you can pretend that you didn't hear the comment and get out of earshot before the next salvo, you've probably won the battle. This is because respect is not the cement that holds our society together; to the extent that anything does—and American society is more atomized and loose-knit than Nepali society—it's the values of personal autonomy and privacy. That guy on the scaffold has a *right* to say rude things to you. You, of course, have a right to say rude things back, but if he doesn't violate the sense of privacy held dear by most Americans, if he doesn't impinge on your personal "space," you probably won't be very bothered by his comments. At least I wasn't, before I went to Nepal, that is. After putting up with eve-teasing in Kathmandu, pondering its meaning for gender and cross-cultural relations, complaining bitterly to anyone who would listen, and always walking around prepared to respond to the next insult, fantasizing about the perfect comeback, I returned to the United States much more aware and wary of even small groups of unknown men and boys. Perhaps partly the need I developed in Nepal for respect for my visible public persona contributed to the increased trepidation with which I regarded groups of men on the street back in Chicago. More fundamentally, however, I think the exasperation and anger I experienced in Nepal brought home to me that euphemisms about "teasing" aside, this behavior, whether it takes place in East or West, is at bottom aimed at the intimidation and control of women. It may have other social functions, but its main effect is to erode women's feeling of ease in public spaces, wherever they are subjected to it.

A few months after I returned to Chicago, I was on my way to the university one afternoon when two youths approached me through an alley—gangly Black kids with baggy pants and untied tennis shoes. They looked in their mid-teens. Probably on the way back to school after lunch, I thought. I was conscious of a nervous feeling as they approached. I wasn't afraid of them, exactly. I didn't fear that they would *do* anything to me. What I dreaded was that they would say something. Something that would force my public, if only tacit, acknowledgment, in this university enclave on the Black southside of Chicago, of the gulf of antagonism between Black and White. In this divided city. In this divided country. As the distance between us narrowed, I felt, just as I had in Nepal, that it was not as a white person but as a woman that I was vulnerable to shame. Oh, what if they said something?

In fact, one of them did say something, just as we passed on the sidewalk. I didn't catch the words but the tone was taunting. I felt myself blush with shame and then with anger. Without really thinking what I was doing, I turned around and yelled at their retreating backs in Nepali: "Why are you insulting me? It's not good to say such things to a woman. How would you like it if someone insulted your sister like this?" Just the things I had wanted to yell at my Nepalese tormentors, but never had.

The boys took off running in their unlaced shoes. Their taunts had been generated by a fear of me! I was still shaking and feeling somewhat surprised at what had come out of my mouth, wondering at the form my response had taken. I was still looking for respect for the public persona I had become so acutely aware of in Nepal. As in Nepal, my claims on this respect found expression not explicitly in racial terms, but more ambiguously, in gendered ones.

Good Morning, Madam

"And what will *you* do in Nepal?" people asked me when they heard that I was planning to join Arjun for the second phase of his fieldwork. I found the question annoying, but also—perhaps this was why it annoyed me—disturbing. It implied that whereas Arjun had a reason and a purpose in living somewhere difficult and remote, I had none. I was anxious about my lack of an independent interest in Nepal. I didn't know what I would find to occupy myself, but I nonetheless confidently told people that I intended to "teach English." Some of the more inquisitive asked me where I would teach, and I was forced to admit that I had no idea.

During my first week in Pipariya, I had brought up the subject of teaching English with Surendra, who was a teacher in the local primary school. He had been enthusiastic and had told me he would discuss it with the other teachers. So it was agreed that I should take over English teaching for Classes 4 and 5 from the regular English teacher. I was self-conscious about "not doing anything" in the village, and I was anxious to begin teaching, but Surendra said why didn't I wait until after the Jithiyā Pāvani was over. "There's no hurry," Arjun said. "This is Nepal." They both saw my teaching at the village school as a casual thing. I didn't adopt this attitude, however; it was with excitement that I accompanied Surendra to school on the first day—not to teach but just "to meet the other teachers." I had met them already the first time I had visited Nepal and had also seen most of them since arriving in the village this time. I recognized this preliminary visit as necessary to my proper introduction to the school, as a teacher this time, not as a tourist.

As Surendra and I rounded the corner toward the school, Surendra's brother-in-law was banging on a rusty triangle of metal with a rod. This man, who was married to Shanthi's sister, was the school "peon"; he performed the functions of a janitor and general factotum. It was just past ten o'clock. Children were running around in the schoolyard, but with the appearance of the teachers, they formed lines for the daily "physical training" drills, a series of knee-bends, arm-raises and leg-kicks that was led energetically by Surendra once we arrived on the scene.

After the calisthenics, Surendra brusquely ordered four of the older schoolgirls to lead in the singing of a patriotic Nepali song. This they did standing crowded close together in front of the columns of their schoolmates. The girls ran through the words of the song "Let us Sing a Song of Nepal" quickly, hurrying over the poet Madan Prasad Ghimire's paean to Nepal in a shy rush. They sang of the greatness of Nepal, past and present, the glory and majesty of her mountains and rivers with their eyes downcast, shoulders stooped. "We are dancing on the mountains raised up high," sang these children of the Tarai plain. "*Jai, jai, jai,* hey Nepal, beautiful, peaceful, and great." The singing abruptly stopped. Admonished by the teachers to walk slowly, the lines of children filed off to their classrooms. Class 1 met under a shelter of corrugated metal supported by eight rough-hewn posts. Classes 2, 4, and 5 met in the three classrooms of the school, and Class 3 met on the covered porch outside.

I accompanied the other teachers into the office, which served as their staff room. The room was dark and dank. The floor and walls were made of concrete, cracking and peeling. Old, discarded books were heaped in every corner, their pages yellowed and curling. Over the door hung dusty portraits of the King and Queen and a smaller painting of the Crown Prince. The faded garlands of flowers draped over the portraits added to the feeling of decay. The room also smelt of urine; the students used the area outside the back window as a place to relieve themselves during school hours.

Urging me to "*basnus,*" the other teachers took their places on two benches set along the wall and several handmade wooden chairs.

The peon went out to ring the gong again. I assumed that this signaled the beginning of the school day. It was 10:30. None of the teachers made any sign of going into the classrooms to teach. Through the bars of the glassless window, I could see the denizens of Class 1 running about outside the confines of their classroom, screaming, laughing, playing, fighting. Following my gaze, Durga Sapkota, the youngest of the teachers and one of two women, got to her feet and went outside brandishing a stout stick, called a *lathi*. The children retreated under the shelter and assumed their places on long, wooden benches after seeing her. Her charges thus chastened and subdued for the moment, Durga returned to the office.

The regular English teacher asked me if I would like to be introduced to my classes. I nodded yes.

Krishna Subedi also carried a stick in his right hand. He slapped this *lathi* repeatedly into the palm of his left hand as he entered the classroom and strode to the front where a blackboard hung on the wall.

"Stand up, Class 4," he barked in English. The command seemed unnecessary; the students had risen to their feet as soon as Krishnasir swung open the door.

"Say, 'Good Morning, Madam'," he directed the class. About thirty voices parroted the greeting.

"Good Morning, Class 4," I responded.

The tattoo of the *lathi* against Krishna's hand continued. "This is Mrs. Guneratne. She is going to teach you English. You should call her 'Madam,' and you should listen to everything she says and behave well in the classroom," he instructed the class in Nepali.

The classroom was dark and airless. A row of narrow, barred windows lined one wall, but their wooden shutters blocked out much of the light even when they were open. The room was furnished with long benches and sloping desk-tables. There was a wooden chair at the front of the classroom for the teacher's use. I almost never sat on it, preferring to perch on the students' desks or on the window ledge as I moved around the classroom asking students questions and checking to make sure they had their books open to the right page.

During my first few weeks of teaching I prepared carefully for my classes, either the night before or in the morning before going to school. One morning when I explained to a university student in the village what I was doing, he reacted with astonishment. "You don't need to prepare for class," he said. "You're the teacher. Only children prepare for class." I soon discovered that this was the prevalent view of the teachers at the school, too. Being a teacher was a status, not a vocation. Teachers spent little time in the classroom teaching. They entered the classroom only to take roll, discipline the students, or assign some lesson, usually an exercise in one of the books supplied by the government. I seldom saw a teacher presenting and explaining material, the method of teaching that I was used to in American schools.

The teachers spent most of their time sitting in the staff room reading the newspaper, talking with friends who dropped by, and occasionally playing games like Chinese checkers and chess that had been donated to the school by an American tourist the previous year.

When I began teaching at the school, I represented a new diversion for the teachers. After completing my two classes, I would sit with them and respond to their questions about America, Sri Lanka, my family, and what I thought of various aspects of life in Nepal before walking back to the house across the paddy fields. At first I found this the hardest and most uncomfortable part of the day. At least in the classroom I was in charge. On the whole I felt my teaching was successful, even fun. I was pleased that the students seemed to enjoy my performances—often I felt I was on a stage instead of in a classroom. I was even more pleased that they seemed to be learning a little English, not just as perfunctory command sentences ("sit down," "stand up,") but as a real language; they were beginning to respond to my English questions, first in Nepali but increasingly in English, and to form sentences of their own.

In the staff room, I was hit from five sides with questions in fast colloquial Nepali. Except for Surendra, one other teacher and the peon (who seldom spoke anyway), the other teachers were all Brahmins. Living with Tharus I was not accustomed to the quick, often truncated and elided Nepali pronunciation of these native speakers. I also felt uncomfortable with all eyes trained on me. In the beginning I tried to excuse myself from their company as quickly as possible after finishing my classes to go home. At any rate, I tried to escape before the tiffin break at one o'clock, when all the teachers walked to the tea shop for a cup of tea and maybe a piece of bread. As my Nepali improved, however, and I became more comfortable in the village generally and with my teaching colleagues in particular, I welcomed the camaraderie of dropping the chalk into the box by the door, replacing my duster, and flopping down on one of the benches to talk or just to sit in companionable silence for a while before heading home. On a few days, I never even made it into the classroom at all, but merely sat in the staff room chatting through my classes.

On these days, some of my would-be students, when ten or fifteen minutes of the class period had gone by and I still hadn't entered the classroom, would venture out to look for me. Spotting me through the bars on the window of the staff room, they would grin shyly and whisper to one another. One of the other teachers would order them back into the classroom.

Discipline was my weak point. The other teachers carried *lathis* and used them freely (though not abusively) to maintain order. When I appealed for advice on how to deal with *badmās* (naughty) students, their advice was immediate: "Hit them." I explained that this method "didn't come" to me. Besides, I was frequently unsure which of my students were to blame for disruptions in the classroom.

My main function as far as the school bureaucracy was concerned was taking attendance during the first class period of the day, which meant I was responsible for doing this in Class 4. This was initially difficult because the children's names were written in the roll book in Devanagari script with which I had only a basic familiarity. The children were accustomed to hearing their roll number read out and indicating their presence by standing up and saying, "Yes, madam." I felt uncomfortable, however, not knowing whether the students responding were actually the ones against whose names I marked a tick. I felt that my *ijjat* (honor) and authority as a teacher were at stake if the children could trick me as to who was and wasn't in attendance. After puzzling over this problem for a few days, I devised a plan.

I passed out some blank index cards that we had on hand because Arjun was using them to compile a Tharu dictionary. I instructed the students to write their names on the cards: English on one side, Nepali on the other. About half the kids did not know how to write their names in English, so I spent most of that class rendering Devanagari names into Roman script.

At home that night I pored over the names and matched them up with the roll numbers of all the students in my class. I also copied the sixty-one names of my students into the notebook I used for making lesson plans and taking notes at school.

When I showed Krishna-sir the pack of name cards the next day, he looked at each individually, beaming as he did so.

"*Dherei dhanyabād,* Madam," he said. (Thank you very much.) "With you teaching them, our students will do very well."

"I hope so," I said.

I could tell that Krishna was genuinely pleased and grateful for the trouble I had taken teaching the students how to write their names and becoming familiar with them myself. While it initially seemed to me that the teachers took their teaching duties lightly, they also seemed anxious for their charges to do well. I realized that the teachers were not shirking their duties by spending time in the staff room, that was just the Nepalese way of doing things.

For three days I used the cards to learn students' names and roll numbers and to help them to become familiar with the English spelling of their friends' names. On the fourth day, while taking roll, I passed out the cards as usual, calling out their names as I did so. This time, however, I told the students they could keep their name cards. I was unprepared for the pleased excitement with which this announcement was met. They seemed to have trouble believing that I was actually giving them their name cards to keep. In fact, several students came up to the window during the next period and asked me again if they could take the cards home. When I responded that the cards were theirs to keep, they scampered off in delight. For days afterward several children wore their name cards pinned to their shirts when they came to school. It looked as if they never took them off.

Teaching gave me a status and an identity in the village not wholly dependent on my husband's role there. In that respect, I suppose it satisfied the concerns of my American well-wishers who had inquired how I would keep myself busy in Nepal. Paradoxically, by the time I had settled into the life of Pipariya and my role as a teacher enough to appreciate how it had broadened my experience and understanding of the village, I had ceased being so obsessed with "having something to do." In fact, I had become quite content with the slow pace of life in which most of my time was taken up with the necessities of everyday living and which afforded lots of time to visit with my neighbors and to experience and enjoy our quiet life there, without trying to accomplish anything in particular.

Being a teacher in the school also gave me an excellent vantage point to observe various kinds of social divisions and conflicts in the village.

After becoming accustomed to the daily routine of cooking, sweeping, agricultural labor, and child care of the women in our compound, I was fascinated by the contrast in the lifestyles and demeanor of the two women teachers in the school. They wore saris to school. They did not wear regular *chappals*, but rather more expensive plastic slippers with a wide strap over the toes and a slight heel. They sat in the staff room and read the paper with interest like the men. Their presence in the tea shop, usually a bastion of male social life, was accepted although they usually chose to sit either on the bench outside or in the kitchen where the tea was brewed on an earthen stove built over a fire pit. Although I didn't know this for a fact, I suspected that their share of household tasks was light. After all, they were away from home for most of the day.

One of the two women teachers, whose husband had left her and gone off to some distant village, was a supporter of the Nepal Communist Party. This was the topic of some comment in Ram Bahadur's family, who supported the opposing Nepali Congress Party. She was the only self-proclaimed Communist among the teachers, although another of the male teachers was suspected of divided loyalties.

Boys outnumbered girls in my classroom five to one. I sometimes tried to imagine which of the little girls who huddled together on the front bench would grow up to take the places of the women teachers in the school.

To me, the most noticeable divide in the school was between Brahmins and Tharus. Two of the seven teachers in the school were Tharus as was the "peon." The representation of Tharus on the staff was not proportional to the population; Tharus made up about 40 percent of the population of Pipariya. I was sure that none of this was an accident. Everything about the school was the result of political maneuvering. The ratio of Tharu teachers to Brahmins in the school more accurately reflected the relative political power of each group. The school was a nexus between state and local power. Brahmins dominated the machinery of government. Therefore their predominance in local affairs was not surprising. It was not unchallenged, however, particularly after the Democracy Movement of 1990, which had had the effect, at least temporarily, of opening the political process.

Among the students, Tharus were also in the minority. Besides outnumbering Tharus, Brahmins were usually better students. As a group, Brahmins placed a greater value on education than did Tharus, although some younger, educated Tharus such as Surendra were trying to change this, seeing a lack of education as one of the main factors contributing to Tharus' status as a "backward" caste. Whereas Tharu children were usually shy and retiring in class, Brahmins tended to be more aggressive and boisterous. They behaved as if they belonged there; Tharus sometimes gave the idea that they felt they were there on someone else's sufferance.

Because of my closer contact with children in the classroom, I began to watch them with more interest when they were not in school as well.

In developed societies, going to school is central to the process of socialization. School is where children not only learn academic lessons, but in a very real sense learn about life in the outside world—the world outside their families. In village Nepal this was not the case. There, school was a realm of, if not unreality, then of limited relevance to their later lives. For the majority of the students I taught and even more so for the many children whose parents didn't send them to school, their lives would be spent farming the same lands, and with more or less the same techniques and resources, as their parents. This is not to diminish the importance of literacy and the ability to manipulate sums. And some of them would go on from the primary school to get a School Leaving Certificate pass that might lead to a vocation other than that of a peasant cultivator. But for these children most of their essential life education would have to take place outside the classroom.

One day as I was returning from the school at midday, I encountered three boys at the *dhāra* who were engaged in one of the favorite pastimes of young boys in the village, hunting birds with home made slingshots. Two of the boys were in my Class 4 although they had been absent that morning. The third boy never attended school as far as I knew. They had killed three birds in one morning: two mynahs and an iridescent kingfisher. When I showed some interest in the birds and asked what the kingfisher was called in Nepali, they displayed this beautiful bird for me. The boys fanned out its wings between their fingers; they forced open its large brown beak.

I called to Arjun to tell him that the boys had killed a kingfisher, and he came from the house to see the trophy.

"How did you kill the birds?" I asked.

One of the boys touched the slingshot in his pocket. "I killed it," he said proudly.

"He killed one, too," he said, nodding at one of the other boys and then, as if to cover over his boastful tone, he added, "they're good to eat."

One of the day laborers who was working for Ram Bahadur hearing this joked, "if they weren't good to eat, why would one catch them?"

After our inspection of the birds, the successful hunters, along with two or three of their friends, all aged eight to twelve, plucked the birds, built a small fire out of rice straw, roasted them, cut them up into small pieces, washed the meat at the well, divided it onto two plates destined for the kitchens of the boys' respective households and delivered the meat into the hands of their sisters or sisters-in-law for cooking. I suppose this was a sort of real-life equivalent of a school project.

Besides the government primary school where I taught, there was another school for young children in Pipariya. It was the Bright Future English Boarding School. "English Boarding Schools" are very common throughout Nepal. In spite of the suggestion of the word "boarding" in the title, these schools are not residential. Similarly, although some of the best ones do conduct their curriculum in English, the bulk of them do not. They are private schools. They are thought to provide better education than the government schools, which they probably do, if only because of the extra motivation and emphasis given to education by parents who deem it important enough to spend money on.

The boarding school in Pipariya was located opposite Tulsi Prasad Ghimire's house. It was a rickety wooden building on stilts. Its three classrooms accommodated about fifty students ranging from "upper kindergarten" (four and five year olds) to eleven and twelve year olds in Class 5. The monthly fee was seventy rupees. The majority of students at "the boarding," as it was called in the village, were Brahmins. Two "masters," or teachers, had responsibility for all the students. They were also Brahmins. One was a young man from a village some way off. The other was a nephew of Tulsi Prasad; like Surendra, he was teaching while studying for his university degree.

I had been approached about teaching at the boarding. I had refused, saying that two hours a day was enough teaching for me, since I had household responsibilities as well. I was also less interested in volunteering in a fee-levying, profit-making school than I was in teaching in the government school. Finally, although I didn't tell the parents who requested me to teach their children in the boarding this, I was reluctant to teach Brahmin children. In my experience I had found them frequently *badmās*. The Brahmin children in the local government school tended to be more obstreperous and naughty than the Tharu students. They were more difficult to control; they got up to all sorts of mischief, clowning and showing off in the classroom. So I begged off teaching in the boarding.

The boarding teachers, like the teachers at the government school, took their tiffin at the tea shop. On the days that I accompanied the teachers for tiffin I often saw my would-be colleagues from up the road. They were always polite and friendly toward me and gradually my awkwardness at having rejected the request to teach at their school wore off.

One day when we went for tiffin at one o'clock, there was a young white woman sitting on the bench outside the tea shop. She was quite plump, fat by Nepalese standards. She was wearing a pair of black cotton tights that clung to her stout figure in a revelation of her shape that would have been unacceptable in a Nepalese woman and should have been unthinkable even for a tourist. On her lap she cradled a bulging day pack.

I was surprised to see a tourist at the tea shop. I couldn't recall ever having seen a Westerner there before. Most tourists would pass the unadorned tumble-down hut without even realizing that it was the social center for the village. I remarked on the foreigner's presence at the tea shop to the other women teachers. The male teachers had stopped to talk to someone on the road behind us.

"She has married a Nepalese boy," Durga told me knowledgeably. "And she's teaching at the boarding."

I was even more surprised. I went up to her and said "hello."

"Hello," she said, in a friendly voice.

I sat down on the bench next to her and introduced myself. "Are you teaching at the boarding school?" I asked.

"Yes, I just thought I'd do what I could to help out," she said in a broad Australian accent.

Her name was Sheila. She had a flat, round face. Her brown hair was cut in bangs and hung to her shoulders. I guessed her age to be early twenties, though she might have been older. Sheila seemed completely unselfconscious and unaware of the sensation her dress was causing. She looked about her with equanimity. She seemed utterly guileless. I was curious to find out more about her alleged marriage to a Nepalese.

"How long are you staying here?" I asked.

"Three months."

Then Sheila asked me the same thing. When I told her I was there for ten months she asked what I was doing. I told her my husband was doing research.

"What kind?" she asked.

"Anthropological," I said.

"Oh, on the locals?" she asked.

I nodded.

This topic apparently interested Sheila. "There's nothing written on the Tharus," she asserted. Without waiting for my response, she asked me if I knew of anyone who could inform tourist guides about the Tharus because some of them were very interested to learn more. She also said that currently information on the Tharus was passed along from one guide to another, but they didn't have any proper sources for this information, it was more or less like myth. If there was someone who could tell them about the Tharus . . . my husband perhaps?

I said that the best way for the guides to learn about the Tharus would be for them to ask Tharus themselves.

"Who knows about Tharus better than Tharus?" I said to her, rather pedantically, I thought. But Sheila didn't seem to take any notice, either of my tone, or of my point.

"Do you know anyone the guides could question?" she persisted. "Someone who knows a lot who would do a good job of explaining Tharu customs to them." If so, Sheila said she would organize a group of tourist guides to come and talk to this person. The guides were all her friends, she explained. It suddenly occurred to me that she was married to a tourist guide.

I told her that the guides, if they were Nepalese, should know whom to talk to among the Tharu community. The Tharus were, after all, their neighbors.

Sheila ignored my objection to her scheme. "I will tell them what questions to ask," she volunteered, adding that she wouldn't be able to interview the Tharu informant herself because she didn't speak Nepali. In fact, it struck me that the only Nepali word I heard her speak was inappropriate in the context. She said "*dhanyabad*" to the proprietor of the tea shop when he brought her tea. *Dhanyabad* means "thank you" in Nepali, but native speakers of the language don't waste the word on trifles like tea. It is an acknowledgment that is saved to express deep gratitude at an unusual act of generosity or kindness.

Nonetheless, the Nepalese woman sitting next to Sheila had been taking a great interest in our conversation, leaned forward on the bench to get a good look at me and, when she heard Sheila's single Nepali word, exclaimed, *"kathi ramro!"* (How nice!) The woman appeared to be accompanying Sheila. When she found out that I spoke Nepali, she addressed herself to me. She and her husband managed the Elephant Lodge Hotel, where Sheila was staying. She invited me to visit them there. *"Aunus, aunus,"* she urged. When would I come, today or tomorrow?

I tried to give as vague an answer as possible. Tomorrow or the day after. *Holā.*

Sheila's Nepalese companion also inquired what my name was.

"Kate," I said several times. She couldn't quite catch this.

"Kite, Kite," said the Australian. "You know, like the thing in the sky." I was amused by Sheila's pronunciation of my name, but I was also struck at her pretension (and perhaps my own) in thinking that we could teach English to Nepalese with only a rudimentary understanding of their language. The English word *kite* is in fact one of the first words Nepalese students are taught, along with flag, stick, cap, and pen. I racked my brain but couldn't remember the Nepali name for that "thing in the sky."

"I hear you've married a Nepalese," I said, my usual shyness in asking personal questions overcome by the irritation I felt at this girl's apparent lack of self-awareness.

"Oh, that was just a joke." She smiled, as if recollecting an amusing occurrence.

"So you're not married?" I queried.

"Well, we regard ourselves as married, but we didn't have a ceremony or anything. What happened was that a few days ago we went —my boyfriend and me—we went to a wedding in his village."

"Is your boyfriend from around here?"

"Yeah, he's a guide at the Elephant Lodge Hotel," she said. "Shyam Adhikari. Do you know him?"

I shook my head no.

"Anyway, we went to this wedding and stayed in the village for a few days. I have this sari that I wear, and when we left they—the women there—they dressed me up, put that red powder in my hair, gave me *tikā* and all the rest of it. When we got back to the hotel they said, 'oh, my god, you got married!' So we said, 'yeah, yeah, we tied the knot.'"

"Are you telling people that you got married?" I asked.

She shrugged. "It doesn't really come up," she said.

"You know," I said. "In the view of people here, you are married. There is no such thing as civil marriage in Nepal. When you came home with *sindoor* in your hair, you were married as far as anyone else is concerned." *Sindoor* is the red powder that is put into the parting of a bride's hair by the groom during the Nepalese marriage ceremony. It is the mark of married women in Nepal.

"I'm sure we'll end up getting married," she said. She didn't sound sure at all.

"Do you plan to go back to Australia?"

"Well, I'm supposed to be going to England to go to university," said Sheila. "I kind of promised my parents. I think I at least owe them that."

"Have you told them about your boyfriend, that you plan to get married?"

"Well, just the usual stuff that you tell your folks when you meet a guy, you know, about what a hunk he is and so on, but yeah, they know about him."

"And what's their reaction to your . . . uh, plans?"

She shrugged again. The last thing I would be writing to tell my parents, I thought, if I were in Sheila's position, was that I had met a "hunk." Then I felt a cold wave wash over me. Did I appear to others as Sheila appeared to me? I, too, had fallen in love with a foreigner, a man of a different country, a different color. And with little more than a shrug for my parents' concerns, I'd married him. Of course, in reality, our circumstances were very different. I'd met my husband at an elite American university, where we had both been students, not on a "jungle walk" where he was the guide. Our educational and class backgrounds, values, and expectations of life were compatible in a way that I could not imagine Shyam's and Sheila's to be. But, I wondered, were these distinctions apparent to other people?

"Of course I'd like to take him to Europe with me," Sheila continued, apparently having decided she wanted to discuss things with me. "But sometimes leaving the country spoils them."

I wasn't quite sure what she meant by this, what exactly she thought would be spoiled in her husband-elect if she took him out of this holiday context, but the conversation had begun to make me feel uncomfortable. After taking my leave of the other teachers and responding one last time to the invitations of the manageress to visit Elephant Lodge, I wished Sheila good luck and went home.

CHAPTER SEVEN

Harvest

Arjun was still in bed. I didn't feel like getting up either, but I had told Bhagavati the night before that I would accompany the girls in Ram Bahadur's house to cut rice that day. It was Saturday, my day off from teaching. I would have liked to putter around the house, perhaps write a letter.

"Bhāuju, Bhāuju," Bhagavati was calling softly from outside the door. It was her day off from sewing training.

"I'm coming," I called back. I got up and quickly pulled down a skirt and T-shirt from the rope hung across our sleeping room and got dressed. I realized with surprise that I was cold. It was the end of October. The weather was becoming cooler by the day. The previous day, for the first time, I needed to put on a flannel shirt in the evening to keep warm. We were using our quilt at night now. The *gauras* (bonfires) that the Tharus made out of rice straw every evening were beginning to look inviting.

This was my second day of participating in the rice harvest. I had gone out with the girls and Indra Prasad's *bahāriyā* servants several days earlier. I had enjoyed the companionship, but had found the work exhausting. My back was still sore.

"I'm taking your hat," I told Arjun. Though the mornings and evenings were cool, the midday sun was fierce. I also smeared sunscreen on my legs, arms, and face.

"Bhāuju!" Bhagavati called again.

"I'm going," I told Arjun.

Bhagavati handed me a sickle with a slightly curved handle, called an *erya*. This tool was designed for cutting rice.

Tharus harvesting rice

We walked eastward along the road past the *Bramathān*. The sun
was climbing in the sky, glowing orange through a thin layer of mist.
Already the chill of the morning had begun to wear off. A little way beyond the *Bramathān* we turned off the road to the south. To get into the
field we had to cross a ditch. Bhagavati ran up the embankment on the
other side easily. I followed suit, less gracefully, wondering briefly
what would happen if I fell on the *erya* I was carrying. We walked
across the fields on a raised *bāto*, or barrier separating the paddy fields
from one another. The other girls were already at work cutting paddy
in a far corner of this section of Ram Bahadur's property. They paused
briefly in their work to stand up and call out to us. These were all Ram
Bahadur's fields. Several fields closer to the road had been harvested.
The cut stalks of rice had been laid out to dry, the heads of grain all
pointing in the same direction.

Some of Ram Bahadur's fields lay on the other side of the *Bramathān*.
A group of about nine itinerant laborers were cutting those fields.
They worked separately from the labor mustered from the household
itself. During the rice harvest, and to a lesser extent during the mustard harvest, groups of itinerant laborers, mostly from the Outer Tarai
or Madesh, traveled through Chitwan looking for work. Some groups
came back year after year and worked for the same landowners. The

group working in Ram Bahadur's other field had cut rice for him the previous year as well. Some groups negotiated a daily wage, somewhere from twenty to twenty-five rupees per person. Others settled on a lump sum for doing a particular piece of work and divided this among their group. Many of the migrant workers were not landless but because their land was poor, they had to hire out their labor to supplement the income they were able to get from farming their own land. Others were working to pay off debts. One old man who spent a few weeks working for Ram Bahadur during the mustard harvest said he was working to raise money to build a house for his son. In addition to paying them a wage, the Chitwan landowners had to put the migrant workers up and feed them. Ram Bahadur's present group of laborers slept in a shelter they had made for themselves out of bundles of rice straw. It was located behind Ram Bahadur's household shrine. They were taken two meals in the fields by the women of Ram Bahadur's household and they ate a third meal in his house in the evening.

Though they couldn't have been working long, the others stopped work briefly when we arrived. In addition to Shanthi, Bikramiya, and Sita, both Bikramiya's and Sita's mothers were cutting rice. Bikramiya's mother told me right off that the work would be too difficult and tried to discourage me from cutting rice. I told her I had done the work several days before and managed fine. The four girls looked pleased at the prospect of my working in the field alongside them.

The older women led the way back into the field to resume work.

"Where should I go?" I asked Bhagavati.

"Here, beside me," she said. The seven of us stretched out in a line working several yards apart from one another moved in a line parallel to the raised path around the field. The swath of paddy I was responsible for cutting included fifteen or so clumps of rice. Beginning at the far right of "my" line of rice, I bent over, grasped a clump of the thick-stalked grass in my left hand, and, using a quick sawing motion, severed the stalks with the *erya* in my right. I had been warned the previous day to hold the rice plants with my palm toward the ground and not the other way around, which seemed more natural. This was to avoid accidentally cutting one's thumb or forefinger.

The soreness in my muscles from the previous day's work in the fields was immediately rekindled. Today I would try to minimize the stress on my back by straightening up every time I had a handful of rice to lay on my growing column of rice on the ground.

The paddy was still wet from the dew. The ground out of which the rice grew, however, was dry, even cracked in places.

The other women worked quickly, severing a whole bunch of rice stalks with a single deft motion. It took me several sawing strokes with my *erya* to get through a single clump. I was frightened to increase the pace of my cutting lest I injure myself.

Once or twice Bhagavati corrected my technique, reminding me to grasp the rice plant with the heel of my hand toward the ground or to cut the rice closer to the ground. Otherwise we worked in silence. Well, not exactly silence: Every once in a while, one of the girls would make a comment and there would be a response, but the work was not conducive to conversation.

At about ten o'clock Tikaurni brought us our *kalavā*. *Kalavā* is the term for rice and the accompaniments that are brought to the field and consumed there. It is therefore distinguished from *bhāt* not by content but by the context in which it is eaten. I was happy to see Tikaurni's tall, straight figure making its way toward us along the *bāto*. I was getting hungry and needed a rest.

Tikaurni was carrying a basket full of *bhāt* on her head. The cooked rice was covered with a layer of banana leaves on which rested some small bowls containing *tarkāri*. She balanced an earthenware urn full of water against her hip. Inside the top of the urn she had nested a *lotā*.

Tikaurni carried the food to where we had sat down on a pile of already-cut paddy. She put the urn on the ground first and then swung the basket off her head. The girls took the banana leaves out of the basket and fashioned them into plates for themselves. Tikaurni had brought a metal plate for me.

The *tarkāri* Tikaurni brought was made from *goñhi*. I had helped prepare these little snails for cooking the day before. Several of us had squatted around a big metal pan containing hundreds of the living snails, harvested from some ditch or pond earlier in the day. On the sharp edge of the bowl we had sliced off the tip and the base of the snails' shells. Now Tikaurni was scooping out handfuls of the curried snails beside heaps of rice. The snails were enthusiastically received by the others, who sucked the meat out of the shell with sharp inhalations of breath. Tikaurni had brought some small bowls of vegetable *tarkāri*, apparently just for me, for I had remarked in her presence while preparing the snails that we didn't eat that sort of animal in the United States. She served me generous dollops of pumpkin and potato curry. She also offered me the snails, and I said I'd try one. It didn't really taste like anything, but I didn't like the way it felt on the back of my tongue.

Tikaurni refilled our plates until we were full. Then she helped to serve the water. I had brought a canteen of boiled water from the house and drank that. I was very thirsty, but I wanted to save some of my water for the hot afternoon. Most of the day still lay ahead of us.

After we'd finished the *kalavā*, we did not immediately return to work. Instead, we sat among the cut rice. Sita and Bikramiya were teasing one another; at one point they were rolling around in the rice straw and laughing.

I don't know how long it would have been before we resumed the cutting if Ram Bahadur hadn't shown up. But as soon as the *jimidār* came into view, walking purposefully along the *bāto*, the girls picked up their *eryas* and resumed cutting. I followed suit.

A little while after Ram Bahadur went off—perhaps to check on the progress of the hired laborers—Arjun showed up with his camera. He was taking photographs, both prints and slides, of the harvest activities. However, Tharu women generally do not like to be photographed while they are working, especially if they are doing something as arduous as cutting rice. When Arjun had tried previously to take pictures of women harvesting, they evinced such disapproval that he had given up. It was not considered *ramailo* to be photographed at work; women preferred to dress up and make an occasion of it.

Bikramiya's mother greeted him with pleasure, addressing him as her son, but neither she nor Sita's mother wanted to have their photos taken. Sita on the other hand was enthusiastic about being photographed; both she and Bikramiya, who also consented, went to put on the head scarves they had left on the *bāto* before Arjun took their pictures. After posing for a few minutes with the scarf over her head, Sita's face suddenly became very serious and she started working furiously. Arjun took several photos of the three of us and started for home. He told me he was being fed in Surendra's house today because I was working in the harvest. He also said he was intending to spend the afternoon helping Bikram Mahato with his harvest.

The afternoon sun was hot. The scarves that the girls had draped decoratively over their heads for Arjun's camera, they now used in earnest to deflect some of the direct heat of the sun from their heads and the backs of their necks. I was glad of Arjun's hat.

Migrant workers threshing rice

The repetitive work was becoming tedious. I tried to estimate the time and the number of hours remaining before we could leave the field and return home, but the thought was too depressing; I knew we wouldn't return to the house before dark. Fortunately this was not my first experience with agricultural labor. I had several times worked picking berries in the summers during my childhood in Oregon, and though our workdays had usually ended by 3 o'clock, I was at least somewhat familiar with the rhythm and tedium of field labor. But did my Tharu companions find this work boring? I had never heard any of them use this concept in talking about cutting rice. They had described the work as hard. They complained about the heat of the sun, but they showed no signs of tiring of it mentally.

I thought back on my initial frustration with the inactivity of the monsoon season. Both the dawn-to-dusk labor of the harvest and the lethargy of the monsoon were part of the same logic of labor in this agricultural community. Both were foreign to my sensibilities informed by the work ethos of an industrialized society. Years later in my research for my history Ph.D., I would encounter the same kinds of reactions as I had had to the rhythms of labor in Pipariya in the writings of nineteenth century European travelers to Latin America, who were simultaneously dismayed with "lazy natives" and outraged by the long "exploitative" hours worked by peasants in the countryside. I was experiencing firsthand the disjunctures in time and work discipline that E. P. Thompson had earlier described for rural workers in industrializing England.

I toyed briefly with the idea of pleading some excuse and going home. Certainly, as Arjun had told me many times, no one expected me to work in the fields. Then I thought of how pleased the girls had looked when I had showed up and of the camaraderie I had felt when we sat together to eat the *kalavā*.

As I continued the monotonous action of cutting the rice and arranging the severed bunches of grain in a line across the fields, my thoughts turned away from the repetitive activities of the moment. I found myself thinking about my life in Chicago before Arjun and I had come to Nepal. My mind moved over the familiar rituals of our life in the tiny apartment next to the Hyde Park Theater where we lived after we were married. As if I were thinking about another life, someone else's life, I remembered getting up in that apartment in the morning, padding my way to the bathroom without even really waking up. I marveled at the convenience of our indoor toilet, how I could pee without having to put on my shoes and without getting cold or wet.

That apartment had been a place of inviolable privacy, where Arjun and I had lived our own self-contained and autonomous life. How different from our permeable hut here in Pipariya and the complex relationships with dozens of people that had enveloped me in less than three months.

Without really noticing, I had begun to hum a song from a tape we used to play in our little Chicago apartment. It was from the musical *Evita:* "Don't Cry for Me, Argentina." Startled out of my reverie by the sound of my own voice, I looked up at Shanthi, who was cutting next to me. She was smiling broadly.

"*Rāmro,*" she said. "Sing another one," she encouraged me. Now that I had an audience I had trouble remembering the other songs on that tape. But after a moment I treated them to a rendition of "I'd Be Surprisingly Good for You," and then "Another Suitcase in Another Hall." I cast around in my mind for other songs I could sing.

When I had exhausted my repertoire of Andrew Lloyd Webber and American folk songs, I asked them to sing for me. After a lot of teasing and giggling about who should sing, Sita sang several songs from recent Hindi films. Then she and Shanthi gave a duet performance of a Nepali film song called *"Kānchilai Gumauney Kathmandu Shahāra."* I asked them to teach me this song, which I had heard before. Unlike many of the songs I had heard in Nepal, I could more or less follow its words, which have to do with a man showing a girl (the *kānchi* or youngest one) around the capital (Kathmandu Shahāra).

We were still singing when Tikaurni brought our afternoon snack: dry *chiurā* (dried beaten rice) and chillies and salt. She also brought another urn of water, which she carried balanced on her head this time. I drank the last of the water in my flask and was still very thirsty. I was tempted to drink some water from the urn but didn't. After this snack we rested for some time in the shade of some trees growing along the southern boundary of Ram Bahadur's field. Several fields away, a group of ten or fifteen harvesters worked steadily. Shanthi and Sita called to some of the girls to come and sit with us. They waved and shouted back but continued working.

My back was sore. I sat on the ground slumped over with my legs sticking straight out in front of me. Touching one of my legs lightly with her hand, Sita said, "Your legs are so nice; they're so fat." Bhagavati laughed. Pinching one of Sita's calves with her fingers, she said, "Sita's legs are fat, too. Mine are thin. They're not beautiful."

I thought how strange it was that I should admire Bhagavati's slim figure and her long elegant arms and legs, and that these very things that my cultural conditioning predisposed me to admire were not found beautiful here. Conversely, my stocky legs and large ankles were thought attractive by Tharus.

I never knew quite how to respond to compliments about my appearance in Nepal. Many of them had to do with the color of my skin. Sita continued in this vein. "You're white," she said. "That's good. We're black; that's not attractive." I responded that in my opinion, they were beautiful looking, but I also tried to look pleased with the compliments they paid me.

They pointed at my freckles and asked what they were called in English. They told me their word for freckle: *tilaka.*

I also complimented Bhagavati on her posture. I said Tharu women move very beautifully whereas my movements were awkward and ugly. I did a parody of myself walking, hunched over. Bhagavati and Sita hooted with laughter; they said they had noticed that foreign women—not me, they insisted—moved in a funny way.

Not long after we had returned to work after our long break, a man came over from the next field. He had come over, he explained, to see what I was doing wielding an *erya*. "I'm cutting rice," I told him.

He could hardly conceal his amusement at the sight of me working. Addressing me as Didi, he told me that he worked as the manager of one of the tourist hotels in the area. He told me his name, which sounded Chhetri to me. He invited me to come and visit him. He instructed Bhagavati to bring me *bholi-parsi:* tomorrow or the day after, in other words, sometime soon. I looked at Bhagavati for direction. She had not ceased cutting the rice while he was talking to me. I, too, became polite but noncommittal.

The man stuck around long enough for me to demonstrate my cutting technique. He looked tickled. Wasn't it hard work? (Yes.) Didn't my back hurt? (Yes.) He said it was difficult for him to do this sort of work; he bent over slightly to imitate the motion of cutting rice. Those were his fields over there; he'd just come to see how the work was getting on. He invited me once more to visit his hotel and went back to his own field. Later in the afternoon, his wife came over to talk with Bhagavati. She looked very pregnant. She and Bhagavati sat by the side of the field and chatted while the rest of us continued to work. She, too, kept darting curious glances in my direction.

By the time the sun began to sink into the jungle, I was too tired for singing. It took all my concentration to continue cutting the rice, gathering it into sheaves, and spreading it in a row on the ground over the short stubs of what had been cut. As darkness neared, the others seemed to pick up the pace a bit. It was dusk by now, a time of day that doesn't last very long in Nepal. We would soon be working in the dark. I began to wonder when we would stop. Finally, Bikramiya's mother announced that she was going to go to the house. Bhagavati told me to go with her. I didn't argue.

My whole body ached. My skin was sticky and salty, but it was too late to bathe. (I had adopted the Tharu attitude that it is unhealthy to bathe after about four in the afternoon.)

I left Bikramiya's mother at her house and went back to our hut. Arjun was sitting on the *wosarā* listening to the radio. Bhagavati and the others returned from the field about half an hour later. Shanthi came to call us to eat. The itinerant workers were eating in the big entrance room. Shanthi led Arjun and me into her bedroom. I was ravenous, but I was so stiff that I had trouble sitting on the mat that Shanthi spread

Migrant workers stacking harvested rice

on the floor for us. She must be tired, too, I commented. She responded that she was hungry. She sat with us while we ate.

"Go and eat," I told her.

"*Ek chin pachhi,*" she said. (In a little while.)

Toward the end of November, when all the rice had been harvested, threshed, and stored, several girls spoke to me about going into the jungle to pick berries. This was apparently something they did every year. They spoke of the upcoming expedition with pleased anticipation. From the mere fact that they deemed it appropriate to ask me to go along I inferred that the trip was regarded as *ramailo:* fun, enjoyable. I accepted the invitation.

On the morning of the berry-picking expedition, Sarasvati came to fetch me to eat at their house at about eight o'clock in the morning.

"We will eat and go early," she told me. Sarasvati, Mangala, Bikramiya's mother, Rukmani, the carpenter's younger daughter Kumari, and I sat in their yard in the sun and ate rice and *tarkāri.*

When we had eaten, the others got out woven baskets to pick the berries into. They also assembled the narrow-mouthed elephant grass baskets used by the Tharus for catching fish. I assumed these were also for transporting berries. I went back to our hut for a plastic bag to pick berries into.

On the road we met about ten other people from the next village, including two men, who were apparently also going berry picking. Mangala told me that the men were going along to scare the rhinos away. I laughed a little nervously. Rhinos are dangerous and unpredictable animals. I had heard many stories since coming to Nepal of people being charged by the animals in and around the National Park. Frequently mishaps occurred when tourists failed to show the proper wariness of the irascible beasts. Recently an Israeli tourist had been gored when he tried to feed a rhino bread. But Tharus, who knew enough to fear and avoid the animals, were also victims of their charges. Two Tharus had been killed the previous year during the grass-cutting season, a brief period when the National Park is opened to the local villagers to harvest elephant grass. Arjun, who had accompanied Ram Bahadur's household into the jungle the previous February to observe the grass cutting, had written to me about seeing the body of one of the rhino victims being carried out of the jungle wrapped in a white cloth.

But the danger of rhino attack seemed remote as we walked along the road toward the jungle. It's pretty difficult to work oneself into a state of anxiety about a danger one has never experienced. Also, the other members of our group were in such good spirits that I caught the excitement of the expedition.

It had surprised me when I first came to Pipariya that the Tharus actively enjoyed their natural surroundings as much as they did. Coming from the United States, I assumed that an urban indoor "modern" lifestyle was a necessary precondition for an appreciation of "nature." I was accustomed to the idea of enjoying "the great outdoors" on weekends and holidays after which one "returned to civilization," refreshed by wilderness, but not, hopefully, beyond being restored to one's normal routine by a hot shower, microwaved meal, and a relaxing evening in front of the TV. It was therefore a revelation to me that the Tharus, who lived much of their lives outdoors, derived a pleasure from the jungle and the beautiful riverside spot where they liked to go for picnics quite as great as any Sierra Club member I'd ever met, perhaps greater.

As usual, many people greeted our group as we walked past their houses. A few more women with baskets joined our entourage. Where the road we had followed west from Pipariya met the Rapti River, we turned onto a cart track that followed the river bank. The jungle, and the Park, lay on the other side. Mangala pointed to some houses as we passed.

"Those are houses of Tamang people," she said.

I was interested. It looked like a sizable settlement. These people must have left the hills and come to Chitwan some years ago, probably in search of land to cultivate.

"How do Tamangs get along with Tharus?" I asked.

"Not very well," Mangala said. "They speak their own language so we can't talk to them." I wasn't sure if she'd understood my question. I was trying to find out if there had been disputes with Tamangs as there had been with Brahmins for taking over land formerly belonging to Tharus.

"It looks like good land," I said, gesturing toward the fields of mustard bordering the river.

"Yes, but it floods easily," Mangala pointed out. "Also the rhinos come and eat the crops here." Indeed, everywhere I looked I saw little huts on stilts where people spend the night to keep an eye out for animals that come to raid the crops in the night. They must have a great problem with wildlife coming across the river from the Park at night to eat their crops. Rhinos were especially damaging to crops because in addition to consuming a lot, their great bodies trampled huge swaths of paddy underfoot as they made broad trails through the fields.

All along the river people remarked on the damage that had been wrought by the flood two months earlier. "The river used not to go this way," someone would say. "Look how the bank has been washed away," said someone else.

After following the Rapti downstream for about twenty minutes, we followed a tributary stream away from the river and the cultivated land into a patch of jungle. We rejoined a road which led, less than a mile further on, to a fording place. We all pulled up our *lungis* (in my case, a skirt) to cross the stream.

"Look how white she is!" shouted one woman when she caught sight of the tops of my thighs above the water.

A group of Brahmin women and girls were resting on the other side of the stream. Beside them sat heavy bundles of wood, some in baskets and others tied to the two ends of a pole to be carried over the shoulder. They looked surprised to see me wading toward them. I realized

I was outside the area where many people recognized me and knew who I was, even if I had never met them.

The vegetation on the other side of the stream was not really what I thought of as jungle. The grass and other scrubby ground cover was cropped short by the cattle brought to graze here. There was a sparse population of sal trees, certainly, but most of them presented an odd and somewhat eerie appearance because their lower limbs had been hacked off for wood or fodder. Thus their only well-developed branches sprouted near their tops.

Gradually, however, this skeleton jungle thickened and deepened into something that more closely resembled my idea of a jungle, though still not a lush and luxuriant one, but rather a stunted, dry scrubby version. The men walked ahead, yelling and beating against trees with sticks.

"They are making noise to frighten the rhinos," Mangala told me.

I realized that we could not see more than ten or twenty feet on either side of the path because trees and plants blocked the view. I looked around nervously. What would I do if I saw a rhino? I'd heard that you're supposed to climb a tree if a rhino charges. I looked at the trees we were passing. I couldn't imagine getting into any of them. I felt a surge of panic. The worst thing was not being able to see.

"If a rhino heard us coming through the jungle, what would it do—run away or come toward us?" I asked Mangala.

"Oh, it would run away," she said confidently. I wasn't so sure. From everything I heard they were ornery and capricious beasts.

No one else seemed the least bit concerned. And yet, they all knew of people who had been killed by rhinos. How could they view a trip into the habitat of these dangerous animals as an enjoyable day out?

I was relieved when we emerged from the obscuring and confining vegetation of the jungle onto the flat, rocky flood plain next to the Rapti. Again there were exclamations over how the flood had changed the course of the river and the appearance of the land adjoining it.

We marched across the sand and rocks of the river bank for a while before turning up toward the jungle again. At the edge of the trees some stickery bushes grew. These were the berries, the object of our outing. The girls and women set to immediately, pulling the reddish-black berries, resembling an oversized huckleberry, from their thorny branches. I have picked many kinds of berries in my day, both wild and cultivated, but I had never met anything as sparse, unyielding, difficult to get at, and ultimately so unworthy of the effort as these berries we had just walked over two hours through rhino country to pick.

As we coaxed the well-protected berries from the bushes, the men kept up their rhino vigil. They picked some berries, too, but I noticed they ate all theirs on the spot. The girls and women ate a fair proportion of their picking, as well, but they still managed to fill the baskets they had brought along in which to carry the harvest home. I asked Mangala what the berries would be used for. She told me they would be dried and used to make a kind of pickle. They also put them in *tarkāri*, she said.

The Tharus complained that there were not as many berries as there had been the previous year. They blamed the flood. Another cause for the shortfall became apparent when, in the course of picking one sparse area clean and moving on to another, we rounded a bush and found ourselves in the company of a large group of *pahariyās*, women, girls and boys. Mangala said they were from West Chitwan, though how she could tell, I don't know. She said they picked the berries to sell in the bazaar.

When the *pahariyās* saw me they stopped picking altogether and stared. A small cluster of girls were the first to lower their eyes, giggling. Mangala said they probably hadn't seen a foreigner before. At any rate, they almost certainly had not encountered one in the jungle.

Because of the paucity of the berries, we quit picking after about two and a half hours. I was glad. My legs and arms were scratched by thorns, I was hot, thirsty, and ready to go home.

We left jungle and rhinos behind and retraced our steps across the broad expanse of sandbank leading to the river. The loop we followed took us closer to the river than we had come on our way to the berry patch. In a depression in the rocky terrain, we came upon a pool of water, apparently a remnant from when the river had overflowed its banks during the flood two months before. We descended into this trough and squatted around the edge of the murky pool. The next thing I knew, both women and men had their *lungis* gathered up about their thighs and were wading systematically in a line that stretched across the pool. They waded through the knee-deep water bent over, with their hands below the surface, apparently dredging the bottom of the pool. In this fashion they moved methodically from one end of the pool to the other. Every few steps several people would bring up a few handfuls of what looked like silt and pebbles from the bottom. Some of these findings turned out to be *goñhi,* the snails that had been eaten during the rice harvest. A lot of it appeared to be plain muck. The *goñhi* were dropped into the elephant-grass baskets. For the first time I realized that the prospecting of this pool was not a pure coincidence but was a planned-for contingency of the expedition to pick berries. This should have made me more patient, but I still had the idea that, berry picking over, it was time to go home. I was happy when, after only two or three passes across the length of the pool, the fishermen and -women waded out of the water, collected their things and we climbed out of the slough again. But if the fishing in that particular pond had been disappointing, it did nothing to dampen the enthusiasm of my companions for the enterprise in general. We went looking for another pond to fish. We found another. And another. In one of these, while the Tharus were sifting through the mud around the edges with their fingers, three water buffaloes made a stately entrance into the water hole. They walked purposefully into the middle of the pool, snorting, and lowered their unwieldy black bodies into the water. They wallowed in the muddy water. Only their heads, topped with curling horns, and the tips of their rumps were visible. We moved on before they did. On gaining higher ground, we saw their driver; he was carrying a stick and walking toward the hole into which his animals had disappeared.

The last hole we stopped at looked too small to be worth bothering with. Although it was smaller, the water seemed both clearer and cooler than the other pools we'd tried. There were only a few *goñhi* in the pool, but there were quite a lot of small fish. These my companions went after with alacrity. After a while most of the adults wandered away. Finally only Mangala, Rukmani, one of the young men from the next village, and I were left. Until this point, I had been a mere spectator. After chasing the fish around the edges of this pool, which was about fifteen feet long and six feet across, Mangala and Rukmani began taking handfuls of mud from the banks and piling it in the middle of the pond to form a sort of dike. Then Mangala took one of the fish baskets and used it to bale water out of one half of the pond. Rukmani caught the tiny fish that were left floundering on the bank as the water they had been tossed up in drained away from them back into the increasingly murky pool. Mangala and Rukmani were clearly enjoying themselves. After watching for a while, I decided to have a go at fishing, too. Tucking my skirt up, I entered the fray. At first I didn't fancy picking up the small fish as they jumped and slithered on the muddy bank. I concentrated on scooping water out of the hole. A fish flopped between my feet. Not wanting to let it escape, I brought my cupped hand over it. I closed my fingers over its thrashing body and it became still. Triumphantly, I carried it to one of the fish baskets and dropped it in. After that I pounced on the leaping fish like the others, letting out cries when they flipped out of my grasp. Finally, though still reluctant to give up the sport while there remained any fish left in the water hole, we picked up our baskets and went in search of the others. We found them resting by the river. They had not been idle either. Almost all the women were carrying big pieces of driftwood they had collected. The girls carried bundles of smaller pieces of wood.

Mangala was still ebullient over the success of our fishing session. She put the basket down on the bank of the river and waded into the river to wash her face and take a drink. I squatted on the bank. Some young Tharu men had also stopped to refresh themselves. One of them said something to Mangala. She became very angry. She strode out of the water and, saying something to Bikramiya's mother, started up the bank toward the jungle. Rukmani and I followed. When we were back on the path and out of earshot of the others, she told me what the boy had said. He'd asked her if she had caught the fish. When she said yes, he'd remarked to his friend that she must be going to sell them in the bazaar, since that's what Musahers did. The other fellow had said something about her being dark like a Musaher.

The Musahers are a *jāt* inhabiting Chitwan who are also found in India. The men who operated the boats that ferried people across the river during and after the monsoon were members of this caste. The Musahers also make a living by fishing and selling the fish they catch in the bazaar. Mangala felt that by implying that she was a Musaher as well as by remarking on her dark skin, the boys had insulted her. She, like most Tharus, considered the Musahers to belong to a lower caste than herself. I don't know whether it was anger or shame that made her leave the basket of fish she had caught on the river bank, instructing Bikramiya's mother to bring it with her when she came.

We waited for the others in a clearing. Then we began the long walk through the jungle back to Pipariya. People continued to collect wood as we walked along and before we crossed the tributary to the Rapti, we met about a dozen men from Pipariya who were carrying long bundles of *khar*, a kind of grass with beautiful silky tassels that are used to make brooms. These tassels, soft and iridescent in the late afternoon sun, bobbed up and down with the jogging gait that the men adopted under their great weight.

The road was full of people leaving the jungle with wood and grass, fuel and fodder of one kind or another. We were passed by several people wheeling Chinese bicycles so heavily laden with wood that their sturdy metal frames swayed under the weight. With horrified amazement, it dawned on me that I was witnessing the much decried deforestation of Nepal. Nothing dramatic: just the faint persistent echo of a hand axe in the jungle, the sound of wood creaking and splitting as someone rends a lower limb from a tree. And this slow, steady procession of poor people struggling under their burdens of wood, just enough to get them through another day.

CHAPTER EIGHT

Village Walk

As I became accustomed to the sounds of normal village life, the calls of people to one another, the cacophony of ducks and chickens, the gravelly grunting bellows of buffaloes and occasional lowing of cattle, the reverberating sucking clank of the tube well as someone pumped its cast-iron handle, I became attuned also to unusual, out-of-the-ordinary sounds or movements in our little world. In particular, I became sensitized to the imminence of a "village walk." A chorus of "bye-bye" and children running toward the road usually alerted me to the arrival of a group of tourists in the village even before I could see them.

"Village walk" was the name used by the nearby hotels to promote a tour of a Tharu village led by their guides who were usually Brahmins, Chhetris, or Newars. Many of the guides, particularly those working at the more expensive hotels, were from Kathmandu. They knew little about the Tharus and had little interest in learning. Yet they led groups of foreigners through the villages, discoursing with authority on the ways of the "primitive" Tharus. The most expensive hotel in the area, the one that had lost the Tamang worker during the flood, regularly sent groups of guests on village walks through Pipariya. These groups usually consisted of six to ten (though sometimes as many as fifteen or twenty) people, predominantly European, North American, and Australian tourists; sometimes there were a few from Hong Kong and Japan as well.

Aside from their cameras, especially video cameras, the most conspicuous thing about the tourists was their footwear. In Pipariya, where people either went barefoot or wore plastic or rubber *chappals,* the number of men who owned a pair of real leather shoes could be counted on one hand. Thin vinyl or canvas tennis shoes were the prized possessions of the village elite who wore them only to go to the bazaar or, in the case of teachers, to attend school. Women did not own shoes of any kind, but only wore *chappals.* In this context, to me, the tourists' shoes looked more incongruous than anything else.

Their clothes also stood out: they all looked new and clean and fresh. By the time I was conscious of making these comparisons, I had already come to the realization that people's clothes in the village were not so much dirty, as I had first supposed, as they were worn out and faded with washing. The kind of hand washing of clothes used in Nepal and the practice of draping them over fences, woodpiles, or spreading them on the ground to dry is very hard on clothes. In less than a year, the clothes we had brought with us to the village were faded, stretched, and developing holes.

In contrast to the worn and shabby clothes of the villagers, the tourists trooped through in sturdy shoes and spotless clothes. In contrast to the posture and bearing of most Tharus, especially women, who stand erect and carry themselves lightly and gracefully, the foreigners often looked clumsy. They were on the whole larger and fatter than Tharus, or Nepalese generally. They seemed to walk heavily, clumping along with large shod feet. And of course many of them looked very self-conscious. Reactions on the part of Pipariya's residents to the village walks were varied and depended somewhat on the age and sex of the villagers. For the children village walks provided entertainment: Here were strange-looking people, wearing and carrying strange things, some of which moreover, they might be induced to part with. Older children were shy. Men generally did their best to ignore the intruders and quietly drifted out of range. The other group that was as unabashed as the children in their curiosity and observation of the tourists were the old women—women like Surendra's mother, who would heft a baby onto one hip and stand around commenting in Tharu on the appearance, equipment, and dress of the visitors. In the encounter of the old ladies and the tourists, it was hard to say who was the observed, who the observer.

It was the girls and young married women who suffered the most from village walks. This was because they were most likely to be the ones who were working around the compound when the groups arrived. Whenever possible, the young married women preferred to watch the interlopers through the tiny slit windows of their houses, but sometimes there was no escape for them from the inquisitive gaze of the foreigners. Tharu women also perhaps best satisfied an exotic image of the Tharu. Whereas many men had adopted Western dress, this was not true for the girls, whose blouses and lungis remained distinctly different from Western apparel.

One day three tourists from Hong Kong—all women in their twenties—had come into the compound while the girls of the household were threshing rice by lifting bundles of it over their heads and thrashing it against a bed frame that had been moved out into the center of the yard. This was a hot and dusty job. The girls covered their heads with shawls to keep the debris out of their hair. Bhagavati and Sita told me heatedly later that evening how the Hong Kong tourists had taken their photographs and had pointed and laughed at them. "We didn't like that at all," said Bhagavati.

On another occasion Mangala and Geeta and I were sitting on a *gundri* outside our hut. Mangala and Geeta were studying English for the School Leaving Certificate exam and I was trying to help them with grammar. The girls spotted the group of tourists before I did. They were accompanied by a young Newar man who had recently arrived from Kathmandu to work as a guide at the most expensive hotel in the area.

"Here come your *didi-bahini-haru* (older and younger sisters)," said Geeta. This was a favorite joke of hers. Once, when several young American women had entered the family's compound, Geeta's father had called jokingly to Arjun, who was at the *dhārā:* "There goes your *sāli* (sister-in-law)." People in the household enjoyed these jokes based on my *jāt* relationship to the tourists, but I felt ambivalent about being identified with them. In particular, I had mixed feelings about answering tourists' questions like, "Are the Tharus superstitious?" "Do they have a church or organized religion?" "Do you eat with your hands?" "Didn't you feel grossed out at first?" "Do you have any American kitchen conveniences?"

On the one hand, as someone resident in the village, I felt I could answer these questions less pejoratively than the Nepalese guides, for whom Tharus were often seen as a "backward" or primitive *jāt*. Perhaps I could demystify to some extent the image cultivated by the tourist trade of these "indigenous" people of the Tarai as "smiling, friendly people forgotten by time and the tide of civilization," as one brochure described them. On the other hand, I was wary of doing just the opposite. By answering a few questions in a superficial way, I was worried lest I actually promote the kind of exoticized view of Tharus that I wanted to combat. And no matter what I said, I was worried that it might appear to the Tharus who gathered around to watch me talk to my "own *jāt*" that I was "telling lies" about them, as they accused the guides of doing.

On several occasions, when asked what they thought of village walks, different people had told us, "We like the tourists, but the guides tell lies about us. They are all from Kathmandu. What do they know about Tharus?"

Now, alerted by Geeta that my "sisters" were coming, I looked up. They had apparently finished their tour of the *jimidār's* compound and were standing at the well looking in our direction. The guide put his palms together in a gesture of *namaskār*. I reciprocated. He said something to his small group of four women and two men, and they started walking slowly toward us. I got up from the *gundri* to greet them. It struck me that Arjun and I were becoming a tourist attraction, too. I suddenly realized I was barefoot. I glanced briefly at the visitors' feet. They were all wearing tennis shoes or, more precisely, jogging shoes (Nike and Adidas). One of the women had on a pair of pristine Reebok "aerobics" shoes. She was wearing shorts. Her legs were sunburned above the knee. The others wore pants. They were all young, twenties and thirties. One couple from Australia; the rest were Americans.

"Hello, how are you?" I greeted them.

"Hi," responded one of the men. "Fine," said another.

I asked where they were from.

They told me their nationalities and the names of their hometowns, which I either didn't recognize or promptly forgot.

"Where are you staying?" I asked, although I knew the answer because I recognized the guide.

"So you live here . . . " said the taller of the two men. He was carrying a camera with a telephoto lens strung on a bright woven strap around his neck. His fingers played nervously with the focusing mechanism as we spoke.

"My husband's an anthropologist," I said. "He's been here for a year. I've been here for three months."

"How do you like it?"

What a question! How could I possibly make a response that even vaguely expressed my reactions to living in Pipariya? "I like it," I said.

"You teaching these girls English?" asked the Australian woman in pants.

I explained that Geeta and Mangala were studying for the SLC exam. "It's very difficult and arbitrary," I said. I picked up Mangala's sample exam. "Listen to this," I said. I read the instructions for one of the sections of the exam. "Change this to indirect speech: 'I'm not going to school, Mother,' said the boy." The translation was rendered even more difficult for the students because there is no indirect speech construction as such in Nepali.

"Yeah, wow, I couldn't answer that," said the other man, shaking his head in exaggerated bewilderment.

"How old are they?" asked the woman in Reeboks, indicating Mangala and Geeta. I repeated this question slowly, in English, for the girls.

"Fifteen years old," said Geeta, eyes fixed on the *gundri* in front of her. "Sixteen," said Mangala.

"Very good English," smiled the Australian woman.

"Where do you get your water?" asked the tall man with the camera.

"From that well you just passed."

They all turned around and looked at the pump as if seeing it for the first time.

"And where do you shower?" asked the woman in Nikes. I indicated the well again.

One of the American women, who had a small instamatic camera strapped around her wrist, had taken a few steps away from the rest of the group to inspect our hut.

"What's it made of?" she asked. I explained how the house had been built and how the walls and floor were periodically resmeared with *māto* by the girls of the household.

"Can I look inside?" said the woman in Nikes.

"Sure, go ahead," I said.

The rest of the group moved toward the house. "Hey, what are these for?" someone asked, looking at the palm prints with which Mangala, Geeta, and Sarasvati had decorated our hut several days before, during the Tharu festival of Soharāyi, observed at the same time as the

Nepalese Tihār. I said that they and the other decorations they had probably seen in the village had been made during this festival.

"Bahini," the guide addressed Geeta. "What are these for?" He indicated the painted decorations on the wall of our *wosarā*. On the first day of Soharāyi, the girls had made prints with their hands all over two walls of our house. Dipping the heels of their hands into paint, they had stamped patterns in purple, blue, and green everywhere. The paint was still fresh and the designs colorful. Geeta had also fashioned balls of *māto* and had hung them on strings from our door frame like a fringe.

"What?" said Geeta to the guide truculently.

"What do these things mean?" he repeated, pointing again at the wall.

"*Hamilai thaha chaina.*" (We don't know), said Geeta sullenly. Could this be the same girl who had joyously taken part in making the decorations for the festival only days before?

"What's Tihār?" someone asked me.

The guide gave a brief description of "the festival of lights," as he called it, listing the various *pūjās* that were performed during the four-day festival, telling of the worship of cows, dogs, and crows.

Geeta started sniggering.

"Why is she laughing?" one of the tourists asked.

"*Galti garyo,*" Geeta said. (He made a mistake.)

"No, I didn't," he retorted in Nepali looking down rather angrily at Geeta sitting on the mat.

Without looking up at him, Geeta repeated what he had just told the tourists about Tihār in Nepali. I was impressed that she had been able to follow his English. But the guide again angrily disputed that he'd made a mistake. Then suddenly his expression cleared and he shrugged. He turned to his group of tourists. "She missed what I said," he informed them. "Shall we go?"

After saying good-bye and wishing me "good luck" the group moved on.

I asked Geeta what was wrong with what the guide said. "He doesn't know about Tihār; he got the days mixed up," she replied scornfully.

On several occasions guides had approached Arjun and asked him to tell them what to tell tourists about Tharus. Arjun always told them to talk to the Tharus themselves. "They're your neighbors," he would tell the Brahmin, Chhetri, and Newar guides. "I'm a foreigner; ask them." But they never did this. Surendra speculated that because they looked down on the Tharus, the Brahmin guides did not want to put themselves in the position of asking them questions. Instead they repeated lore passed down from one generation of guides to another, regardless of whether the information was accurate. The Tharus continued to complain of "lies" being told about them.

For a brief period of time I actually went out of my way to meet tourists who came through the village. This was when Surendra, Jamhaurni's son Thagawa, and some other young men were raising money for a "Tharu Youth Club" and asked me to help them by inviting tourists on village walks to make contributions.

After discussing the matter with Surendra, I wrote up a one-page description of the aims of the youth club: to encourage Tharu youth to study, whether or not they were in school, to preserve Tharu culture and administer a fund for use for Tharu religious occasions. Arjun made a sign-up sheet with columns for names, home country, and amounts given by tourists who made donations.

The next time a tour group came through the village I was washing rice at the pump. I hurried back to the house, covered the pot to keep the mice out of the grain, and went to meet the group with my sheet of paper.

I met them outside the shed where rice is pounded into flour. A group of at least ten, mostly middle-aged Americans were leaning into the shed where the pounding was taking place much to the embarrassment of Bhagavati and Sita who were operating a large pounding tool, called a *denkhi*, with their feet. This giant mortar and pestle apparatus consisted of a heavy, seven-foot-long beam resting on a wooden fulcrum. Underneath the other end of the beam a downward protruding piece of wood had been carved into a tip, which had been sheathed with some kind of metal. When the girls lifted their feet in unison off the lever end of the post, the metal fell into a hole carved out of a piece of beautiful hard redwood sunk into the floor. Both girls held onto the roof beam over their heads for support and balance as they manipulated the pounding beam with their feet. They took turns using a long stick with a fabric-covered foot to push grains of rice and partially milled flour into the indentation in the floor. The flour that is produced by pounding the rice in this fashion is used for making several kinds of unleavened *rotis* (breads).

Indrani had once called me into this pounding house when she and the *bahāriyā* servant were using the *denkhi*. She had invited me to have a go at operating the machine with my foot. I had found that the apparently simple action of lifting the beam with a downward thrust of the foot took both skill and strength. I had tired after only a few moments. Yet I frequently heard a regular thumping rhythm emanating from the hut that went on for hours.

In the old days, Indrani told me, before the advent of the commercial mills, the Tharus had produced all the flour they required this way. She said that in the time of Ram Bahadur's father, there had been eight such rice-pounding ensembles for that household alone. At that time there had been many people in the house, she said. (As opposed to now, when the household was composed of only twenty members!)

She claimed that the process of making flour at the modern mills took the protein out of the flour. Flour made in the traditional way was better, but today's commercial mills made work easier for women. Before there were mills, women not only ground the flour by their own effort, they also pressed the oil out of mustard manually. "We were harnessed like oxen," to a pole attached to a millstone, she told me. "Just the unmarried girls did this kind of work." She made a joke about the milk in mothers' breasts being pressed out by the effort of straining against the pole that drove the press. One day's hard labor yielded only a liter or two of mustard oil. "Things are better for women now," she concluded.

Standing outside the millhouse, I greeted the tourists, made the usual small talk about where they had been and where they were going and made my appeal for money.

"What do they need money for?" asked a balding middle-aged man with a paunch and a video camera.

I explained that in addition to building a club house, the young men wanted to buy some sports equipment: football, volleyball, Chinese checkers.

"Why do they need money to build a house?" the man challenged me. "I thought if you wanted to build a house here you just built it. The wood's there; grass is there, mud's there," he said.

I told him to look around him and notice how few trees, outside the National Park, there were. "Wood is very precious," I said. "It's expensive." I didn't mention that a lot of wood is poached by villagers. Anyway, that doesn't change the fact of its scarcity.

Ignoring my request for money, the man, who seemed to be the accepted leader of the group, changed the subject. "If the door's open, can I just look in?" he asked me, taking a few steps toward Ram Bahadur's house.

This reminded me of a story Surendra had told us. Once, while his father was alive, the guides would occasionally take tourists right into the house. One day several tourists had walked into the kitchen in their shoes, an act of disrespect and pollution. One of them had stuck his finger into some *tarkāri* to taste it. The old *jimidār* became so angry that he threatened the foreigners with a stick. After that the guides didn't bring them into the house.

"No, I don't think they'd appreciate you going into their house," I told the tourist. He turned away from me and started filming a group of children who had gathered to stare at the visitors. I went back to the house in defeat.

The next day another group came. This time, my request for money for the youth club met with more success. When the second group, numbering about twenty, came into our yard, I was serving tea to Indra Prasad, Ram Bahadur, and Surendra. I made my brief appeal. Most of the group responded positively, and I could see some of them reaching for their wallets even before I'd finished talking.

"If you'd like to ask any questions, here's Mr. Surendra Chaudhary," I said. I could hear Arjun prompting Surendra to "explain *garnus*."

Surendra got up from the *gundri* on which he'd been sitting on our porch and addressed the group in English. He talked about their desire to preserve Tharu culture, to encourage kids to study; he talked about the "hand and mouth" problems of poorer Tharus and also implied that the club might give some money to promising Tharu students whose families could not afford to send them to school beyond Class 5, when the fees for attending the government schools increased steeply.

He also told the tourists how the group had already raised over 5,000 rupees by singing and dancing in other villages and at nearby hotels over the Tihār festival. This is a common way for organizations to raise money, whether it's for repairing the local school, improving a road, or, as in this case, starting a club.

When Surendra finished speaking, Arjun again invited people to ask questions.

I was watching from the *wosarā*. Several of the women gravitated toward me. The group was mainly women, though most of them were older, retired, I guessed. Were there any Americans in the group, I

Village walk: tourists gather to listen to Surendra outside our hut

asked. No, they were mostly from Australia; two nice young women from Vancouver, British Columbia, one very tall blond with a punk hairstyle; the other a short plump cheerful woman of Chinese ancestry.

"Do you do the same work that women here do?" the blond with the punk hair asked.

I tried to explain that while I did many of the same tasks involved in cooking, keeping the house, and washing the clothes that other women did, because we were still considered guests in the household I was discouraged from work that was considered dirty or difficult.

I had had a discussion with Menaka on this subject shortly after I'd arrived in the village. I told her that I was embarrassed to have other girls and women working around me while I did nothing. "That is not how it is," Menaka had told me. Here the work is divided up; my brothers' wives, they do the cooking; Sarasvati and Mangala wash dishes; each one has a task. You should teach the children English, teach Shankar, Dip Narayan, Kishore. That should be your task."

"Do you pay the villagers rent?" was the next question.

"No," I said. "They won't take rent. They are extremely hospitable people. We paid for the materials to build this house, but the labor was provided free and we stay here without paying."

"Where do you get your food?" Another good question.

I responded that Ram Bahadur's family insisted on giving us rice and very often vegetables. I was beginning to realize that we sounded like parasites. For a moment I wondered if this were in fact the case. We were certainly acting in accordance with the norms of hospitality and friendship operative in Tharu culture and our acceptance of their gifts of food was made at their insistence. But were we actually taking advantage of them? As so often when I got into conversations about our experience of Nepal with other Westerners, I felt caught between two conflicting cultural perceptions of the subject being discussed. Accepting the easy hospitality of the Tharus had become natural. But I had not lost my own culturally informed sense of what were proper relations between guest and host, especially when the former was much wealthier than the latter. I hurriedly added that we also made trips to the bazaar to buy food.

Meanwhile Arjun had agreed to let the visitors see inside our hut.

"I didn't realize the floor was so . . . spongy," said one woman. I explained that there were several layers of straw underlying the mud-dung mixture.

"Is this the kind of bed they sleep on?" one of the middle-aged Australian ladies asked, lifting the *gundri* on our bed and tapping the wood bed with her finger.

"Some people have beds like this," I said. "Others, especially children and unmarried girls, sleep on this kind of straw mat spread on the floor."

"The roof's higher than I thought," commented another older lady. "Does it keep out the rain?"

"Fairly well," I said. "Actually, this roof hasn't been tested by the monsoon yet."

"Oh yes, the monsoon," she said. "That must be really something." I nodded silently in agreement.

Outside, the woman who had remarked on the texture of the floor was asking Mangala and Geeta their names. Mangala was standing behind Geeta with her arms around the younger girl's neck. They were both smiling broadly and only a little shyly.

The woman demonstrated how she had learned to count to ten in Hindi while they'd been traveling in India. "*Ek, do, teen,*" she began. "Are the numbers the same here?"

"Virtually the same," I said.

German tourists visit the jimidār's compound

"We like Nepal so much better than India," she said. "It's such a relief to get here. Nepalese people are so friendly."

Arjun and Surendra appeared to be engaged in discussion with several people about the impact of tourism on the Tharus, and what Tharus thought of village walks. Meanwhile, the Newar guide was hanging around the periphery of the group looking slightly bemused.

After spending about an hour at our hut, our visitors took leave of us and started on the walk back to their hotel. They thanked us profusely for showing them our house and "telling them about Tharus." Several of them wished Surendra good luck with the youth club. They had given generously: four hundred rupees in all. Surendra seemed pleased with the interaction with the tourists, as well as their donation to the club.

While they did not participate in the discussions with the tourists, Ram Bahadur and Indra Prasad had watched the interaction with interest from the vantage point of our *wosarā*.

In general, we observed that the most meaningful interaction occurred when tourists came through the village by themselves, without a guide. These cross-cultural meetings sometimes proved just as enlightening for the Tharus as for the tourists. Arjun once acted as an interpreter between several villagers and a Dutch dairy farmer who came wandering through Pipariya by himself. The conversation had quickly turned to the care of cows. Among other things, the Dutch dairyman had told the Tharus that milk production could be increased by feeding cattle sugar cane. This had interested the Tharus very much. Sugar cane is grown in the Tarai—though not in Chitwan—and while these men were unlikely to begin feeding it to their animals, it was the kind of mutually relevant information that went some way to bridging the distance and difference between Nepal and the Netherlands.

On another occasion I was returning from a trip to the bazaar when I met two college-aged American women. Just as I was about to pass them on the road through Pipariya, one of them stepped off the road, bent over, and took a photograph of something in the ditch.

I was curious. "Are you photographing plants?" I asked her.

"Marijuana," she giggled. On second glance, I noticed a healthy cannabis plant growing there in the ditch. The same weed flourished among our tomato plants, and indeed grew wild all around us. It was occasionally picked, dried, and smoked by some of our neighbors, mostly old people.

A bit further down the road I met Jamhaurni's son Thagawa and a group of other young men. They were looking after the retreating figures of the Americans with curiosity.

"No guide," Thagawa commented to me approvingly in English as I stopped to greet them. "They are pure tourists."

CHAPTER NINE

American Gurau / Tharu Tourists

The entrance to the American Embassy's recreational compound on Kantipath is through a thick black metal door in a long stretch of white wall. The compound, known as Phora Durbar, is located opposite the National Panchāyat (parliament) building. The door in the wall is wide enough to admit only one pedestrian at a time. There is also an entrance for cars. Inside this metal gate, mechanical steel barriers can be maneuvered to block vehicles.

I pause at the sentry box to show my plastic laminated Embassy photo ID to the khaki-uniformed Nepalese guard. This identifies me as a "USEF spouse."

"Thank you, Madam," the guard says, waving me into the compound. I walk across a spacious blacktop parking lot. There are about twenty vehicles parked here. To my right are two fuel pumps marked "diesel" and "gasoline." In front of me is a playing field. There's a baseball diamond marked out, a volleyball net set up against the far boundary of the compound. A lone jogger in shorts and sweatshirt is plodding around the periphery of the field. The atmosphere in here—the tall trees, the mown lawn, the hot, still, humid afternoon—reminds me of summer on the campuses of the Claremont Colleges, where my parents work.

A red brick path from the parking lot leads to a dining facility, swimming pool, and locker room. The flower beds along the path are tended by a veritable army of Nepalese groundsmen. My destination is a building that looks like a suburban ranch house. This is the medical unit for the American diplomatic community, including the Peace Corps.

On the solid wood door of the clinic, the hours of various services are listed: visits by appointment, walk-ins, inoculations, emergencies. I open the door and step into the air-conditioned reception area. I sign in on a clipboard at the desk. There's one column for Peace Corps, another for Embassy staff, the US Information Agency, Lincoln School, and USEF.

"It will be just a few minutes," the receptionist, a young Nepalese woman with polished English, tells me. I sit down in one of the blue vinyl chairs, such as one might find in any doctor or dentist's office in the United States. I flip through an old *US News and World Report*. Under my chair is a box of toys for kids to play with. At the far end of the room there's a topographical map of Nepal. Passport photos of the two-hundred-odd Peace Corps volunteers are linked by strings and colored pins to the sites where they are posted. I walk over to the map to see if there's anyone in our area. As usual I seek out the faces of the volunteers I've met in Nepal.

Beside the map a water cooler dispenses ice-cold water. On a shelf by the water cooler, a towering stack of stool specimen cups suggests that the ailments most frequently treated at the clinic are gastrointestinal in nature. "No Stool Specimens Accepted After 3 pm Except in Emergency," warns a sign. In addition to their intended use, Arjun and I have discovered that these sturdy (and presumably sterile) wax-coated cardboard containers make very good bowls for eating yogurt and muesli, our standard breakfast fare at USEF, where we have no real bowls of our own. I pick up a supply for whichever need should prove more urgent.

The only other patient in the waiting room is a girl of about fourteen. She is dressed in T-shirt, baggy pants, and white high-topped tennis shoes with fluorescent yellow laces. Untied. This must be the latest fashion among teenagers in the United States, I reason, because if the American diplomatic community in Kathmandu knows anything, it's how to keep up American standards in this alien place. There are Betty Crocker cake mixes and microwavable macaroni dinners in the commissary and video screenings of American movies at Phora Durbar every week.

The nurse emerges from her office and indicates that she's ready to see me. There are two nurses on the staff here. They've both been in Nepal for years. I have tremendous respect and admiration for them. They're also a lot of fun.

"So, how are your feet?" the nurse asks, opening my chart. The last time I'd been in, to get a gamma globulin shot, I'd complained of badly cracked dry skin on my heals from going around in *chappals* in the cold dry conditions of Pipariya.

"Oh, they're fine now," I tell her. Actually I still have one crack on my left heel, but it is no longer painful. "I'm here for my Hepatitis B shot," I say. "I think I was supposed to get it two weeks ago, but we just got back from the village a few days ago."

"No problem," she says. "Climb on the table."

I step through the accordion door separating her office from the examining room.

"I think we have scabies," I tell her as she expertly inoculates me. I show her the red spots and hard scabs on my stomach, back, and inner thighs. When Arjun and I had first begun scratching and noticed the red welts on our bodies, I had reacted with near panic at the mere thought of being infested with some kind of tiny insect. Our consultation of *Where There is No Doctor* had only increased my distress when our symptoms seemed to fit the description of scabies. When I was in sixth grade in a small logging and farming community in Oregon, we whispered about the "dirty" kids at school who were sent home with scabies. Now I was less hysterical. Like a lot of other discomforts in Nepal, I'd learned to live with them. It was like sleeping with the rats skittering about in the hut. It didn't bother me that much anymore.

The nurse inspects the areas I show her and asks me questions. "I've never seen scabies before," she finally admits. "Let me get the doctor."

She returns almost immediately. Behind her is the Embassy doctor. In his mid-forties, he's athletic looking in spite of a pronounced slouch in the way he moves.

The nurse shows him the scabs on my body. "Not on the extremities," he says. "Unusual for scabies. Maybe they're fleas."

"I've seen them," I say. "They're definitely not fleas. I know what fleas look like."

"They don't hop?"

"No, they're very small and black with hard bodies. I've watched them burrowing under my skin."

"Maybe body louse," says the doctor. He's talking to the nurse, not to me.

Then he turns to me. "You need to get some insecticide for your bedding. Black Flag should work."

"She can't get that here," says the nurse. There's a hint of exasperation in her voice.

"Well, some other kind of bug spray, then. What is your bedding, anyway?"

"A *sirak*," I say. Both look blank. "It's a quilt with a sheet cover. The cover can be washed but not the quilt." This is the most common kind of bedding in Nepalese homes. "And a straw mat," I add.

The doctor rolls his eyes. "That will have to be sprayed," he says.

"Do you have anyone who comes into your house?"

I suppose he means servants. I tell him that people stay in our house to keep an eye on our things while we're away. I can tell before the words are out of my mouth that I've said the wrong thing.

"Why do they do that?" the doctor asks sharply. "Why don't you just lock the house and go?" Suddenly I realize that there is a huge disparity in what house connotes to each of us. Embassy personnel in Nepal are compensated with large secure houses. The doctor probably has a guard at his house, too. And a heavy door that can be bolted, and bars on the windows. Somehow I can't explain that by house I mean a mud hut with chicken wire over the windows and a thimble-sized padlock securing the elephant grass and plastic door.

"If you continue to let infected Nepalese come into your house and sleep in your bed, I don't see how you can get rid of this. When we stay in hotels or go trekking, we always turn over the mattresses and spray them with bug spray," the doctor continues. "And we sleep in our own sleeping bags," he says pointedly.

I'm beginning to feel like I am in the sixth grade again, embarrassed and guilty. It is clearly my fault that I've got these things. Secretly I'm thinking that the bugs aren't so bad, after all. We can endure them for a few more months. To the doctor I say, "Yes, I'm thinking it may not be possible for us to get rid of them, given the way we live."

This is apparently a position inimical to modern medicine.

"You really should get rid of them," the doctor says. "They carry disease. Typhus . . . " he mentions some other diseases I don't recognize. "You can get very sick." He describes some symptoms of these illnesses for additional effect.

I nod.

"And you should tell the Nepalese you're living with how to treat them, get them to treat their own clothes and bedding with insecticide."

Some of the skepticism that I feel must be apparent. The doctor rushes on. "You may think this is changing their culture; I would say it's advancing society. Tell them they can get sick from the bugs and how they should treat them."

He pauses. Is he waiting for me to disagree? He seems to be expecting an answer. Suddenly I have a vision of myself as I must appear to this man, sitting on his examining table, hair greasy and stragglylooking from weeks of washing it at the well with laundry soap, unshaven legs dangling from under a crumpled and faded skirt. It occurs to me that maybe he thinks anthropologists are opposed to cultural change. I attempt to counteract this idea with my next response: "I just don't think this is a problem people in our village will treat with pesticide."

"Pesticide is readily available in this country," the doctor says. "It may be more toxic than what's available in the United States. It may not meet EPA standards . . ." he fixes me with a meaningful glance. "It may cause environmental damage, but it's available, believe me." The guy must have me pegged as an environmental nut, too. This is what comes of not shaving one's legs. I'd forgotten about all the minute markers of social attitudes in the United States. In Nepal, I had so far been liberated from being "placed" by members of my own culture.

I don't explain to him that what I mean is that people won't spend limited disposable income on something that they regard as a minor nuisance and for which they have their own treatments anyway: bathing frequently and thoroughly airing bedding in the sun. But the doctor seems to sense some resistance even in my compliant silence.

"This is what we're here for," he begins, a little tentatively at first, but with increasing conviction as he warms to his topic. "To advance society, to educate people, to improve health."

I'm scratching my head. I can't believe I'm hearing this. It's like a meeting of some nineteenth-century missionary society.

"You have 'em in your hair, too?" the doctor asks.

"No, no," I say quickly, "I just scratch my head when I'm talking to someone who makes me feel nervous." I realize this is the most honest thing I have said to this doctor yet. But it probably completes this guy's picture of me as a social incompetent: fleeing my own society to "live like a native" (he'd used those words, too) in Nepal. He gives the nurse some instructions about flea powders and insecticidal lotions and goes back to his office.

I am still sitting on the examining table pondering the tensions in the American expatriate community and our different experiences and perceptions of Nepal when the nurse returns from the medical unit's well-stocked dispensary with a handful of bottles and tubes. She closes the door and leans against it. She looks at me and raises her eyebrows. I explode into giggles.

"I know what you mean because I live like a Nepalese, too," she says. "It's one thing if you live in an Embassy house," she says, "but this is just a part of being here. I have a woman who comes into my house, a good friend of mine. She's always told me to put clothes and bedding out in the sun. I never understood why, but now I know. A few months ago I got head lice. I tried the medicine we prescribe here, but it didn't kill the eggs, so they came back again. Finally I had to get a good friend to sit down in the sun and pick them out of my hair, one by one, just like you see women doing all over the country. It's the only thing that really works." I nod. I'm grateful to have someone whose outlook is closer to mine. Then we drop the subject. She gives me the instructions on the flea powders.

She hands me four boxes. Kwell Cream (registered trademark): active ingredient lindane 1 percent. The cream is packaged in confidence-inspiring two-color boxes. Classic American pharmaceutical. The packaging conveys professionalism, seriousness, scientific knowledge, precision, everything central to the cult of Western medicine. The Latin words and laconic instructions communicate magic and mystery just as the bearing and incantations of the village *gurau* do. My medicine is manufactured in Puerto Rico. I wonder how effective our EPA standards are there.

Arjun was on the phone when I returned to USEF from the medical clinic. I sat on the sofa across from the receptionist's desk to wait. Before I could relate my experience with the doctor, he said, "Guess who's in Kathmandu!"

"I don't know," I said.

"Geeta and Bhagavati," he informed me. "Ram Bahadur wants to take Geeta to the Teaching Hospital." She had been suffering from recurrent abdominal pains during the last few months. "They got here last night."

I responded to the announcement of the arrival of my friends from Pipariya with mixed feelings. On the one hand I was glad they'd come. Neither of them had ever been to the capital before. The visit should be exciting and eye-opening for them. I was also interested to see how they would react to life in the city. At the same time, I was conscious of feeling that their arrival was an intrusion on my time to myself, my vacation from Pipariya, my rare opportunity to write and read, in the private, self-sufficient, anonymous world that we lived in when we came to Kathmandu. And I also wondered what they would make of our more Westernized lifestyle here. In the village even the few clothes and belongings we had brought there with us were considered "*dherei sāmān-haru*," a lot of stuff. In Kathmandu we had clothes and other possessions that had never been seen in the village. I was anxious about their perception of this wealth. In short, I was a little worried, embarrassed even, to meet our village neighbors on what was more like my own ground.

"Where are they staying?" I asked Arjun. This was another concern, while we enjoyed automatic hospitality in Pipariya, living for months on end with Ram Bahadur and his family, we were constrained in reciprocating this hospitality by the fact that we were staying in USEF. The same was true for our ability to feed them. Though we did have access to a kitchen in USEF, we didn't have the equipment necessary to cook for and feed guests. Even if we had enough cooking utensils and facilities, I doubted whether I was up to negotiating the purchase, slaughter, cleaning, and cooking of one of the live chickens I passed in cages on the street every day. But we would have to feed our guests meat; that is the true measure of Tharu hospitality and respect for guests. A vegetarian curry, no matter how tasty, was inadequate. Anyway, in spite of my affection for Ram Bahadur and his family, especially toward the women of the household, I had to admit that I was not really prepared to go to the trouble of cooking for them. It was too much of a hassle.

As it turned out, it was Geeta and Bhagavati who continued to play the role of hosts to us.

They were staying with family friends in a Newar village outside Patan. They invited us there to eat the next day. Once again I was humbled by the generosity of our Tharu friends.

The next morning we went to meet Sunder, the head of the family with whom Geeta and Bhagavati were staying, who worked as a driver for an international aid agency. We had first been introduced to Sunder and his family a few weeks before when they had come down to the Tarai to *gumné* (visit), on holiday. They had stayed with Indra Prasad, whom Sunder had met years earlier through a job in Chitwan. It was at that time that he became friends with Indra Prasad; subsequently he had brought his wife and three daughters to visit several times. No one in Indra Prasad's family had visited them in Kathmandu before though.

We went to Sunder's workplace to meet him. He took us to the staff canteen and gave us each a glass of hot milk. Then he put us into a taxi driven by a neighbor and we set off for the village, which was about seven miles south of Patan. It took us two hours to get there because a gravel truck had tipped over on the narrow road to the village. The taxi finally dropped us (free of charge) at a little lane on which Sunder's house was located.

It was mid-afternoon. Bhagavati and Geeta were sitting in the middle of the lane in a patch of sun, trying to absorb some warmth. They looked up with spontaneous smiles of welcome when they saw us getting out of the taxi. Sunder's wife was also sitting outside chatting with some other women. She welcomed us kindly but didn't accompany us inside. Her two daughters, both in their early teens, sat with us, but it was clear that we were Geeta and Bhagavati's guests.

The house was three stories high and narrow. The first room we entered had a huge pile of *māto* with a well of water in the center of it. I guessed that this was maintained for repairing the ground floor.

A set of stairs, more like a ladder, led up to the second floor where the family slept on mats rolled out on the floor. The second-floor room had a glass window (a sign of prosperity) and a raised bed.

We sat on the bed and were served tea. We chatted about Kathmandu and what was happening in Pipariya. Bhagavati told us excitedly that one of Indra Prasad's servants had eloped with Bikramiya's brother.

When both Sunder's daughters were out of the room, Bhagavati asked us quietly how we liked the village.

"*Ramailo lāgyo,*" Arjun said.

"Really?" Bhagavati asked. She leaned over and whispered, "I don't like it." I was surprised at her vehemence.

"Why not?" I asked.

"We can't talk to anyone here. They speak only Newari, all the women of this village. They don't even speak Nepali."

Sunder's daughters both went to school so there was no one for them to talk to during the day. They couldn't communicate with the girls' mother at all. "She's embarrassed she can't speak to you," Bhagavati said. "That's why she stayed outside."

Bhagavati was far from done with her complaints about the village. "It's very cold here," she said. I had already noticed that she was not adequately equipped for Kathmandu's cold. She was wearing a diaphanous sari, one of her best, covered with a synthetic cardigan sweater. As fashion among Tharu village girls dictates, only the top button was fastened. She had neither socks nor closed shoes; only her plastic, open-toed *chappals*.

"There's nowhere to bathe," Geeta added, making a face. "And the water's so cold. We went to a stream one day to bathe, but it was filthy. There was *goo* (shit) everywhere. People here only wash part of their bodies; they don't bathe thoroughly like we do at home."

"And there's no latrine," Geeta continued. "It's so dirty everywhere." She made a face of distaste. I got the idea that she meant there was human excrement everywhere.

I realized that even though we were only a few miles from the country's capital, some things were not very different from other remote villages we'd visited in Nepal. And because of the higher population density, some of the same problems of rural areas, such as water and hygiene, were worse in the valley than outside it in more "undeveloped" areas.

Bhagavati had made us a delicious meal. After a week of the inferior fare served up in Thamel restaurants and our own shortcut cooking, we devoured her food with enthusiasm. She kept pressing more chicken on us until my accumulated desire for meat was sated. Accustomed to our peculiar food habits, Bhagavati had even boiled water for us. We drank it still warm. Bhagavati and Geeta claimed that they had no ill effects from drinking the water in Kathmandu. However, on his return to the village later that week, Ram Bahadur had to get the bus to stop three times as he was suffering from diarrhea.

After the meal, eaten sitting cross-legged on burlap mats on the packed-earth floor of the kitchen, we climbed back up the stairs to view the family photo collection: pictures of Sunder with various people he'd met in his career as a driver, photos of the girls dressed in traditional Newari costumes at festival time, and several dozen snapshots of dancers performing for a film in Patan's Durbar square.

At about four o'clock, Sunder's friend arrived in his taxi, and we got in. Before we left I arranged to meet Bhagavati and Geeta and Sunder's daughters the next day to *gumné* with them. What did they most want to see in Kathmandu, we asked. "Pashupathinath," they immediately responded.

"What about the airport?" Arjun asked. Yes, Bhagavati, especially, wanted to see the airport.

Earlier that day Sunder had told us how his daughters had accompanied Bhagavati and Geeta on the bus into Kathmandu to go sightseeing. When they'd got off at Ratna Park, the bus terminus, they had looked around for the famous Rani Pokhari, or Queen's Pond, which is located right behind the bus stand and is a major landmark, literally of the you-can't-miss-it variety. They had returned home to the village saying the Rani Pokhari was "lost." They hadn't seen it. Sunder was very amused at this. To me it suggested how overwhelming and incomprehensible the city and its famous tourist sites were to these girls, even to Sunder's daughters, who lived in the valley. But even though they lived in the Kathmandu Valley, with commercial jets flying low over their village to land, they had never been to the airport (why should they go?) and obviously found the city itself an alien place. I was in many ways less lost and out of place in the capital than they were, these Newar girls, whose ancestors had lived in this valley for thousands of years. It reminded me of a Ghurka soldier we had met on a bus. He was on six-months leave after a tour of duty that included Britain and Hong Kong. He had brought his aged parents down from the mountains to Kathmandu for the first time in their lives. He told us his mother kept asking in disbelief whether Kathmandu was really part of their country.

Gumné is the infinitive of the verb "to visit, to travel, to wander about." *Gumauné* means to show someone else around, to effect his wandering about a place. It also means coming to something by a roundabout way. I resolved to do whatever I could to give the girls a good *gumauné*. What I did not anticipate was what a different perspective I would gain on the city through acting as their tour guide.

I was ready with water for tea boiling and a plate of biscuits when Sunder drove into the USEF compound in an official vehicle the next morning to drop the girls off. After a cup of tea, he departed with my assurances that I would take care of the girls and see them home at the end of the day.

Before catching a bus to Pashupathinath, I took the girls to see the Royal Palace and then to look in the shop windows along the fashionable shopping street, Durbar Marg, where exclusive clothing boutiques and the offices of international airlines line the streets, and Nepalese sometimes appear in a minority among the cosmopolitan well-heeled pedestrians. All four girls, not just Bhagavati and Geeta, looked confused and uncertain as we stepped onto the street at the intersection of Kathipath and Tridevi Marg; overloaded buses, scores of "tempos," and squadrons of swiftly pedaling cyclists tore around the traffic circle in endless succession. I took Bhagavati's hand; it rested comfortably in mine, and we crossed the road. As we walked along the front of the palace grounds under the massive iron fence that separates the King from his subjects, people turned to stare at our little procession: four village girls and an American walking along hand in hand.

None of my companions showed much interest in the palace, although Geeta stopped to stare at the uniforms of the guards outside the south gate.

When we had safely crossed the road onto Durbar Marg and were strolling down the wide sidewalk, I said "This is where the people were shot by police and soldiers during the *andolan*." On April 6 of the previous year, police guarding the entrance to the palace had fired on unarmed demonstrators marching to press demands for multiparty democracy in Nepal. Estimates of the number of people who had died in the brief but bloody revolution ranged into the hundreds. This elegant broad avenue had been the scene of its most violent confrontation. Bhagavati and Geeta nodded seriously and looked around them. There were no signs of the violence and death now.

A number of "jungle" lodges located in and around Chitwan National Park have offices on Durbar Marg. Some of the offices have huge photos of wildlife, Tharu villages, and the kind of accommodations they offer posted in their windows. Bhagavati and Geeta paused in front of several such window displays looking at the pictures of their familiar terrain as well as the anomalous resort swimming pools and the luxurious "Tharu village" style tented camps, which didn't look like any Tharu village any of us had ever seen.

Walking with Bhagavati, Geeta, and Sunder's daughters I was aware as never before of the differences in class, caste, and ethnic identity of the other Nepalese we passed. Most of the Nepalese we met along Durbar Marg were middle or upper class, members of Nepal's urban elite. The women wore fine saris, lipstick, carried stylish purses, and had gems in their ears and noses. The men wore Western-style suits or Nepalese national dress and *topis*. There were also some workers, men and women, struggling under yokes balancing heavy loads that swayed in two baskets as they walked. These men wore shorts, or *lungi* and T-shirt. The women were draped in worn saris, soiled blouses and wore *chappals* or went barefoot. All of them looked my companions up and down. I had the distinct impression that from this quick glance they gleaned all the information that they required to place strangers in their society.

To get to Pashupathinath I decided to take a local bus. If Arjun and I had gone by ourselves we would probably have taken a motorized "tempo," but there were too many of us. I didn't want to appear profligate by taking a taxi. Besides, I figured, they were used to taking buses. I began to regret my decision as soon as we squeezed ourselves into a bus heading for Gaushala, and I looked round at the startled and anxious expressions of my friends. Most of the other passengers were men and boys. I wondered if I had dragged the girls into a situation that they considered inappropriate. What about my assurances to Sunder that I would take care of his daughters and give them a good time? I should have taken a taxi, I thought, as I wondered where Pashupathinath was in relation to Gaushala. And how would we find the temple once we got there anyway? I didn't have any more time to worry because the conductor was saying "Gaushala, Gaushala," and I motioned to the others to push their way out through the rear door. I gave the conductor a five-rupee note and looked around for someone to ask directions to the temple complex. I asked a few people who gestured toward the other side of the street and informed me that it was "just there." I shouldn't have worried. I knew the temple complex was located in a gorge where the Bagmati River ran, so it would have to be downhill. Once my confusion and concern over subjecting my charges to the crush of the bus had subsided, I noticed a number of people selling devotional items—colored powders, leaves, and incense used for *pūjās*—as well as items of personal adornment—hair tassels, pins, and *bindis*—lining a road that ran off down a steep hill. We crossed the intersection and started down this road. The further down the shady monkey-inhabited avenue we walked, the more concentrated the pavement entrepreneurs became, until, within sight of the temple complex itself, the sellers of devotional pictures and bead necklaces sitting cross-legged with their wares spread out on mats in front of them gave way to well-stocked shops and stalls.

We were indeed following the curving road down into a gorge where the holy waters of the Bagmati River flowed, a dirty trickle of water as it runs past the most revered Shiva shrine of Nepalese Hindus. Under the bridge, women were washing clothes just as they might in any other bit of water in the valley or throughout the country for that matter. Downstream several funeral *ghats* were in use; groups of men stood around two separate piles of burning wood on which the bodies of their deceased relatives were being cremated. In the middle of the shallow stream of water, the leftover timbers from another such funeral pyre had lodged and were creating ripples where the current flowed around them. Pointing at the fires, Bhagavati asked me what they were for. I was surprised that she didn't know. But according to Hindu custom, only the male relatives attend the cremation. The *ghats* upstream, closer to the temple were reserved for royalty according to a self-appointed guide who attached himself to us as we crossed the bridge that connected with hundreds of stone steps leading up the hill on the opposite side of the river. The wind blew a cloud of smoke over us. I fancied I could smell burning human flesh and wondered that I did not react with revulsion. I had felt much more distaste and horror when I had glimpsed not a corpse, but the feeble dying body of an old woman who had been carried by her family to die on the filthy (but holy) banks of the Bishnumati River as I had walked back from a visit to the Buddhist stupa Swayambunath one day. I think what had disturbed me about the scene of the dying woman brought to breathe her last on the banks of the river, thus speeding her soul on its journey, was a violation of a sense of privacy that I felt. It did not fit my idea of a peaceful death. And it looked so uncomfortable, such a physical ordeal to be dragged to that stinking place to die among the rubbish and scavenging dogs.

The others stopped to buy flowers and sweets in preparation for their *pūjā*. Non-Hindus are not allowed to enter the main temple at Pashupathinath. This did not rule out Sunder's daughters, Newar Buddhists, however. Buddhism and Hinduism have long shared temples and devotees in Nepal. Anyway, there was no one to stop them. I, on the other hand, as a conspicuous foreigner was turned back long before our small band of pilgrim-tourists reached the entrance to the temple. As I walked up the paved banks of the Bagmati with my young companions, I was arrested by the gravelly voice of a middle-aged Brahmin woman.

"You can't take the American in there," she admonished Bhagavati. Bhagavati looked as if she might press the issue. For a moment I was alarmed lest she insist on my being admitted to the temple. I quietly disengaged my hand from hers and returned to the bridge to wait for them to complete their *pūjā*. As I stood on the bridge looking upstream at a new temple built by the Japanese and watching debris float by in the water, the young man who had earlier offered his services as a guide approached me again. We had a short, friendly conversation preparatory to his proposal to show me the Shiva shrines arrayed on the bank opposite the main temple. I told him as politely as I could that I wasn't very interested in religious shrines and had only accompanied my friends who were now inside the temple. This was close to the truth. While I am interested in how religion enters into the everyday life of people and enjoy the beauty and mystery of religious places, I do not feel compelled to find out what they "mean," to know their histories or to identify their style, period, or architecture. He seemed to accept this, but remained on the bridge to chat until Bhagavati and Geeta came up. Bhagavati showered marigold petals on my head and gave me some of the sugar crystal sweets to eat. I guessed that this was the *prasād*, or food offered to and blessed by sacrifice to the god. She asked me which braided thread necklace I would like to wear. They had bought a number of them, apparently intending to take some back to Pipariya as gifts. I chose one in which red, black, and white threads were braided together. Bhagavati fastened it around my neck.

For the trip back to USEF I had resolved to take my friends in a taxi. We engaged one half-way up the hill from the temple.

The girls seemed anxious to return home to the village. Perhaps they had found the day's outing as tiring as I had. However, I didn't want them to leave before I could feed them a meal. Since I didn't have access to the kitchen at USEF during the day and it would have been a big production to cook a proper meal for them anyway, this meant taking them to a restaurant. But which one?

Thamel is full of restaurants, of course, but almost all of them cater to tourists. They serve foreign food—Italian, Chinese, Mexican, Israeli, American, British, German—at prices higher than the average villager can afford. I also wanted to take them somewhere they'd feel comfortable. One solution was to take them to a "hotel," that is, a Nepalese eating house serving cheap *dāl bhāt* in a small room with only a curtain to separate it from the sights, sounds, and smells of the street. There was such a hotel just around the corner from the USEF where we'd occasionally drunk tea; I'd seen them cutting up vegetables there to make *thukpa*, a thick Tibetan soup, and it had looked good. But Bhagavati and Geeta balked.

"We don't eat *momos*," they said.

I could have reassured them that there were other things on the menu besides *momos*, which were made from buffalo meat and therefore considered unclean by Tharus. But the tiny hotel was already full of young men having an afternoon meal, so we continued down the road, into the heart of Thamel. Bhagavati immediately assumed the role of my protector, as she did when I accompanied her into the bazaar. She froze the sassy carpet salesmen with an icy stare when they called out to me, "Hey, Madam, buy carpet . . . change money." One boy carrying a wooden box filled with shoe polish and brushes followed me for about twenty feet, pleading, "fix shoes, Madam; I give good price."

"*Pardaina*," Bhagavati told him haughtily: We don't need it. The shoe shine boy dropped away. "What did he offer you?" Bhagavati asked me.

We ran a final gauntlet of money changers, beggars, carpet salesmen, and shoe shiners and entered into the wide paved entrance to the Kathmandu Guest House, one of Thamel's oldest and best known hotels. I had decided to take my guests to the Ashta Mangala, a purportedly Tibetan restaurant where Arjun and I often went for *thukpa*. I had frequently seen other Nepalese (albeit upper class) eating there, and I hoped that its dark, subdued atmosphere would make the girls feel comfortable.

As soon as we entered the compound of the hotel, which also accommodated a few clothing stores and trekking agencies, I sensed something was wrong. A guard whom I had never noticed before, yelled after us to ask where we thought we were going. I yelled back that we were going to eat. He came running after us. I stopped. Bhagavati and Geeta didn't even look around. "We're going to *gumné*," Geeta said defiantly. I admired her spirit. I was more meek in my response. I explained that we were going to have lunch at the Ashta Mangala. The guard apologized to us. "It's my job; I have to ask," he explained in Nepali.

I led the way down the steps leading into the cool, dark rooms of the Ashta Mangala. One of the young waiters greeted me with a smile of recognition. "*Namaste*," he said, exaggerating the stress on the last syllable.

I ushered my friends into one of the booths. The waiter brought five menus. The girls turned the plastic-coated booklets listing Nepalese, Chinese, Tibetan, and Western dishes over in their hands not knowing what to do with them. After taking the taxi back from Pashupathinath, I realized I didn't have much money.

I asked the girls if they wanted tea or soft drinks to drink.

"Soft drinks," they said.

I ordered five soft drinks and five bowls of vegetable *thukpa*.

We sat in silence and waited for the meal. Geeta and Bhagavati looked uncomfortable. I heard Geeta whisper to Bhagavati that this was a "tourist hotel." Meanwhile the waiters were sitting by the entrance to the kitchen smirking and whispering.

The bottled drinks arrived. I'd decided that I might not have enough money to pay for our meal, so before the waiter had taken the cap off mine I told him that I didn't want it. He wordlessly carried the bottle back into the kitchen.

When he brought our soup, the younger of Sunder's daughters said she didn't want it. I told the waiter in Nepali, "She won't eat it."

"Oh, no," he said in English. "It is yours. You pay."

The girls picked suspiciously at their noodle soup. I realized that the adventurousness or at least open-mindedness with which I had been brought up to approach different kinds of foods was alien to these girls, who had eaten rice and *tarkāri* and little else their entire lives. Or maybe they considered the whole establishment unclean.

After lunch we walked through Thamel, Chetrapati, and Asan on our way to the Ratna Park bus stop where they would catch the bus back to their village via Patan. The girls loved looking through the glass windows of jewelry shops in the tourist ghetto. They were less interested in the color photographs of the *andolan* arrayed in the window of a photo developing store.

"You have all these," Geeta said. In fact Arjun had purchased some of the photos of people involved in the *andolan*, some of them badly beaten and bruised, others dead. One young "martyr of the revolution" had been shot and then run over by a truck. A gruesome photo shows her naked torso, one arm blown off and her chest stitched hastily back together, apparently after an autopsy. Her face is spattered with blood, but otherwise intact. It is a beautiful young girl's face. Her lips are parted revealing perfect white teeth. A bead necklace hangs around her neck. There were also photos showing the jubilant aftermath of the King's declaration that he would restore multiparty democracy.

When we got to the bus park, a bus for Patan was just about to leave.

Assuring me that they could get home on their own, the girls stood on the back steps of the crowded bus and waved good-bye.

The next day was Saturday. We met Sunder, Bhagavati, and Geeta in Kamal Pokhari and took a local bus out to the airport. Tribhuvan International airport is smaller than most municipal airports in the United States and gets far less traffic, but for Nepal, it's a big deal. It's "modern"; it connects Nepal with the outside world, the gate through which foreign tourists and development agencies enter with their money.

Built in the late 1980s, the main terminal building is made of red brick. Except for the bathrooms, the airport is relatively clean. The main attraction is the observation deck overlooking the runway. There is an entry fee of five rupees just to get into the terminal building and another two rupees to access the observation deck.

I would have paid quite a bit more to stand on that platform overlooking the runway in the pleasant midday sun with a breeze blowing. More than watching the planes, I enjoyed watching the other people on the deck, mostly passengers and their families, as well as a few like us, who had come to visit the airport as a tourist attraction in its own right. Most of the Nepalese were members of the urban middle and upper classes. The men were well turned out in Western dress, here and there set off with a *topi*. The women were wearing saris though a few younger women strutted about the platform in high heels and short skirts. Squatting along the railing and leaning against the wall of the terminal, there were a few poorer-looking Nepalese, also in their best clothes.

The special-day-out clothes, especially the frilly dresses and shiny shoes of the little girls who played tag on the deck, and the general atmosphere of excitement reminded me of going to the airport when I was a child in Oregon. Going to meet my mother's parents or other relatives from England meant a sixty-mile drive to the Portland airport. Such trips were a rare expedition. We all got dressed up to go. People dressed up to fly then, too. Air travel was relatively more expensive and exclusive.

We walked out onto the observation deck at about one o'clock. The regular flight from Bangkok was due in at two. We sought out a place along the railing, and Arjun and Sunder pointed out various features of the airport and the planes to the girls.

Outside a barbed wire fence surrounding the air field, in the shadow of huge storage drums with Nepal Oil written on them in Devanagari, sari-clad women gathered fodder for their cattle as I had seen women doing all over the country, bending over at the waist to cut clumps of grass with a hand sickle. They collected the grass in a basket, which they carried on their backs supported by a sling over their foreheads.

Sunder, who seemed to meet people he knew wherever we went with him, was talking in Newari with a man wearing an airport ID badge. A few minutes later they both disappeared through a door marked "Emergency Exit Only. Do Not Enter."

The rest of us shared some buns and biscuits Arjun and I had bought at a bakery. I noticed that I was the only non-Asian person standing at the railing. (By this time I was balanced precariously atop it.) The other *videshis*, mostly tourists in jogging suits and sweatshirts, were seated at tables in a cordoned-off area of the deck around which several signs reading "restaurant area" had been positioned forbiddingly.

Geeta muttered that she needed to pee. Bhagavati looked inquiringly at me. I pointed to the "Ladies Toilet." They both started toward it, and after a moment's consideration, I followed them. There were two stalls in the bathroom. One contained a squatting toilet, the other a Western-style commode. Bhagavati ushered me into the squatting one. She and Geeta took turns on the sit-down toilet. Once again it seemed they were trying to take care of me in a place where I was actually more at home than they were. I thought it ironic that they had sent me into the Nepalese toilet while they struggled with the unfamiliar Western one. I grinned as I squatted over the enamel basin: if they only knew how awkward it had been the first time I had used one of these things!

Even more than the water faucet trickling water into a marble-esque sink, Bhagavati and Geeta were fascinated by the hot air blower that came on automatically when one passed one's hands underneath it. While they were still testing the hand dryer, the siren signaling the approach of a plane sounded.

"Quick, the plane's coming," I said. We all rushed out onto the deck. In her haste, Geeta had forgotten to pull down her *kurtā*, the loose tunic that she wore over her *surwal* "pants." When she realized this state of disarray she was mortified. With eyes cast to the ground and her hand clamped over her mouth in embarrassment, Geeta alternately giggled distractedly and berated Bhagavati for allowing her out of the bathroom without noticing her *surwal-kurtā*. Bhagavati, too, was giggling. Sunder, who had reemerged from behind the forbidden door, asked me what was going on. "I don't know," I said, thinking I might embarrass Geeta even more by telling him. Geeta was so overcome with embarrassment that even when I spotted the plane and pointed it out to her, she couldn't raise her downcast eyes to look at it. The thing uppermost in her mind, plane or no plane, seemed to be that she had come into the public view in an inappropriate state of dress. When the plane came in to land, the embarrassment was forgotten—briefly—as the girls stood awestruck at the sight and sound of the powerful machine, its wheels screeching and trailing dust on contact with the tarmac.

We stood at the railing to watch the passengers, mostly white and carrying a lot of luggage by Nepalese standards, as they disembarked and were ferried across the tarmac in five blue buses. The girls were amazed that so many people could fit inside the plane.

Sunder scolded me for not bringing a camera to photograph the girls at the airport. Then they could have shown everyone at home their picture in front of a big plane; how *rāmro* that would have been. I felt a bit regretful about this, but I hadn't wanted to make a production out of going to the airport, and I thought the girls might have felt shy or embarrassed if I'd shown up with a camera. Once again I'd misjudged the culturally different causes of embarrassment.

Bhagavati wanted to wait for the Bangkok-bound passengers to board the plane and see it take off. None of us had any objection. As passengers walked along the covered ramp connecting them with the loading point for the buses, some of them looked up to the observation deck and waved to people standing there to see them off. Bhagavati was engrossed in watching the spectacle.

Geeta commented that we would be getting on such a plane to fly home in a few months.

"Maybe even this plane," Arjun said.

"You should take Bhagavati on the plane with you to America," Sunder said. His tone was light, joking, but I thought I detected an edge to it. In some way I felt he was alluding to the limits of our involvement with Nepal, and with them.

CHAPTER TEN

Wedding Season

Arjun jokingly greeted it as "the season of mists and mellow fruitful-ness." The gray and foggy mornings of January gradually gave way to the cool, dewy mornings of February, whose dawn mists burned off quickly. The Tharus still lit and squatted around their *gaurās* at night, and rekindled the piles of smoldering ash and rice straw in the early morning, but the function of the *gaurā* seemed more social and less an urgent necessity to chase the chill away from hands and feet.

The mustard harvest was in. The humid heat and lashing, unremit-ting rain of the monsoon were several months off yet. February and March were wedding season for Tharus, as—with some variation—they are for most ethnic groups in Nepal. During this two or three month period between the major harvests, when the weather is con-ducive to travel and farmers have a bit of cash and some spare time from agricultural tasks, almost all arranged marriages take place.

Marriages among Tharus fall into two categories: formal, arranged marriages (*bihé*), and elopements (*udéri*). Arranged marriages are fur-ther distinguished by the rituals that accompany them as either *purāno* (traditional) or *naya* (new) in which a Brahmin priest officiates.

Before malaria was eradicated in Chitwan and the *pahariyās* began moving into the area from the hills, Tharus had married according to their own customs. Now that Brahmins lived among them and Tharu families sought the expertise of the priests for important ceremonial occasions, they had begun to integrate Brahmin rituals into their weddings.

Not long after we returned from Kathmandu, I had the opportunity to observe my first Tharu wedding. The bride was from a moderately well-off family who lived in a village on the way to the stream where we had gone to bathe during the Jithiyā Pāvani. The family had invited old Mainahaurni to the wedding in the traditional way, by presenting her with a piece of areca nut. Although not invited to take part in the celebratory *bhoj* (feast), Mangala and Sarasvati along with many of the young people of Pipariya went to observe the wedding. They invited me to accompany them. I agreed with some excitement. I had been looking forward to seeing a Tharu wedding.

Mangala and Sarasvati came to get me after dinner. Mangala carried a metal plate with compartments for rice, *dāl, tarkāri,* and the like, as a gift from her family. As we walked along the road to the bride's house, we met many other people going the same way. A wedding is a big deal in the village; everyone goes to look.

The path from the road into the bride's compound was decorated with streamers and a big red banner with *swāgat* (welcome) on it, and another saying *subha bihé* (auspicious wedding). People hanging around the entrance to the compound seemed to be in a festive mood.

Shortly after we arrived we heard the *janthi* (groom's party); a rented loudspeaker in the bed of a tractor-trailer blasted Hindi film songs as the groom and his kinspeople wound their way through Pipariya.

When the tractor turned into the bride's place and drove under the welcome banner, I got my first glimpse of the groom. He was a tall, slender boy, in Nepalese dress, including a long jacket and *topi*. He looked to be in his late teens, although a scarf wound round his neck so that it covered his mouth made it difficult to tell. Mangala told me it was unlucky for the bride to see him smile before the wedding, hence the scarf over his mouth. He didn't look like he was in any danger of smiling to me. In fact his whole party on the truck looked solemn; perhaps they were just tired from their journey and from the blaring Hindi music. Several young girls in the trailer, perhaps the groom's sisters, were carrying gifts for the bride. One held a *nanglo* on her lap on which there were arranged various items of clothing and cosmetics. In the dark and the crush of people to see the *janthi*, I couldn't actually see the items on the *nanglo*, but it is customary for it to contain a red or pink shawl, a red sari and underskirt, plastic comb and hair ornaments, and bangles and perhaps some other jewelry. One of the girls also carried a length of white cloth for the bride's mother, to symbolically compensate her for the trouble and sacrifice she had undergone in bearing and raising the girl.

The groom and his party were greeted with a ritual in which the bride's mother threw some water on the groom. The water was deflected by an umbrella held protectively over the groom by one of his male kinsmen. The mother did this with much embarrassed good humor.

By this time, everyone in the groom's party had climbed down from the tractor. After some more socializing while things were prepared for the marriage ceremony, the focus of attention shifted to a small enclosed area in the compound that had been erected specially for the wedding. The enclosure (*jagyā*) measured about six feet square. Four wood posts supported a bamboo structure from which a cloth "roof" hung. The posts were decorated with strips of colored paper and banana stems. The flat earth floor of the *jagyā* had a little mound in the middle. The Brahmin priest had decorated this mound with flour mixed with *abīr* to give it a pink color.

People were pressing in around the *jagyā*. We joined the throng. The bride and groom entered the space, the bride walking slowly with eyes downcast. She was dressed in a red sari, part of which she had pulled over her head, and a pink shawl. Her hands were stained with reddish brown patterns such as I had had put on my hands during the Jithiyā Pāvani.

Ritual items assembled for the wedding included five *lotās* painted with red and yellow vertical streaks. These held water; their mouths were stuffed with mango and peepul leaves. One of the *lotās* and a decorated clay oil lamp rested on a large mound of uncooked rice. A basket made of leaves contained rice mixed with yogurt and *abīr.*

While almost all arranged marriages take place during the wedding season, people elope at any time of year. When they had visited us in Kathmandu, Geeta and Bhagavati had excitedly related the news that Kumari, one of Indra Prasad's servants, had eloped with the son of one of the servants in Ram Bahadur's house. For poor people such as these, elopement is sometimes the only form of marriage they can afford. In this case, the groom, who worked in a tourist hotel, had paid the bride's father some money and Ram Bahadur had loaned him more money to buy a goat to celebrate the union.

I was sorry to have missed all the excitement that must have accompanied the elopement. When we returned to Pipariya two weeks after

the event, things had returned to normal. Kumari had taken up resi-
dence in the one-room hut that her in-laws shared near to Ram Bahadur's house. Her new husband had already returned to the hotel
where he worked. Kumari spent most of her time around the hut,
washing pots that had previously been the work of her mother-in-
law, brushing her hair, talking, and laughing with her new sister-
in-law, who was her long-time companion. Mangala's elopement had
meant the transfer of a servant from Indra Prasad's household to that
of Ram Bahadur. However, Ram Bahadur observed that so far she had
made no move to contribute to the work of his household. "They say
she'll work, but when?" he complained, only half-jokingly.

The second wedding I attended was of another of Indra Prasad's servants, a sixteen-year-old girl from a poor Tharu family whose house
lay on the way to the school. She was to be married into a family from
a village located three hours away by oxcart. This was a very different
affair from the wedding I had seen with Sarasvati and Mangala. With
some small adaptations it was a traditional (*purāno*) Tharu wedding.

After such a marriage is arranged by the parents, or by a go-
between, and accepted by the young couple, the groom's parents invite the male members of the bride's family to a feast. According to
Surendra, this is a way for the groom's family to show respect. In the
past it was customary for the boy's father to present the girl's father
with a large piece of meat, these days the piece is smaller, and some
have dispensed with this aspect of the *bhoj* altogether. Formerly fish,
ghee, dal, and milk were required for the *bhoj*. Nowadays, the meat of a
castrated goat is considered sufficient. Poor people may even substitute duck or chicken.

The *bhoj* provides an opportunity for the prospective groom to meet
his future male in-laws, who bring him presents including a turban,
new clothes, and money. The date for the wedding is set at the *bhoj*.
Formerly the presence of the *chaudhary* and the *jimidār* was required at
a *bhoj*. Today the family's Brahmin priest is also invited to set an auspicious day for the wedding at which he will preside.

After the *bhoj* has been eaten, the marriage is considered finalized.
Neither side can back out without incurring a financial penalty.

According to the traditional Tharu wedding customs, the groom
does not go to the bride's house for the wedding. Instead, six young
people, three boys and three girls, from the groom's family go to the
bride's house to bring her home with them. The girls carry gifts of

bangles and other similar items for the bride. In the old-style Tharu wedding, the groom's kin did not eat at the bride's house, but rather were fed by someone else in her village. After doing *pūjā* to her household gods in the morning, the girl was picked up and carried on the back of one of her close male relatives, such as a brother or uncle, and placed in the cart that would carry her to her new home and husband. Some of her friends from her own village accompanied her on this trip. They were fed by the groom's family. At the groom's house another *pūjā* was performed. After that the bride entered the house and the wedding was over.

Three young men and two girls came to collect Suneetha from Pipariya. They arrived after dark. They had taken a bus along the east-west highway as far as the bazaar and then caught a ride from there on the back of a tractor. According to custom, they were put up at another house in the village.

The next morning Arjun and I went to Suneetha's house. We arrived at about six o'clock. There were a handful of villagers milling around outside, but the atmosphere was very different from the "new style" wedding I had attended at night. There was no Hindi film music. Everyone seemed subdued. Suneetha was sitting on the *wosarā*. She was draped in a new blue sari and a pink shawl embroidered with gold-colored thread. She sat on a *gundri* surrounded by her friends. She had one corner of her sari drawn over her head and she was sobbing against Mangala's shoulder. In front of her sat a *nanglo* with its little bundle of gifts for her. Beside it was a *kalash*, an essential item for a Tharu wedding. The *kalash* is a container with an oil lamp burning inside it. It was decorated with mango leaves and red and white streaks of paint with strips of red and white cloth tied around the mouth of the vessel. The two girls had brought this from the groom's house and had to keep it burning until they had brought the bride home. There was also a metal plate containing water. One by one Suneetha's relatives knelt in front of her. They bathed her right foot with water, which they then "drank," catching a few drops as they ran off her toes and touching these to their lips. Then they presented her with a gift of money or a metal plate, which her friends took and packed away carefully in a tin box. After the gift giving was completed, the white cloth was presented to the bride's mother.

Suneetha was supported by her friends as she made obeisance to the household gods, both inside and outside the house. She appeared

Bride's kinsman washes her feet

so overcome with grief that she was unable to walk unaided. Her female relatives were also crying, though not as uncontrollably as the bride. After the *pūjā* to the household gods, Mangala supported Suneetha with one arm and held an umbrella over her with the other as the bride's mother tossed a *lotā* of water over them. Mangala seemed to be enjoying herself. She laughed as she deftly swung the umbrella to deflect the splash of water from the *lotā* held by Suneetha's mother. Mangala was wearing a ready-made dress and cardigan bought in the bazaar. She held her head erect and her eyes darted unabashed around the gathering of spectators. She presented quite a contrast to her sobbing companion. I wondered what her wedding would be like. Mangala was sixteen. She was preparing for the School Leaving Certificate exam, but even so, it probably wouldn't be long before her father and brother began looking for a suitable husband for her. Since her family was wealthier, more educated and "modern" than that of Suneetha, I could guess that her wedding would probably be a more elaborate "new style" affair. Still, like Suneetha, she would be leaving Pipariya for an unknown household in a different village. For the first time she would have to take her turn at cooking for her husband's family.

Mangala's marriage was still in the future. Here and now, Suneetha was about to leave her *maiti*, the house where she had been born and

Auspicious ritual: bride's mother splashes her with water

lived her whole life. In the final ritual performed at her house, Suneetha was picked up by her elder brother, who carried her on his back to an oxcart draped with a red sari. The cart was one of five that would take the bride and her friends to her new village.

Suneetha sat slumped against the side of the cart, sobbing. No one else seemed in the least perturbed, however. In fact, the rest of the young women and children in the cart looked about them with mild excitement at the prospect of a festive visit to another village. Suddenly, I felt angry. Angry and disgusted that this young girl, whom I had seen so happy with her companions in the field, was being taken away from her family, bundled like a sack of rice into an oxcart, and sent to an unknown husband. As a new wife, her status in the family would be low. Under the direction of her mother-in-law, she would cook, plaster the floors with *māto,* and work in the fields. I hadn't felt this way at the other wedding I'd observed. Somehow the more elaborate rituals, the burning fire, the special clothes and loud music, even the darkness, had obscured the transaction that the ceremony symbolized: a girl was changing hands, from one family to another. The Nepali word for this kind of marriage is revealing: *kanyadān*—the gift of a virgin. On this gray-cool misty morning, the simple rites of leave-taking and the unmistakable anguish of the bride seemed to unmask

Oxcart leaving Pipariya for the groom's village

for me this basic fact of Nepalese women's lives: they would be alienated at an early age from their own families and go to make their adult lives in the homes of strangers. I repeated the usually comforting words "this is how it is here" and reminded myself that Indrani, Mainahaurni and Baghaurni had endured a similar dislocation and seemed happy enough now. But my mantra of relativism seemed powerless against the image of Suneetha slung over her brother's back as he carried her out of the house where she was born to the awaiting oxcart.

After three days in her husband's village, Suneetha returned to her natal home for a visit. I glimpsed her on her second morning home as I passed on the road. She was sitting in the family's compound with her mother, combing her hair and chatting. Gone was the anguish of the wedding morning. Suneetha looked serene, but also, I thought, more subdued than I remembered her, as if she had left something of herself back at her new *ghar*. Her husband came to fetch her less than a week later. Such visits to the *maiti* are common among Tharus, especially if the distance to the new village is not great. Sometime between May and July, the bride's father typically brings his daughter home for an even longer visit, which may last until just before the Emosā Pāvani in mid-September, at which time the groom visits the bride's village once again to bring her back.

As a salve to the memory of the prostrate bride in the oxcart, lacking control over her own destiny, rendered incapable even of independent motion, another image remains strongly associated with the wedding season in my mind. It is the image of carefree Tharu girls careening around the village on bicycles.

One of the first things that Shanthi told me after we returned from Kathmandu was that she was learning to ride a bicycle. She had expressed her desire to learn before we'd left, but she'd also given me the impression that Surendra was opposed to her acquiring this skill. The sight of a woman on a bicycle embarrassed him, she said. So I was surprised that she'd persevered. She wanted to show me how she could ride. She brought a borrowed cycle to the *dhārā* where I was preparing our first meal after returning. I held the seat while she got on and balanced. Then I gave her a push, and she was off to a wobbly start. Once she started she rode steadily (and a little too fast, I thought) as she peddled the borrowed bicycle around and around the *jimidār's* house.

Shanthi's face was exultant as she flew past the *dhārā*. I experienced vicariously her liberation and joy of movement. Now that she'd learned to ride a bike, Surendra seemed proud of his wife. He coached her and encouraged her to practice on a long, straight stretch of road leading out of Pipariya. He and Shanthi laughed a lot over her bike riding. Perhaps he was still embarrassed.

Bicycle riding had become quite the rage among Tharu girls in our village that year. Previously, only the daughters of the *jimidār* and the schoolmaster had learned to ride. Indrani could also ride. In fact, she had just acquired a new lady's bike, the only one of its kind in the village, which she used to travel from village to village carrying out her "motivating" work for the Family Planning Association. Maybe it was this new bike that triggered the craze. After we returned from Kathmandu, I saw several girls from the poorer Tharu households careening gleefully through the compounds, *lungis* hitched up, hair flying, and faces flushed with excitement as they took turns pushing one another and shouting encouragement.

On the occasions when I borrowed a bicycle to ride into the bazaar, I rejoiced in the relative ease of movement as I pedaled serenely past people plodding along the dusty road. I even felt impervious to their stares because I was moving too fast to have to engage or avoid them.

The sight of village girls, especially *bahāriyās,* on bicycles pleased me because it represented their control over—even if only temporary— a valuable piece of property, one that was associated with male agency and freedom of movement.

I woke up early on the day of the Nepali Congress women's picnic. Geeta and Mangala came to help me drape my sari. The girls in both households had been asking when I would wear the sari that I had bought one day on a trip to the bazaar with Shanthi. I had decided that this political rally cum picnic would be a good opportunity to wear it in public.

I had ambivalent feelings about wearing the sari. Sometimes I wondered why I had spent 180 rupees on five and a half yards of loosely woven cotton that I would hardly ever wear. I didn't even like its pink color. I had been overwhelmed by the variety of patterns and styles and pressured by the shopkeeper; Shanthi had chosen the small pink floral design. I had bought it because the sari is an attractive form of apparel. I had long admired its graceful lines and beautiful swishing pleats and fall on my mother-in-law and sister-in-law in Sri Lanka. The cheap, sometimes gaudy saris the women of Pipariya wore for special occasions seemed just as lovely in their own context, and I coveted one of these timelessly feminine garments for myself.

Several times during visits to Sri Lanka, my mother-in-law had good-naturedly helped me to drape a sari. This was just for fun. I had worn it outside the house only once, to dinner at my sister-in-law's house. I felt a bit like a little girl playing dress up, aware that I was just pretending but confident that I looked glamorous, even if it was just a game.

At the same time I couldn't imagine wearing it "for real," at least, not in public. I felt foolish to be seen in it. I thought how strange the sight of a white woman in a sari must appear. It seemed strange to me. When I'd seen white women in saris, my reaction had been: who's she trying to fool? That's not her dress. I would be an anomaly, an impostor.

A few months earlier I had bought a *lungi* in Naryanghat and had taken to wearing it around the compound. The *lungi* was practical. It suited the movements and pace of the tasks I performed around the house: washing, sweeping, and more than anything, squatting. Its length and tubular shape made it easy to squat with modesty. And I knew that it pleased people, especially women, to see me wearing it.

But none of this explained my desire to wear a sari. Although I had long ago forgotten my original impression of the sari as a confining garment—I had seen women in saris engaged in every kind of activity, from cooking and working in the fields to motorcycle riding—this did not apply to me. However adept South Asian women might be in their saris, I could not pretend that the sari was comfortable for me. I was aware of the cloth pulling against my legs as I walked. I was in constant fear lest the whole thing come unraveled. Most of all, I didn't know what to do with the fall, the loose end of the sari that is gathered into pleats and worn over one shoulder. But if people were pleased to see me in a *lungi*, I knew from brief dressing-up sessions, they were delighted to see me in a sari.

I enjoyed being included in the feminine camaraderie of dressing up, sitting around in a dark bedroom in the company of other young women and perhaps their little brothers while they helped one another to dress and do their hair. I didn't know how to drape the sari, but even if I had, I think I would still have submitted to their deft hands tucking the collected pleats in at my waist and turning me around by the shoulders to arrange the long piece of gauzy cotton.

Part of their enjoyment in dressing me in their clothes, I'm sure, was at my expense: the sari transformed me into an oddity at the same time validating their form dress and putting it somehow out of my reach. My wearing it was an indication of my desire to be like them and at the same time a demonstration of difference between us.

Once when I had been waiting for a bus in the bazaar and began talking with a group of guides who were waiting there for some tourists, they had asked me, since I was living in Nepal, why didn't I grow my hair long and put *sindūr* in the parting, wear a sari, and get my nose pierced? Didn't I think those things attractive? Yes, I did, I answered, but I wasn't a Nepalese woman, therefore those things were not appropriate for me. "Why?" One of the guides persisted. Changing my tack I said that if I got my nose pierced, people in America would stare at me. "Plenty of people come here from America and stare at our women," someone countered. I couldn't tell whether he was teasing or whether the thought of staring foreigners angered him.

The privilege of staring and perceiving, of appreciating another human being from a different cultural aesthetic is a tourist pleasure. In a mild form, I think that's the pleasure I afforded the Tharus when I "dressed up." Seeing me in sari allowed them as well as me the titillation of appropriating something exotic.

I had chosen today's picnic for my debut in sari because it was a women's event. My sense of belonging as one of the women, as *bhāuju*, as *didi*, was less secure outside the small social world of our compound. I was aware that I was still viewed as an outsider, albeit a familiar one, by the rest of the village, especially by the Brahmin population. Still I felt relatively comfortable about wearing the sari to the political picnic because many of the organizers would be women I knew. If I was going to be stared at by people, at least they'd be women.

The picnic was the initiative of the local Nepali Congress Party to motivate women to take part in the upcoming elections. It had been planned by some of the prominent women in the village: the wife of the Brahmin priest, the wives of several political leaders, and one of the female teachers in the school. Indrani was the only Tharu who was included in the leadership organizing the day's events.

I had not realized that there would be so many people involved with the picnic until I stood—now somewhat self-consciously because of the sari—in front of the newly constructed Nepali Congress Party office across from the tea shop, waiting to be joined by women and girls from every Nepali Congress household in the village and even from a few known Communist Party families. Its political importance aside, this was a major social event in the village.

Since Indrani was one of the local female leaders of the Nepali Congress Party and one of the organizers of the picnic, she and her household showed up at the assembly point early. I was part of this group. We waited in front of the Nepali Congress headquarters while women joined us from all over the village. Each woman had paid ten rupees (the price of a balcony seat at the cinema) to attend the picnic. The money had been used by the organizers to pay for the food that would be cooked as well as other supplies for the picnic.

We waited for over an hour in front of the political headquarters for women to assemble. The mood was festive. Women were dressed up, mostly in red. They had left their work at home for the day. But there was an air of the significance of the event as they squatted in the road to visit with neighbors and friends and wait for enough people to arrive to begin our procession through the village.

Finally, the organizers apparently decided that a critical mass had congregated, and we all set off on a relaxed march through Pipariya, led by an oxcart carrying the ingredients for the lunch and a banner urging people to vote for the Nepali Congress Party. There were other banners, too, and many girls carried the Nepali Congress flag as we walked. I felt a little uncomfortable about appearing in such a blatantly partisan political event. On the other hand, it was well known that Ram Bahadur's family were ardent Nepali Congress supporters; our close association with this family would probably lead people to assume that that was where our sympathies lay anyway.

Our colorful procession wound through the village. Then we followed a track through some scrub jungle to a clearing by the river where boys from the village brought cattle to graze. On the far side of the clearing, the river defined where the Chitwan National Park began, dense and dark and green, in contrast to the stubby yellow grass of the over-grazed common area that was our destination.

All along the way women came out to join our procession, and people gathered along the road to watch. Although I was walking with people I knew, I was surrounded by women who were unfamiliar to me. Most of the women going to the picnic seemed to be Brahmins.

As we made our way across the clearing I wondered where we would stop. As was usually the case when I accompanied Tharus anywhere, I didn't know exactly where we were going until we got there. The oxcart halted close to the river. Women began unloading huge cooking pots and baskets of potatoes and rice. I stood on the riverbank staring into the jungle on the other side. At closer range, it looked less dense and untouched than it had appeared from further off. It was easy to see where branches had been hacked off trees on the other side.

Soon five women from our group hitched up their saris, waded across the river, and disappeared into the jungle to collect wood for our cooking fires. They reemerged a short time later with bundles of wood balanced on their heads.

The part of the river where we now stood was where villagers came to perform their funeral rites. The body of the deceased was brought to the river wrapped in white cloth as soon after death as possible by the men of the family. Women did not participate in the funeral, although they observed separate purification rituals such as going to bathe at another place in the river. Here, in this clearing, was where the male kin would build a funeral pyre and cremate the body, commit the ashes to the water, and bathe themselves before returning to the village.

Bhagavati pointed my attention downstream to a place where the earth had been turned over. She told me a man had been buried there and observed that his ghost might be around. Who was he? I asked. She said no one knew, he hadn't come from around here; in the absence of any kin to perform the funeral rites and cremate the body, some local men had buried him. In such cases it is believed that the unhappy ghost of the dead man lingers at the site of the burial.

Ordinarily, this was a place that only men came. But today the clearing was full of women. The short-cropped grass was covered with women standing or squatting in groups, talking, laughing, apparently at ease and content in one another's company. A few male leaders of the Nepali Congress Party had showed up to dig three pits in which to make the cooking fires, but they seemed very much in the background, drab and out of place among the crowds of animated, gaily dressed women. Here in the open, the women moved with relaxed enjoyment, not only of the beauty of the river and jungle but also in the pleasure of a change from the daily routine of the home and the opportunity to be with other women.

Along with the visiting, preparations for the meal were going forward. As I looked around me, everyone appeared busy doing something. Seemingly without direction, groups of women busied themselves with different tasks: peeling and dicing potatoes, washing rice, cutting onions. I asked one of the organizers what I could do. She reminded me that I had agreed to take photos, so I took some pictures of the food preparation.

The women around me were not diffident and retiring as they appeared in public places like the bazaar, nor were they the passive participants submitting to fate that they seemed in wedding ceremonies. For this day at least they were confidently in possession of this liminal area between the village and the jungle. The activities in which they were engaged brought together the rhythms of the everyday and the impersonal, somewhat mysterious rituals of national politics: banners, marches, processions, speechmaking. The speechmaking, which

Preparing biriyani for the Nepali Congress women's picnic

would follow the meal, was the centerpiece of the day's activities. Some university students as well as the mature women leaders of the Nepali Congress Party had been asked to make speeches to "motivate" others to vote for the party and to get involved with the election. Throughout the day, not least during the speechmaking, I was struck by how self-sufficient the women were. It wasn't just that they organized and carried out the day's activities (except for digging the fire-pits) without any help from men; it was also the feeling of self-containment, adequacy, and preference for female company that seemed palpable among the gathering.

For months I had been analyzing, struggling with, accommodating myself to the status of women in Nepal, the drudgery of the lives of village women I lived among, the circumscribed movements of urban middle-class women, the separateness of the sexes in almost all spheres, from the set-apart benches of my few fifth grade girls to the fact that women were expected to eat after men.

As a foreign white woman I was not subjected to the same exclusion from the male sphere that shaped the reality of women's lives in this country. One of Arjun's professors had described his wife's status in the Indian village where they had lived as "honorary male." While I could understand the appeal of this characterization of the status of an anthropologist's wife, I felt it did not do justice to the complexity and ambiguity of our sexual roles. I have always thought honorary male to be a suspect category anyway. It negates the possibility of a woman's female identity while at the same time reinforcing the idea that her identity as male is not real; it is "honorary." Honorary male certainly did not accurately describe my status in Pipariya. Arjun and I constituted our own social category in some respects, but from the beginning, I sensed that to be accepted by Nepalese women, I had to accommodate myself to the roles defined for them. I had not sought to associate myself with men or with their social world in the village. I had hung out with women, participated in their work, and listened to their views. In short I had tried to identify myself as much as possible with women's lives in the village. This is not to say that I lived the life of village women; as an outsider, a Westerner, I had choices about what I would do and how I would behave. My female identity was circumscribed but only partly defined by local norms.

By the time I attended the Nepali Congress picnic I knew better than to describe Nepalese women as meek or passive or to assume that in spite of the structural control that men exercised over them they were not capable of autonomous, even dominating action. However, what I had perhaps not fully appreciated before the picnic was the strength of women's relationships with one another and the feeling of sufficiency in an exclusively female social world such as this picnic represented. In a sense, the celebration of female company at the picnic was an affirmation of the separateness of women's everyday lives.

My experience of women's organizations in the United States, from the Ladies' Guild of the Lutheran seminary where I worked, to my observations of sororities in college, even to my attendance at baby showers, suggested that the mere fact of exclusion of men rendered these all-women affairs incomplete, even comical. All my life I had had the feeling that men were in the background somewhere doing something more interesting; exclusively female activities were irrelevant and even ridiculous. The only exception I could recall was my experience of women's athletics in college, but even here, I was aware of their provisional nature and the difficulty of translating that power, independence, and purpose into other spheres of life.

Cooking the lunch, which was a single-dish *biriyani*, took several hours. Serving it to all the women present took the organizers another forty-five minutes. Everyone had brought her own metal plate, which

Brahmin women eating at the picnic

she washed in the river and placed in front of her where she sat or squatted on the ground. The Brahmin leaders of the day came around with the cauldrons in which the rice dish had been cooked and ladled a portion onto each plate.

People separated along ethnic lines to eat. The majority of the semi-circles that women formed into to eat consisted of Brahmins. On the periphery, smaller groups of Tharus and Tamangs squatted together.

After eating, women washed their plates and drank from the river. Then it was time for the main program of the day, the *pūjā* honoring the portrait of the Nepali Congress leader with red *tikā* and flower garlands and the speeches by party activists. I found I had trouble understanding much of the oratory, as each successive speaker exhorted her *"didi-bahini-haru"* (older/younger sisters) to vote for the Nepali Congress Party to ensure prosperity for the country and freedom for all its people. Several speakers seemed to stress the promises that the Nepali Congress had made to better women's lives, and Indrani declared that her party would help disadvantaged people such as the Tharus. I was impressed by the demeanor of the speakers, both old and young, Brahmin and Tharu. There was not a hint of nervousness in their voices; they spoke forcefully and confidently to their assembled sisters, who sat and stood in a knot around the portrait of the party leader and the Nepali Congress flag. The speeches continued for over two hours. Although some girls wandered away, most people paid rapt attention to what was being said and clapped appreciatively after every speech.

After the last speaker had had her say, the audience broke up into smaller groups for dancing. Again these groups formed along ethnic lines. As I sat on the periphery of a group of Brahmin dancers, I was urged to take my turn in the center of a circle of onlookers. I declined. I was sure that I could not reproduce their sinuous arm movements and fearful that the Brahmins would greet my efforts with mocking laughter. Instead I gravitated to a smaller group of Tharus who were performing their distinctive dance, singing and clapping and shuffling around in a circle. Some Brahmins also came over to watch the Tharu dance. I noticed them pointing at the dancers and smirking. I reflected, not for the first time, on the difference between the exuberant, individualistic, performance-oriented dancing of the Brahmins, and the slow, plodding, patterned Tharu circle dance. I admired the Brahmins' dancing in the same way that I admired their often brash, unapologetically outgoing behavior, but I was more comfortable within the Tharu circle of the dance. At Indrani's invitation, I joined the dancers, most of them women from my own compound. After stumbling a few times, I struck the same rhythm as the other women and followed the lead of Bhagavati to my right, bending at the waist and straightening up as she did, clapping with loose-hanging arms in unison with the rest of the dancers. I sensed the faint ridicule of the Brahmin women who gathered to watch. Characterizations of Tharus by the dominant group flitted through my mind as I went through the heavy methodical steps of the circle dance: stupid, backward, "ox-like." I felt a mixture of resentment against the Brahmin attitude as well as a sense of pride at joining in the circle dance. It was the first time I felt identified with Tharus—significantly, it was in opposition to another group.

The dancing finally broke up with some embarrassed laughing, though less than I had observed when the dance had been exposed to the male gaze during the Jithiyā Pāvani.

The final ritual of the picnic was a boisterous game of "playing *abīr*" in which we all smeared one another with red powder from several large boxes that had been purchased by the organizers to supply the *tikā* for the portraits of the party leaders as well as for this rambunctious ending to the day's festivities. Then we loaded everything back into the oxcart and prepared to depart. It was close to five o'clock by the time our procession headed out of the clearing. Everyone seemed in high spirits, a number of Brahmins broke into song and even paused to dance on the way back to the village. I was exhausted. My sari was coming unraveled. The pleats that Geeta and Mangala had carefully arranged in the morning had lost their crispness and sagged into loose folds that threatened to trip me up. The fall that had hung jauntily down my back on the walk out of Pipariya was wound around my neck like a scarf. I couldn't wait to get back to our hut to get out of the cumbersome garment.

CHAPTER ELEVEN

Janam-Janam

In the Tarai, specially among the Tharu people, the Holi is a time for great excitement and riotious revelry.
—*Kesar Lall*, Nepalese Language, Folklore and Practices for Foreigners

The image that the village presents to an outsider, that of a harmonious, homogeneous community, is a romanticized view. As one might expect in any small, tightly woven community where people are involved with every aspect of one another's lives from birth until death, the bonds of kinship and friendship are strained by resentments, jealousies, differences of personality, as well as by struggles over property and the conduct of village affairs. There are also conflicts that result from differences in caste and social position.

The longer we remained in the village and the more we came to be considered *bhitra-ko mānche* (insiders), the more we became aware of the tensions in the village. At the same time that we found ourselves increasingly taken into the confidence of the *jimidār's* family, we were also becoming aware of the gap between their interests and concerns and those of the poorer members of the community, those who lacked access to land and depended to one degree or another on the landowning families for work or other kinds of patronage.

I am not usually very interested in festivals, religious observances, or the kinds of "rituals" that are often the grist of anthropological fieldwork. However, in spite of my determined indifference to *pūjās* and festivals, they often brought about revelations in my understanding of village life and in particular seemed to highlight tensions in the community that otherwise remained hidden from us in the course of "everyday" life. The festival of Holi, or Phaguvā, which is the name by which Tharus know it, was indeed, as Kesar Lall says, a time of unsurpassed revelry; it also provided me with insights into village relations at all levels.

Phaguvā falls some time in late February, early March. The festival continues for several days. It celebrates the loyalty of a devotee to the god Vishnu and the punishment of an evil king and his sister Holika. According to the story a king named Hiranyakasyap so pleased Brahma by worshipping him that Brahma offered to grant the king a wish. The king's wish was that he might be immortal. Brahma consented and the king, thinking he was immortal, decreed that all should worship him as Ishvar, an incarnation of Vishnu. The people of his kingdom obeyed his decree. However, when Hiranyakasyap's son Prahalad returned from studying in a far-off place, he refused to worship his father as Ishvar, saying he would only worship the true Vishnu as Ishvar. When the king learned that everyone recognized him as Ishvar except his son, he ordered people to persecute Prahalad. Hiranyakasyap had a sister, Holika. For her Ishvar showed such favor that the fire could not burn her. One day Hiranyakasyap directed Holika to take Prahalad and sit in the fire. Holika ordered wood to be brought and piled on one place. Holika then took Prahalad and sat with him on the pile of wood. She told the people to set fire to the wood. Instead of burning Prahalad, however, the fire consumed Holika; Prahalad was left unharmed. It is said that Prahalad was saved by Vishnu because of Prahalad's devotion to him.[1]

In Tharu villages, people celebrate Holika's fiery end with symbolic bonfires in which she is burned in effigy. During Phaguvā, people exchange gifts of *rotis* and other foods, and young people "play *abīr*," that is, they smear one another with colored powders or squirt one another with water, also dyed if possible.

The day before the festivities I walked to the bazaar with Sita to buy ingredients to make "American *roti*" to give to our friends and to get some *abīr* with which to daub Shanthi, Bhagavati, Mangala, Sarasvati, and Durga as well as anyone else who came to "play *abīr*" with us. Sita was going to the bazaar to buy material and get a new blouse sewn for the holiday. As we walked out of his compound, Ram Bahadur directed me to take her to see a film. This was an easy request with which

[1] Adapted from "The Story of Holi." In R. Caldwell Smith and S. C. R. Weightman, *Introductory Hindi Course* (Mussoorie, India: Landour Language School, 1979), 304–305.

to comply; I love Hindi movies. From the first one I had seen, in the company of about a dozen girls from our *tole* during my first few weeks in the village, I was hooked. Films in the bazaar represented a rare diversion from our everyday routine. But even today, I think I would gladly walk six kilometers to see a Hindi movie.

We got to the bazaar at about half past eleven. We went directly to the cinema hall to buy the tickets. It was understood that I would buy the tickets for both of us. I bought balcony seats for ten rupees each. The next showing was at noon. I pocketed the tickets, and we walked into the center of the bazaar in search of blouse fabric for Sita.

Sita had definite ideas about the kind of material she wanted. Black with little red appliquéd tufts on it. These little tufts were called *bhutos*. Both Tikaurni and Bhagavati had blouses made of this kind of cloth. We went to several shops selling fabric, but Sita could not find what she was looking for. I pointed out that the film would be starting soon and that we should go to the theater. On the way back to the theater, Sita stepped into a shop selling ready-made clothes: T-shirts, jeans, and polyester skirts and pants. She spoke rapidly and authoritatively in Tharu to a smiling young man behind the counter who greeted her as *didi*. Her final words as we walked out of the shop were a repetition of some order followed by the exhortation *"ho!"*

We hurried back up the road to the theater. Situated about a mile apart on the east-west highway, the two cinema halls were the biggest and most substantial buildings in the bazaar. We headed for the older, slightly smaller of the two. A few people squatted at the entrance to the theater's walled compound selling peanuts in cones fashioned out of newspaper. Others crowded around the ticket office. Otherwise there were few people in the compound. It was early and a working day.

On Saturday afternoons the area outside the theater would be crowded with people, either waiting to enter for the next film or lingering afterward to socialize. Groups of girls and boys standing separately, many dressed in their best clothes for the outing to the bazaar. A few courting couples, or more commonly, courting couples contained within larger constellations of young people. When Surendra and Shanthi had eloped, they had gone to the bazaar to see a film in the company of one of Shanthi's sisters. After the film they had sent the girl home with the news that they had boarded a bus together bound for Birganj.

We entered the cinema through an arch to the left of the ticket office. The cinema had a small foyer, with three sets of wooden double doors opening into the main viewing room on the ground floor and a concrete staircase leading up to the balcony seats on the right.

We quickly climbed the stairs. It was past noon and I didn't want to miss any of the show, not the advertisements, nor the previews of other films, and certainly not the opening song and dance sequence of today's attraction.

The projection room opened off a small platform at the top of the stairs. The door was open. Inside two youths sat slumped in chairs on either side of an ancient projector. A standing fan was making ripples in great lengths of celluloid that unfurled across the floor. As we passed the door, one of the young men stood and began manipulating one of the film reels loaded onto the projector.

The cinema sold two classes of ticket. The general admission, which afforded entry to the main floor, allowed one to sit on wooden seats fixed to the concrete slabs. "Balcony" tickets, which cost more than twice as much, entitled one to climb the stairs and sit in one of the same wooden seats arranged in rows overlooking the main floor. The view from the balcony was better. But its real advantage was the four fans mounted from the ceiling that served to stir up the heavy stale air inside the theater. On my first visit to the cinema I had sat on the main floor. It was during the monsoon and very hot and humid. When the four doors that let in a little light and air had been closed, I had felt a moment of panic, shut in the hot dark hall packed with people. The balcony was more pleasant because there were fewer people. Sita and I found the seats corresponding to our ticket numbers and sat down. Then we both looked around to see if there was anyone we knew. Sita seemed more relaxed in the theater than she had in the bazaar. She leaned forward to greet a couple of young men from the next village. Most of the movie-goers seated in the balcony that afternoon were young men. I couldn't see onto the ground floor very well from where we sat, but the main hall didn't seem full either, certainly not as crowded as it had been on my first trip to the theater.

After a few moments the doors closed and it became dark. I heard the clicking and musical whine of the projector starting up in the little room behind us. Then the ads came on. I had seen both the ads before. They fascinated me as much as the films. The first one was for laundry soap: "Puja," the kind people used for washing clothes at the tube well and on the rocks of the river. The ad featured a fair-skinned sari-clad young middle-class housewife, happy and relaxed in her modern home. A small boy, fair-skinned and carefree, dressed in clean, brightly colored shorts and shirt, established the woman's status as a mother as well as the mistress of the laundry. Not that she did any washing on screen. Indeed, the soap never even shed its wrapper, and it was difficult to imagine the elegant woman on the screen lathering and slapping clothes about. The part of the ad that most interested me was the view of the bathroom: tiled and spacious, clean, well-lit, boasting a pristine bathtub, toilet, and bidet.

The mass-marketed Hindi movies churned out at a tremendous rate by the largest movie industry in the world and distributed across South Asia are more than the sum of plot and character; they are extravaganzas of dancing, singing, breath-taking scenery, gorgeous costumes, and amazing feats of bravery.

Each of the cinemas in the bazaar showed one film at a time. The current offering was called "Janam-Janam," which translates as something like life-after-life. It was a story about a kichkanyā, that is, the ghost of a woman who died young. The heroine of the film had jumped to her death from the roof of the house of a rich and powerful man who had ordered her to be abducted and brought to his house while her husband was away on business. Rather than suffer dishonor at his hands she had committed suicide. The young husband was devastated to learn of his wife's death and took revenge on the wealthy landlord. This part of the story took place in colonial India at the turn of the century. In the second part of the film, the young husband was reborn as a post-independence civil servant who is sent to the same area. He is haunted by the eerie singing of the kichkanyā in the woods around his official residence and slowly uncovers the history of the tragic young woman and begins to understand his connection with it.

This was the fifth Hindi film I had seen while living in Pipariya. As always I found myself transported by the extravagant costumes and beautiful scenery. To understand the phenomenal success of Hindi movies and their appeal in villages across India and Nepal, one has to understand the contrast between those villages and the glamorous world depicted on screen. Certainly one could never understand the hypnotic power of Hindi films by viewing them on a VCR in the comfort of an American living room, or in a middle-class Indian living room, for that matter.

Emerging from the dream world of the movie, we resumed our search for the blouse fabric. We returned to the shop where Sita had given the terse instructions to the Tharu boy. He showed her two bolts of fabric that he had secured from somewhere. Neither met with her approval. We continued on to the largest fabric shop in the village. I wondered why Sita hadn't begun her search there.

The shop's walls were lined with colorful bolts of material. Three men sat cross-legged on a cloth spread on the floor. Ten or twelve clients sat on a wooden bench along one wall. It was clearly a busy afternoon.

I sat near the entrance between a group of men and two Tharu women. Sita found a spot on the other side of the women. The attention of the shopkeeper not already engaged in showing material to customers focused on me: What did I want, a sari perhaps? I indicated Sita. "She wants material for a blouse," I said.

He got up from the floor and went into a back room. I saw him go back and forth several times with different samples of cloth, but I was paying more attention to the other transactions taking place in the shop. And I was enjoying looking around at the patterned *lungis* and bolts of cotton material without feeling any pressure to buy.

Sita had apparently made up her mind. The shopkeeper cut off about three quarters of a meter and rolled the piece up in a tube, which he wrapped in newspaper. Sita took the package and shoved a crumpled handful of small notes toward the man.

He didn't count them. He was waiting for Sita to give him more. She perceived this and pushed a few more bills across the floor. He collected these also, but still didn't count them.

She handed him another five rupee note. Then she sat back, watching him anxiously.

"*Pugdaina*," he said. (This isn't enough.)

Sita looked very embarrassed. She gave him a few more notes. Ones and twos.

"*Bahini*," the shopkeeper said in tones of exasperation. "This still isn't enough."

It suddenly dawned on me that Sita couldn't count. She had no idea how much money she had given him, or possibly even how much he had asked for.

She mumbled something about the cloth being expensive.

"What do you expect?" retorted the shopkeeper. "Good cloth is expensive. Do you want it or not?"

Sita seemed to want the cloth.

I went and sat by her.

"Do you have the money?" I whispered to her.

She claimed to have the money, but said that the cloth was expensive. I didn't want to interfere if Sita had decided she didn't want the material after all, or if she thought the shopkeeper was trying to cheat her and was trying to get the price reduced.

Meanwhile, the shopkeeper said she still owed him thirty rupees. Sita held out a ten and a pair of two rupee notes.

He remonstrated with her. "*Bahini,* you don't know how much the cloth costs. You village Tharu [girls] can't count."

Sita was so embarrassed that she literally turned her face away from him into the bank of fabric lining the wall. I had the feeling that if she could have run away or crept in between the bolts of cloth, she would have.

The transaction had come to a standstill. "I'll give you the money," I whispered to Sita. She repeated again that it was too expensive.

The shopkeeper said he'd settle for fourteen rupees instead of the sixteen still owed him. I handed him fifteen.

He berated Sita again for being ignorant and not knowing her numbers. He made no movement to give me any change. Sita picked up her small parcel and we escaped with what was left of our dignity.

The next stop was the tailor. This man brusquely informed Sita that he was going to his home in another village for *Holi* and that he couldn't sew her blouse. We went to another tailor's shop. In the second shop, which was so tiny that one of the three tailors working there had to sit at a machine positioned outside the door, the people were more friendly. Still, they said they couldn't have it ready for her by the next day as she had hoped, but only by the day after. I couldn't help suspecting that the reluctance to undertake work for her as well as the downright rudeness that we had encountered in the fabric shop were due to the fact that Sita was a poor Tharu servant girl, who spoke Nepali with difficulty and was young and unassertive. I recalled my first trip to the bazaar with a group of girls from Pipariya and how it had appeared that they had been bullying the man in the stationery shop. Now that scene made more sense.

Next we went to a "fancy store" to look for some *bindis* that Shanthi had requested Sita to buy for her. Sita referred to these decorative felt dots as "*tikās*," much to the derisive amusement of the shop's Brahmin proprietors. One of the shopkeepers also corrected Sita's Nepali. When I realized what was going on it occurred to me that although I regarded her as fluent, Sita's Nepali was probably not much better than mine.

The final transaction in which I was aware of the contempt to which Tharu village girls were subject in the bazaar was when we went to buy oranges. After finding out the price of the fruit and asking for a kilo, Sita rather anxiously and uncertainly demanded that the man selling them give us a bag to carry them in. He looked at her with amused condescension and said haughtily, "Of course I'll give you a bag," as if it were unworthy of mention. These were all small things. The social niceties of commercial interaction, yet they represented the point at which the two *jāts* came into contact, and in a way condensed the differences in status, wealth, and power into the minutiae of market transactions.

When Sita and I returned from the bazaar I was not surprised to learn from Arjun that we had been invited to eat at Ram Bahadur's house. I was looking forward to a respite from cooking during the festival; we were almost always invited to eat with the *jimidār* when they had meat.

That night a *pūjā* was performed and Holika was burned in effigy. A band of stick dancers made their way around the village, finally ending up on the compound of Indra Prasad's house. There they danced in a circle, each man or boy holding two sticks in his hands, which he tapped against one another and then lifted to meet the sticks of the man in front and behind him in the circle. This was the most exciting dance I had seen in Pipariya. Unlike the slow, plodding repetitive circle dance of the women, in which they danced turned in on themselves with their heads bowed and arms drooping toward the ground much of the time, the men were turned outward, seeking and winning the admiration of the crowd that had gathered to watch them. They danced with great energy, their heads held high, hopping and jumping from foot to foot as they leapt forward to meet the sticks of their fellow dancers with a reverberating thwack. Not for the first time I reflected that women seemed merely to participate in dances; men performed them.

After more than an hour of vigorous dancing in the *jimidār's* compound, the dancers were given *rakshi* and meat to eat by the women of the households that had "hosted" them. Then everyone drifted off to bed.

During festivals such as Phaguva, employers gave their *bahāriyās* and day laborers the day off and were also supposed to feed them meat and give them *rakshi* to drink.

"Last year we didn't have enough *rakshi*," Mangala confided in me. "The workers became angry because of this. On holidays we have to feed them well." But not too well, apparently. Mangala criticized one young bride in another house who had decanted too much liquor and meat to the young men who had come singing and dancing in groups during this Phaguvā. "It should be for *tikā* only," she said, but this girl had "given out all the *rakshi*," according to Mangala. So they had had to make more. The unfortunate young woman had also exhausted the family's share of the goat that had been killed and divided by the residents of her *tole*.

"Did you notice that they killed a chicken this morning?" Menaka asked me pointedly. I nodded. In fact, I had eaten some of that chicken. "Her mother-in-law was scolding her because she served all the goat meat to the guests last night. She doesn't know how to do things." Mangala's implied criticism was that the girl was too ostentatious in her generosity and that she hadn't managed the resources of the house well.

"*Ke garné?*" I said. (What to do?) "Many people came to the house last night. They had to be fed. What else could she do?" Mangala sighed as if she despaired of making me understand. "She gave too much," she said.

I was interested in the fine distinctions that Mangala was suggesting in Tharu hospitality between generosity to guests and ostentation and dangerous waste of the household's precious festival food preparations. I would have liked to pursue the subject, but I did not want to jeopardize my neutrality by criticizing the girl who had given too much to the dancers or by taking her side against Mangala and what appeared to be the village norms of behavior in this matter. I knew from previous bits of gossip about this girl that Mangala had favored me with, moreover, that she was disliked by the women of the *jimidār*'s family; she was from a poorer family and they thought her uppity. "I don't talk to her anymore," Mangala had told me once. "She thinks she's a *thūlo mānche* [a big shot]." But I liked talking to the girl, finding her outgoing, adventurous, and fun-loving. So I didn't say anything.

On Phaguva I walked to the tea shop in the morning to buy the eggs to make my "American *rotis*." These were in fact a watered-down (literally watered down since I had to substitute water for milk) version of a traditional family recipe for "Swedish pancakes." On my way back I borrowed a flat round piece of iron from Indrani on which to fry the pancakes. I then went to ask Baghaurni for the *ghee* she had made from their buffalo's milk. When I had told her of my intention to make my special *rotis* during Phaguva she had insisted that I take *ghee* from her. I suspected her interest in securing a good share of the end result; I had made the pancakes once before and they had been much appreciated in their household. This was fine with me; I was intending to make plenty to give to all our neighbors and friends.

My ingredients and implements assembled, I spent the rest of the morning mixing the batter and squatting in front of our temperamental stove, pumping the valve in the pressure chamber at intervals to keep the flame going. In the afternoon I distributed plates of pancakes to our neighbors and to some of the other people in the village who had shown special hospitality toward us.

I was interrupted at one point in my cooking by a visit from Geeta and Sarasvati, but I suspected that their intentions were not altogether innocent and was ready for them. I poured two fistfuls of *abīr* into the pockets of my skirt before I went to the door.

As soon as I stepped outside the hut, the two girls grabbed hold of me and smeared the gritty, paint-smelling powder all over my face. I immediately retaliated and we disengaged from a messy embrace to laugh at one another's red faces.

"*Kathi rāmro*," Geeta exclaimed. "A white person with a red face!"

In the afternoon I had another visit from Durga and her sister-in-law, who was married to one of the prominent village leaders of the Nepali Congress Party. They had come to "play *abīr*." They had also brought a plate of *sel roti*, a slightly sweet bread, shaped in a ring and fried, somewhat like a donut. I submitted to being covered again with powder, this time of various hues: blue and green as well as red. Then I repaid the compliment. I invited them in for a cup of tea and some of my *rotis*. They sat on the bed while I tended to the tea preparations in the kitchen. The mood was relaxed and festive, and the conversation flowed easily and enjoyably. I felt a kind of subdued elation at my participation in the holiday.

Our conversation was interrupted when the light elephant grass door of our hut squeaked on its hinges and opened slightly. A dark stringy stubble-faced old man staggered into the room. He listed toward the bed. He sat down with a thump next to Durga. She wrinkled her nose in distaste. I could smell the liquor from the kitchen, so it must have been very strong to Durga who was enveloped by his breath as he spoke.

"*Bahini,*" he said in a wheedling tone. "This is Phaguvā. I have come to your house . . ."

"This isn't my house," retorted Durga.

The man looked taken aback, even in his drunkenness. He turned to me and repeated his appeal. "You know me, *holā,*" he began.

"I don't think she knows you," interrupted Durga.

I looked hard at the old man trying to decide whether I had seen him before or not. I thought I recognized him as a man who had recently come to work for Indra Prasad as a day laborer.

"This is Phaguvā," he continued, slurring the words. "So I have come to your house to ask for some *rakshi.*"

"This is a *derā,* not a house," Durga said. "There is no *rakshi* here."

The old man turned his bleary eyes on her. "*Bahini,*" he said. "When I was a young man, I met the King."

Durga raised her eyebrows and the tone of her voice in mock amazement. "Ho?" (Is that so?)

He nodded solemnly.

I was feeling it was my responsibility as a hostess to get rid of this intruder on my pleasant visit with Durga and her sister-in-law. I stood at the window and looked toward the *dhārā.* "Look," I said, "Arjun's taking a photograph. You should go there so he can take your photo."

"Yes," Durga chimed in. "Go quickly and have your picture taken." This had no effect on the man. Perhaps he hadn't understood.

"*Bahini* . . ."

Durga tried another tack. "Listen," she said. The *jimidār* is calling you."

"*Jimidār?*" The old man sat up involuntarily.

"Yes," said Durga. "He is calling you. The *jimidār* wants you to go. *Jānus.*"

The man slumped over again. "Bah," he said, or the Tharu equivalent. He made a dismissive gesture in the direction of the supposed summons by the *jimidār.* "Let him call me. I'm not going."

I was interested in the power of the alcohol to take away this laborer's accustomed servility and submissiveness in the face of a supposed order from the *jimidār*. Realizing that we were not going to be so easily rid of our drunken guest, the other two women and I turned our conversation to other topics and tried to ignore him. But the relaxed atmosphere that had prevailed before his arrival was destroyed.

The door squealed again, this time flying all the way open as Arjun stepped into the room. He immediately sized up the situation and said in a urgent voice, "Quick, the *jimidār* is calling you." For the first time, the old man looked agitated. He stood up and lurched out of the room in a flat-footed retreat.

We all laughed. "I just said the same thing," protested Durga. "Why did he listen to you and not to me?"

"Who was he?" I asked.

"One of Indra Prasad's *bahāriyā* servants," Arjun said.

Later I said to Arjun. "It's a little sad really: that old man came to the house of wealthy people looking for some hospitality which was his due during Phaguvā. Instead he got laughed at. I wonder if he was too drunk to remember how you tricked him into leaving the house." We agreed that we would probably never know. The social distance and respect of the village hierarchy had been broken down for one day during the feasting and merry-making of Phaguva. But the lapse of the usual deference would pass with the laborer's drunkenness and the holiday itself.

By the end of March the hot season was upon us. The change in the daily temperature was gradual, almost imperceptible. The mornings became less and less crisp. The winter morning fog thinned and then vanished altogether. The mornings and evenings were still cool, but by midday the sun was blistering and in the afternoon, between one and half past three, it was so hot that we didn't feel like doing anything besides lying in the hut and reading. Everyone who could, meaning everyone except servants and itinerant workers, retired indoors during the hottest part of the day. If I left the hut during the afternoon to go to the tube well or to do some other errand, the force of the hot air outside our hut took my breath away. As the afternoon wore on, the temperature of our hut inched its way up, until, by three o'clock there wasn't much difference between inside and outside. We lay on the bed, not even able to read.

At three-thirty or four o'clock we would come out to bathe, and the village would begin coming back to life, people stirring to carry out the evening tasks.

Ram Bahadur had hired four men to help harvest and thresh the *dāl*. Three of these men from the outer Tarai were young and not distinguishable in any way from the dozens of young men who had passed through the village already that year to work in the rice and the mustard harvests. The fourth man was old. He looked ancient, stooped, toothless, and worn. He may not have been older than forty-five, but he had the cadaverous skinniness of an old man. His ribs were clearly defined under his dark wrinkled skin. So was his collarbone. Unusual for a laborer, he wore thick spectacles. He must have been nearly blind without them. He spent the whole afternoon sifting piles of harvested *dāl* plants through the ropes of a bed frame that he moved around on the threshing floor behind Ram Bahadur's house, trying to capture what little shade there was. All his movements were slow and deliberate as if they pained him. He frequently sang as he sifted the *dāl* plants. He also coughed a lot. Sometimes I would hear him coughing in the early hours of the morning as he lay on a pile of rice straw in the oxcart where he slept. He probably had tuberculosis. I pondered what misfortunes must have led such an old and infirm man to seek work as an itinerant laborer. He was too old for the work. Even Indrani said so. She told me he had a house and land of his own, but that he was working to earn money to help his son build a house. I doubt he lived to see the completion of that house.

During the heat of the day, people who could stayed indoors, and the village was quiet. But after dark when the enervating energy of the sun faded into a soft warm glow, the village came back to life. Arjun and I would drag the string bed off our porch and listen to the sound of a light breeze in the leaves of the sisal trees which stood against a brilliantly clear and cloudless sky. And people would come to talk with us. Or we would seek them out as they sat under the stars in their own compounds.

Indrani frequently came to visit; she said I would be leaving soon and then we would have no more opportunities to "*guff garnu*" (chat). The subject of my imminent departure from the village was a frequent topic of conversation. One day the carpenter's wife asked for a photograph of me to keep after I left the village. Hearing this, Indrani scoffed, "What good is a photograph? Can you talk to a photograph? Can it make a response? No."

The younger women assured me that they would long to see me after I left. "How will it be?" Bhagavati mused. "When you went to Kathmandu for a short time, how we wanted to see you!"

Bhagavati also asked me if I would forget all my Nepali when I went back to America. I confessed that I probably would forget at least some of my Nepali.

"What about Tharu," she asked. "Would Arjun forget his Tharu language?"

"Yes, probably," I said.

She thought for a moment and said, "but Arjun-*dāi* has written our language in so many copybooks. I don't think he will be able to forget." I was impressed by this observation. I agreed with her that with the help of Arjun's notebooks, we would be able to remember some Nepali and Tharu.

Some of the confidences that women shared with me seemed to be prompted by the approach of my departure. I had shown interest during my stay in Pipariya in the work of the local Family Planning Association. Indrani knew that in me she had a receptive audience to tell how she had to endure scolding and insults in her efforts to "motivate" women in the area she was responsible for to practice contraception. A common response from women with whom she discussed forms of birth control was the belief that a decrease in their ability to produce children would be accompanied by a deterioration of health and strength generally.

"This is what women say to me when I talk to them about family planning," Indrani told me. "They say to me, will you feed my children? Will you provide clothes for them and send them to school? Then who are you to tell me what to do!" She told me that she had advised the young woman who had come to work as a *bahāriyā* since Sita returned home to have her tubes tied after her third child. The woman had railed against Indrani in the usual way. Now, still in her early twenties, the woman had five children. She and her husband had to work as servants in someone else's house. They had no land. They couldn't send their children to school. The woman had finally gone for the operation. She had been afraid that it would weaken her, make her unable to provide for her family.

One of Indrani's duties as a community worker was to accompany people she had "motivated" to the local family planning clinic for tubal ligations and vasectomies. I asked her which was more common, sterilization of men or women. Women, she responded. Wasn't it a more dangerous operation, I asked. Yes, Indrani said. Sometimes women died as a result. And the vasectomy, by comparison, was a more straightforward operation, wasn't it, I asked. Indrani agreed.

"So why do men send their wives for the operation?"

Indrani shrugged. "Men are afraid," she said.

I told her I thought it was the same in my country.

One beautiful clear evening I went to sit with Baghaurni and her family. Baghaurni's sons were studying by the light of a kerosene lamp on the *wosarā*. The eldest one was singing a Hindi film song. I started to sing American popular songs. As usual when I started to sing the strange songs, people stopped what they were doing and gathered around me. They urged me to sing more songs. As I usually did, I responded to their demands for more songs with a request that they sing Tharu songs for me.

Finally, the old woman Mainahaurni began singing a song about pressing mustard seed as they had done when she was a young girl. Sarasvati whispered to me that this song was very old. When Mainahaurni finished, Sarasvati told me that times had been very hard then. Baghaurni added that women had only been able to sleep "for a moment at a time." There were no *chappals* in the old days. People had strapped pieces of wood to their feet with homemade rope. In those days anyone going to Kathmandu, which she referred to as "Nepal," had to walk. And there were no proper roads. Only trails. People had to walk through the jungle, then over the mountains. It took three or four days. They took pots for cooking, oil, salt, and *chāmal*; everything they needed to cook along the way. They slept in the jungle. Old and young agreed: Life had been hard in the not-too-distant past.

April is a month of *hurrees*—howling winds that sweep across the Tarai plains, blowing clouds of dust over the fields and darkening the sky. These blasts of wind are accompanied by thunder and lightning and usually succeeded by pelting rain or huge hailstones.

One day it was so hot that it melted a candle we had stuck through the wire mesh on our window for safe keeping. At about four o'clock a fierce *hurree* swept through the village. First we heard a far-off roll of thunder. The sky to the north became dark. The clouds were rolling toward us. The air was still hot, in spite of the movement. Then the rain started. Lashing rain, more like squirts of water than rain drops. I was just walking out to the *dhārā* to wash some pots. Arjun had been on his way to conduct an interview. Both of us had to retreat to the shelter of the *wosarā*, where we sat on the string bed and experienced the drama of the storm. We were engulfed by swirls of dust. The *wosarā* was covered with debris: clumps of grass and earth, branches, sticks, and leaves.

When the wind and the rain let up somewhat we decided to walk up to the irrigation channel to view the condition of the village and the fields around it after the storm. Arjun tried to capture the dramatic color of the sky on slide film. It had now become quite cool. The temperature had dropped about twenty degrees.

While we had been sitting on our *wosarā* at the height of the storm, we had noticed a number of children running past our house shouting to one another. We had assumed they were running for cover and shouting in excitement at the *hurree*. As we walked past the mango grove near the irrigation ditch, more children ran past us, and as we returned through it, we saw that the mango orchard was full of children collecting the still unripe fruit that had fallen from the trees during the storm. But they had not stopped at collecting the fallen fruit from the ground; children could be seen in the branches of the trees. Some of them had clambered twenty feet off the ground in the grand big-leafed trees. The grove rang with the excited chatter and cries of the children. Many of them were hidden from view; their presence discernible only by the swaying of branches and the shuddering of the mango leaves as they tried to shake off the fruit loosened by the *hurree*. Some of the children were already leaving the orchard, munching on the windfall fruit: still unripe mangoes, green, the size of apricots. We met Sarasvati on the road and she gave us some of the fruit. They were sour as crabapples.

Several days later we accompanied a Sri Lankan friend who was working in the area into the carefully laid out garden of the luxurious (by local standards) Narayani Safari hotel where we sat in white deck chairs at a table between the swimming pool and the tennis courts. The mango trees in the hotel garden had also had their fruit shaken prematurely from the boughs. Surveying the green mangoes strewn upon the mown lawn, I was struck by the contrast between the mango orchard in the village where the children had braved the storm to collect the fallen fruit and this secluded garden with its trees grown merely for show, where the unwanted fruit lay untouched under the carefully pruned trees.

The last day in April was also my last day in the village. Arjun would remain in Nepal for another month to observe Nepal's general elections in the village. I was returning ahead of him to spend some time with my family in California and get started on my own dissertation project.

At about half past six on the morning before I was to leave Pipariya, the peon from the school arrived on his bicycle to summon me to the school. Since the weather had become hot, the schedule had shifted; school now began at six and ended at about ten-thirty. I had been going at about seven o'clock to teach Class 5, but I had given up on Class 4; I couldn't get up in time to make it to the first class period, which was when they had English scheduled. No one seemed the least bit perturbed that I had redefined my teaching duties. Krishna-sir had gone back to teaching the younger students and I concentrated all my attention on the students in Class 5, who had begun the year with me in Class 4. I felt they had adapted to my more spontaneous and interactive approach to English teaching and was pleased with their apparent comprehension of the language that had seemed an arbitrary and meaningless system of symbols and sounds when I had first begun teaching them seven months before.

I had said good-bye to my students several days before, explaining that I was returning to America and would no longer be teaching them. I had also taken leave of the teachers though I had said I would come by the school one last time with Arjun so that he could take a picture of the teachers as a group.

The peon told me to come quickly to take the picture as the children were going on a tour to a nearby factory, and some of the teachers would be accompanying them. I had been boiling a pot of water to make tea. I abandoned this and set off across the fields to the school. Arjun said he would come after taking the picture of another family in the village to whom he had promised a portrait some time back.

When I reached the school, the teachers were sitting in the office. As usual, a number of children had left their classrooms and were playing outside. It appeared that no classes were taking place that day because of the trip. I made my way through the shouting, darting children at play, who now took no notice of me. Inside the office, the teachers greeted me nonchalantly. I explained that Arjun had gone to photograph someone else and said he would come to the school soon. *Holā*. We sat largely in silence. After about half an hour the peon brought a kettle of tea and seven glasses from the tea shop. He also unwrapped three packets of glucose biscuits and passed them around on a plate. As the peon was pouring the tea Arjun showed up. Several other men arrived as well. The peon went in search of more glasses. I realized that this was a good-bye party in my honor.

The headmaster decided to call a holiday. He directed Krishna-sir to call the children together outside. The peon rang the rusty triangular gong and the children assembled on the ground outside the building. I stood behind Krishna-sir as he addressed them.

"Our Madam is leaving our village tomorrow. She is going to America," he said.

I felt hundreds of young eyes trained on me. I wondered what the idea of "going to America" might mean for them, many of whom had never been further than the bazaar.

"Madam won't be teaching here anymore," Krishna-sir continued. Then he paused. "Has she not taught you English?" he almost shouted.

It was a rhetorical question that was immediately met by the expected response: "Yes, she has," chorused a hundred youthful voices.

"Has she not taught you well?" Krishna prompted his young audience.

"Yes, she has!" they responded.

Krishna-sir turned to me. I understood this was my opportunity to speak to the students. I stepped to the edge of the covered porch and told them that I was sad to be leaving the village, but that I would not forget them when I returned to the United States. I told them to study hard and be good students and I wished them all well in their studies and in the future. Krishna-sir had to intervene several times to help me express these wishes, as my Nepali proved inadequate.

The other teachers had come out of the office and were standing behind me on the porch. When I finished speaking, Durga stepped to the front and, dipping her thumb into a box of *abīr*, pressed a wide *tikā* mark into my forehead. Then she applied the red powder to the part in my hair: *sindūr*.

I smiled and turned to face the children again. Krishna-sir directed them to *namaskār* me, and they obeyed, raising their hands in the familiar gesture of respect and goodwill. "*Namaskār*, Madam," they shouted. My throat was becoming tight. I put my hands together in *namaskār* as well. Then, smiling through my tears, I shouted, "bye-bye."

This was an English word known to even the youngest students. My farewell was met by a torrent of "bye-byes."

Krishna-sir's announcement that a holiday had been called and that school was dismissed was met with even greater shouts of excitement and delight. The children set off a great cheer as they began to disperse in all directions. The older children who were going on the field trip hung around the school, however. A tractor-drawn trailer had pulled up in the schoolyard. I assumed this was what would take the students to the factory. The boys began climbing on the vehicle. A few girls, who were also going on the outing, sat quietly to one side, watching them.

Next the photograph. We carried the heavy wooden chairs out of the office and set them up on the grass in front of the school.

After sitting for a portrait of the teachers, and saying good-bye again, we wandered off to Sita's house where we had promised to take a photograph of her and her brothers. Arjun wanted to get all the photo taking done before he accompanied me to Kathmandu. He would get the photos processed there and be able to present them to people before he left the village a final time.

Sita had given up working as a *bahāriyā* in Ram Bahadur's house and had returned to her *maiti* to live. I had not seen her for some time. Bhagavati and Shanthi had told me that she had become thin because she didn't get such good food at home as she had when she lived in the *jimidār's* house.

Sita was waiting for us in the front of the small neat hut where her family lived. She was dressed in her best sari and the new blouse made of the textured *bhuto* material whose purchase had caused such embarrassment a month earlier. I didn't notice any difference in her weight and was prepared to think that the other girls' comments about her appearance were caused by disappointment and disapproval that she had left their household and their conviction that she would have been better off staying with them. Sita's mother, with whom I had cut *dhān* during the rice harvest, sat huddled under a blanket on the *wosarā*. Sita told us she was sick. The house was neat and well-swept, inside and out. Sita led us around to the back where she and her brothers posed in a field of corn that reached their shoulders. They waded into that field of green until only the purple of Sita's sari and the blue of her brothers' school shirts were visible above the corn plants. It would not make a good portrait, but it was a beautiful sight, and knowing that this was how the Tharus liked to pose for their photos, in a field of corn, or mustard, or potatoes, we didn't interfere.

After Arjun had taken their picture, Sita and I stood awkwardly in her front yard. She asked me all the same questions: When would I return? Would I forget her? I assured her that we would try to come back to Pipariya as soon as we could and that I would not forget her. Arjun and I returned to our hut.

The rest of the day was taken up with packing and going around the village to say good-bye to people. "Don't leave without coming to see us," had been a common request, and I tried to honor it.

I was not surprised that Ram Bahadur had invited us to eat on my last evening in the village. I was a little surprised, however, when I saw him dismounting from his bicycle and untying two large live white ducks that he had apparently purchased in the bazaar for the feast. I had assumed that they would slaughter one or two of their own chickens or ducks for the occasion. Later when I went into their house to return something, Surendra's mother was butchering the fowls in the entrance hall.

Besides the ducks, Ram Bahadur had bought a bottle of beer. He plied both Arjun and me with beer and *rakshi*. I had an upset stomach and didn't feel like drinking, but Ram Bahadur urged me, saying that I must be happy and dance on my last day in his house. I said I would be happy and dance even without the drink. After the meal we moved out onto the *wosarā*. I made a presentation of some small gifts to the women and girls of the household. They also gave me presents of bangles. And then to everyone's delight, I danced. They concluded that I must be drunk after all. Ram Bahadur asked Arjun to bring a tape recording of a song and dance performance organized by the Nepali Congress at the school several days earlier. He directed Arjun to search for a particular song that the political dance troupe had performed. When Arjun found the one he was looking for, the *jimidār* got to his feet and, lifting his arms above his head rotated his body and moved his feet in little mincing steps. We all laughed. After he'd collapsed on the *gundri*, I got up again and did my best imitation of the kind of dancing I'd observed the Brahmin girls doing at the Nepali Congress women's picnic. More laughter, and again the opinion that I must be drunk to be dancing in this way. Other people were exhorted to dance. Then Ram Bahadur, Indrani, Bhagavati, and Geeta escorted us back to our hut. They seemed reluctant to leave us. Ram Bahadur and I took turns dancing in the confines of our hut. Finally, they said good night and returned through the darkness to the big house.

Ram Bahadur woke us up at four o'clock in the morning. He was very businesslike: informing us he was getting ready the oxcart that would take us to the bazaar. The drunken dancing of our farewell feast seemed forgotten. Baghaurni called us to drink tea with them a final time before our departure. Various people had asked us to stop along the road for a final farewell. We were both a little concerned lest we miss our eight o'clock bus in the bazaar.

As it turned out, we had to wait hours for the bus. It was coming from Birganj and had to stop to change two flat tires. Waiting was a normal part of bus travel in Nepal, and we sat down patiently with our luggage. In contrast to my restlessness and self-consciousness when I had first arrived in Chitwan nine months before, I surveyed the goings on in the bazaar with familiar interest. I didn't even wish for anything to read. I was quite happy to observe life around me and to greet the occasional acquaintance who came up to us. I didn't go out of my way to tell people that I was leaving the village for good this time. I was trying not to think about how long it might be before I returned to Pipariya and I didn't want to encourage any kind of emotional leave-taking, in myself or anyone else.

A group of tourists on their way back from the National Park to Kathmandu were waiting for the tourist "luxury coach" from Sunauli. This also seemed to be delayed. They lounged around outside the office of the commission agent who'd sold them their bus tickets snacking on fruit and biscuits and occasionally complaining pointlessly about the tardiness of the bus to the man in the office.

A little boy of eight or nine came slowly toward the group of tourists. He had the most woeful and self-pitying look on his face I had seen for some time. There was nothing about him that warranted his abject demeanor as far as I could see. His clothes were ragged and his feet were bare, but neither of these features distinguished him from the hundreds of children who were running around the bazaar. I attributed his dejected and miserable attitude and his dragging doleful movements to his occupation: begging.

He stood just outside the circle of tourists.

"Hello, one rupee," he said.

"What you need is one handkerchief," said one of the men in an Australian accent. I wondered why foreigners were so upset by the sight of a Nepalese child with a runny nose. He gave the boy a piece of toilet paper.

"It's no good; he won't know what to do with that," said a British woman disparagingly.

As if to contradict her prediction the little boy took the toilet paper and could be seen wiping his nose and upper lip with it as he walked in the direction of an underutilized garbage can, around which orange peels, paper, and other kinds of debris were strewn thick on the ground.

"There, he's using it," said the donor of the toilet paper. His tone of pleased astonishment reminded me of commentaries on the human-like activities of monkeys I've heard in zoos.

The little boy clearly knew something about pleasing his prospective benefactors. He made his way back toward the group and propitiated them again, this time with a clean nose.

I heard them discussing giving him a banana. "Give him a green one," said another Englishman, who seemed to be the life of the party. "They make one sick."

The boy eventually made his way round to me and I gave him my standard lecture on how begging is not good work and refused his entreaties for "one rupee." He stared balefully at me for a moment, and then melted away to try his luck with some other tourists who were waiting for the bus.

A short time later two other young boys presented themselves in front of me. "Hello," one said.

"Hello," I responded.

"One rupee," demanded the bigger, more forward of the two boys. He was wearing imitation leather pants and a T-shirt. I was intrigued by the pants. They looked like vinyl and must have been very hot to wear.

"Meaning," I queried him in Nepali, "that I should give you one rupee?"

They nodded.

The smaller boy had his arm around the bigger one's shoulder.

"No, I won't give you a rupee," I said.

"I have nothing," said the boy in the vinyl pants.

"What? You have no mother, no father?" I asked skeptically.

They shook their heads.

"Only my older brother," said the smaller one.

The boys sat down on a bench opposite me. The more aggressive one reached out to touch my new glass bangles, a present from Geeta. They seemed to have forgotten about their initial aim in initiating our conversation.

"How many bangles?" he asked, fingering them.

"Four," I said in Nepali.

"Four," he said in English. "Black color."

I put out my other wrist. He counted the eleven bangles. "Eleven," he said in English. Using his index finger, he traced the numeral eleven in the dirt, carefully adding the tails on the ones at a jaunty angle.

"C-a-t: cat," he continued proudly.

"Meaning . . ." I prompted.

"Meaning birālo," he said.

"D-o-g: dog," I said.

"Meaning kukur," he responded.

"P-i-g: pig," I said. He didn't know that one, so I told him the meaning. He also demonstrated that he knew the English words for pen and book, two basic elements in primary English language education in Nepal. At this point I also learned that he was in Class 5; the younger boy was in Class 3. The boy with the vinyl pants showed me a plastic watch that he'd bought for fifty rupees, a pretty large sum for a boy with nothing.

He made one final gambit to part me with my money. When he found out that I was waiting for the bus to Kathmandu, he informed me that there would be pickpockets on the bus and I might as well give my money to him beforehand as have my pocket picked on the bus. I didn't recognize the Nepali word for pickpocket, and appealed to Arjun for a translation. Realizing that we were traveling together and perhaps sensing that Arjun's Nepali was better than mine, the boy who would have saved me from pickpockets asked Arjun who I was.

"She's my wife," Arjun replied. Both the boys looked incredulous, but apparently this subject didn't hold as much interest for them as it did for more prurient adults, and they moved on to other questions.

"Where had I been staying? Had I been into the park?" I explained that we had been living in a village. They didn't know where Pipariya was.

"Where do you live?" I asked them.

"Just there." They pointed inconclusively up the road.

The boy wearing the leatherlike pants informed me that they were on their way to see a film in Narayanghat.

"Which film?" I asked.

He told me the name, which I didn't recognize. It's a Nepali film, he told me.

"I saw 'Janam-Janam,'" I told the young movie buffs. They had seen that one, too. And "*Maine Pyār Kyā*" (I loved). I hadn't seen this movie, but Arjun had told me that its soundtrack had featured in almost every *janthi* (bridegroom's procession) during the previous wedding season.

Having exhausted the cinematic offerings of the bazaar, the boys were trying to raise money to see films in the nearest big town. When the next local bus stopped on the road, they ran to get on.

Our bus was nearly four hours behind schedule when it reached us. We had reserved seats, which was a good thing, because it was crowded with people. We picked our way as carefully as we could over the passengers sitting on their parcels in the aisle and wedged ourselves and our luggage into our seats. I rested my arm on the sill of the open window and looked out at the familiar countryside as the bus rattled along the east-west highway toward Narayanghat. In a few days I would be back in California with my parents. What then would I remember of my life in Nepal? And what would people in Pipariya remember about me? Although I knew from experience that one cannot determine memories in the way that one enters data into a computer for future retrieval in some complete, whole, and ordered form, I willed myself to take a mental photograph of the passing scene and not to forget. To the south, beyond the shops and dwellings lining the road, the midday heat shimmered over the verdant fields of maize. In the distance, the jungle cloaked the rolling Churia Hills in darker, cooler greens and greys. To the north, the most majestic mountains on earth reached as far as the eye could see.

The bus gathered speed along the narrow highway through the bazaar. Cyclists, boys driving buffaloes, and women walking with bundles balanced on their heads took a few steps off the road as the bus rushed by. I felt the hot Tarai air spiced with smells of food from roadside tea shops hit my face.

As we left the outskirts of the bazaar, I caught the strains of the eerie theme song from "*Janam-Janam*" blaring from the cinema hall. It seemed an appropriate accompaniment to the transition from what had, in many ways, seemed like another life.

GLOSSARY OF THARU
AND NEPALI WORDS

My rendering of Nepali and Tharu words into English has privileged simplicity over an attempt to capture exact pronunciation. I have anglicized the plural form of Nepali words by adding the suffix "s." I have used macrons to indicate long vowel sounds (for example, ā is pronounced as in aardvark).

-haru   Nepali suffix used to make words plural

abīr   powder, usually red; used as *sindūr* and for applying *tikā*

achār   Nepalese pickle

andolan   movement, agitation; refers here to the popular movement of 1990, which restored multiparty democracy to Nepal

aunus   come (polite command)

aushadi   medicine

badmās   naughty

bahāriyā   a servant who lives with his employer, is fed and clothed by him and is paid every year with a few hundred kilograms of unmilled rice

basné   to sit or stay

basnus   sit down (polite command)

bāto   path, road

Bhagwān   god

bhāt   cooked rice

bhāuju   elder brother's wife

bhitrā   inside

bhoj   feast

bholi   tomorrow

bhutos   tufts on fabric

bihe   An arranged marriage performed according to prescribed rituals; the most prestigious form of marriage

bindi   decorative dot worn on a woman's forehead

bistaré   slow, slowly

Bramathān   Tharu village shrine

chāmal   uncooked rice

chappal   rubber slippers, or thongs, "flip-flops"

chaudhary   formerly, the term for a high-ranking revenue collector in the Tarai; today, a common "surname" for Tharus

chiso   cold or wet

chiurā   rice that has been soaked in water, beaten flat and dried

chor-dinus   leave it (polite command)

dāi   older brother

dāl   lentils

dahi   yogurt

Dasain   ten day festival observed in Nepal in October

denkhi   pestle and mortar apparatus used for pounding grain into flour

derā   apartment, flat

Devanāgari   script in which Hindi and Nepali are written

dhān   unprocessed or unharvested rice

dhārā   a tap, a source of water

dhanyabād   thank you

dharma   religious duty, moral duty

dhoti   a cotton garment worn by men, wrapped around the waist, passed between the legs and tucked in behind

didi   elder sister

dukkha   trouble, pain, sorrow

eryā   sickle used for cutting rice

garnu   to do

garnus   do (polite command)

gaurā   bonfire made of rice straw

ghar   home, house

ghar mukyā   head of the household

ghāt   landing place or crossing place on a river; often a site for cremation

ghee   clarified butter

gīt song

gobar cow manure

goñhi small snails found in rice fields that are eaten by Tharus

goo human excrement, shit

gundri mat woven out of rice straw; used for sitting or sleeping on

gurau Tharu shaman

hāthi elephant

holā the subjunctive form of the verb "to be"; maybe

Holi Nepalese festival

hunchā OK

hurree wind storms that sweep across the Terai in March and April

janam-janam life after life, reincarnation (Hindi)

janthi wedding procession of the groom to the bride's house before the wedding

jānus go (polite command)

jāro cold

jāt caste, tribe, kind

jimidār formerly a large landowner responsible for collecting taxes at the village level; although the office was abolished it is retained as an honorary title

Jithiyā Pāvani Tharu religious festival observed by women

kalavā the term for rice and the accompanying food that is brought to the field and consumed there

kathā story

ke garné? what can one do?

khānā food

khānu to eat

kichkanyā ghost of a young woman who dies violently or unjustly

lāmā Mahayana Buddhist monk

lathi stick or cane

lotā drinking vessels, usually made of pewter or stainless steel

lungi a tube of cloth worn around the waist

mahut elephant driver

maiti natal village or home

makāi corn (maize)

māto a plaster of mud and cow dung used for building and repairing houses

māyā love

mehedi stain used for creating patterns on women's hands

mīth   relationship of ritual friendship

mītho chā   it is tasty

momo   Tibetan steamed meat dumpling

Musaher   a Tarai caste

namaskār   a politer form of *namaste*

namaste   Nepali greeting meaning "I bow to the god in you"

nanglo   a flat woven tray used for winnowing grains

narāmro   not good, bad

padalé   flatulence, fart

pahariyā   Tharu term for people from the hills (*pahar*)

pāni   water, rain

parsi   day after tomorrow

patidār   patriline

pauroti   bread

pāvani   Tharu religious observance

Phaguvā   Tharu festival corresponding to Holi

ping   swing

pūjā   worship

rakshi   distilled rice liquor

rāmro   good

rangi-changi   multi-colored

roti   unleavened bread

sādhu   holy man, ascetic

sāg   cooked greens

sāmān   goods, baggage

sāthi   friend

sindūr   the red powder that is put into the parting of a bride's hair
   by the groom during the Nepalese marriage ceremony; the mark
   of married women in Nepal

sirak   quilt with a removable cover

Soharāyi   Tharu festival corresponding to Nepalese Tihar

surwal-kurtā   loose pajama style pants and tunic

swāgat   welcome

tapain   you (polite form)

tarkāri   vegetables or a vegetable curry

thāhā chainā   I don't know

thūlo   big, great

thūlo mānchhe   a big shot, an important person

tikā sign of auspiciousness, a mark made on the forehead with a paste of rice, yogurt, and red *abīr* powder

tole group or cluster of houses; neighborhood

topi Nepalese hat worn by men

videshi foreigner

wosarā the covered porch on Tharu houses